The Rise of Fiduciary Capitalism

The Rise of Fiduciary Capitalism

How Institutional Investors Can Make
Corporate America More Democratic

James P. Hawley
Andrew T. Williams

PENN

University of Pennsylvania Press

Philadelphia

10 9 8 7 6 5 4 3 2 1

Published by
University of Pennsylvania Press
Philadelphia, Pennsylvania 19104-4011

Library of Congress Cataloging-in-Publication Data
Hawley, James P., 1944–
    The rise of fiduciary capitalism : how institutional investors can make corporate
America more democratic / James P. Hawley, Andrew T. Williams.
        p.   cm.
    Includes bibliographical references and index.
    ISBN 0-8122-3563-0 (alk. paper)
        1. Institutional investments — United States.   2. Stockholders — United States.
    3. Capitalism — United States.   4. Democracy — United States.   I. Williams,
    Andrew T., 1943–   .   II. Title.
    HG4910 .H43 2000
    338.7′4 — dc21   00-039285

To Diane and Linda
for their love and support

Contents

Tables

Introduction

Ever since the modern corporation came on the American business scene between 1890 and 1910 it has been the focal point of both intense criticism and praise. Since its emergence it has undergone three waves in its mode of ownership and control. At inception corporations were disproportionately owned and controlled by their owner-founders (most notably John D. Rockefeller, Leland Stanford, and Henry Ford), although stock was publicly traded. Men such as these were either the "captains of industry" (as supporters dubbed them) or "robber barons" (as critics christened them). Yet in the majority of large corporations, by the 1920s de facto control had passed or was rapidly passing from the founding entrepreneurs or their direct agents to professional management who, unlike the owner-founders, did not personally own a significant proportion of the firms they managed. The influence of original owners and their descendents was declining while the absolute number of shareowners grew rapidly, as did the proportion of the general population that owned shares as a major form of investment. Shareholding was increasingly diffused, albeit mostly among the top most income brackets and wealth holders of the population. The 1920s witnessed the emergence of what one noted historian characterized as managerial capitalism, which replaced what could be called corporate entrepreneurial capitalism. Unbridled managerial capitalism held sway for about fifty years, from the 1920s through the 1970s.[1]

However, beginning in the late 1960s, coming of age in the 1980s to early 1990s, and continuing to the turn of the twenty-first century, a third wave of ownership began to transform the nature of corporate ownership and control once again. During these thirty years shareholding has rapidly reconcentrated, but this time not in the hands of individuals. Rather, shareholding has now been concentrated in the hands of major institutional investors, the most important of which are public and private pension funds and mutual funds. This change has been remarkable. Since 1997 these institutions, along with the insurance companies, now own more corporate equity than all the individuals in the country combined. The change is all the more stunning when one notes that individuals owned almost 80 percent of corporate equity as recently as 1970.[2] These fiduciary institutions are legally and ethically bound to prudently serve the interests of their beneficiaries and investors, although there are significant differences between public pension funds and privately owned mutual funds. This book argues that unbridled managerial capitalism is coming to be replaced by fiduciary capitalism, an emergent form of hybrid ownership in which large fiduciary institutions of various types have come to own about one half of the total equity in the U.S. market.[3]

Fiduciary capitalism began to effectively challenge corporate managers' heretofore unquestioned domination of corporate behavior and governance. This occurred in two phases. The first phase began in the early 1980s and was mostly associated with the hostile merger, takeover, and acquisition movement. Hostile takeovers developed and made use of the market for corporate control as the primary means to remove top corporate management, and to restructure firms. This phase came to an effective end around 1987–88 with the collapse of the savings and loan industry, which had supplied significant capital for the takeovers. The next phase, following closely on the collapse of the takeover period, and with longer staying power, was corporate governance activism, which was initiated by state public pension funds such as the California Public Employees Retirement System (CalPERS), the State of Wisconsin Investment Board (SWIB), and the College Retirement Equity Fund (CREF), a cooperative retirement fund for college professors that is the largest U.S. pension fund.

In the 1930s, Adolph Berle and Gardner Means wrote about the separation of corporate ownership and control, arguing that the increasingly dispersed ownership of most large firms gave managers de facto control. This relegated the shareholders, the nominal owners, to mere suppliers (or renters) of capital with little or no influence on firm behavior. Now at the end of the 1990s, with the emergence and growth of large fiduciary institutions a partial remarriage of ownership and control is occurring for the first time since the early twentieth century. Yet this "remarriage" is partial in the sense that large institutional owners are themselves fiduciary representatives of the ultimate investors and beneficiaries, such as pensioners or investors in mutual funds. Thus, an added bureaucratic-organizational link between what can be termed the beneficial "owners" and the firms they "own" mediates this ownership or agency chain. Fiduciary institutions of all types may increasingly be active owners, but they, like the corporations they "own," are run by professional managers.

Early in the century Berle and Means observed the emergence of the professional manager—individuals trained to exercise the control of the earlier generation of owner-managers, but without a significant ownership stake in the company. Now we observe the emergence of professional owners, individuals academically trained to exercise the rights and responsibilities of the ownership of equity and other assets on behalf of the ultimate or beneficial owners. These professional fiduciaries, in their role of active and involved "owners," have begun to redefine the terms of the partial reunification of "ownership" and control of publicly traded U.S. corporations. This redefinition has potential advantages as well as pitfalls. The potential advantage is a more expansive and inclusive ownership of firms that might foster greater long-term vision on the part of firm managers. The pitfall is the greater concentration of financial power in the hands of fiduciaries (especially private sector ones) that have as little or even less accountability than corporate managers once had.

The Rise of Fiduciary Activism and the Growth of the Universal Owner

Some of the largest and most powerful of these fiduciary institutions have begun to assert their rights as active "owners" in the form not only of buying and selling equity, but also of voting proxies, initiating proxy resolutions, and formally and informally pressuring corporate managers and boards of directors to pursue particular policies to their liking and change other policies not to their liking. Major and early examples of this were the "corporate coups" of 1992–93 when large public pension funds and CREF (with quiet but active support from some mutual funds like Fidelity) were able to dislodge the incumbent CEOs and many members of the board of directors at such venerable but then economically underperforming firms as IBM, Westinghouse, GM, and Sears.

Thus, emergent fiduciary capitalism and the fiduciary activist institutions, which define its nature, began to transform the role of owners and managers, as well as their relation to financial markets and, indeed, the role of financial markets as a factor in corporate managers' behavior. The growing importance of corporate governance in the United States during the 1990s reflects these underlying developments. Fiduciary institutions have begun a major historical redefinition of the terms of the partial remarriage of ownership and control.

Market and Nonmarket Means

But there is greater significance to the emergence of fiduciary institutions than closing the gap to some degree between the separation of ownership and control. These fiduciary institutions are very large in absolute size. (CREF, for example, typically owns 1–2 percent of many large firms, and in 1997 the largest twenty-five institutional investors as a group owned 28 percent of the largest twenty-five U.S. corporations.)[4] What is striking about the corporate governance activities of these large fiduciary activists (disproportionately public pension funds) is their use of a variety of nonmarket means to achieve their ends. While the hostile takeover and mergers and acquisitions movement of the 1980s relied overwhelmingly on the market for corporate control (using means such as tender offers, greenmail and the like), the corporate governance movement of the 1990s has relied primarily on formal and informal voice to achieve its ends. To a large degree the use of voice results from the very nature and size of institutional investors' portfolios. They are, on the whole, both too big to sell the holdings in their portfolios that are seen as underperforming (the "dogs" that exist in any large portfolio), and even if they chose to sell, they would typically be selling into a declining market, all too often of their own making, since the largest institutions themselves move markets. Compounding this problem is that most large institutional portfolios look like the portfolios of other large institutions. Therefore, finding a potential buyer at a reasonable price is difficult. For example, if a large institution wants to divest itself of the 1–2 percent of the outstanding shares of a poorly performing firm it holds, it likely would need to sell to another institution, which would likely also desire to sell. The market becomes locked. Therefore, large institutions holding widely diversified portfolios make increasing use of the portfolio strategy known as indexation.

An indexed investor does not pick its stocks since it is too large to selectively purchase only the "best," or even just "better," stocks. Its size demands that it buy what is essentially a cross section of the whole market, for example, the Wilshire 2000, the S&P 500, or some predetermined section of it. For example, CalPERS (the large California public pension fund and the largest public pension fund) owns about 1,400 stocks, holding between 0.5 and 2 percent of the outstanding stock for each company in its portfolio. It buys and sells shares only to maintain a predetermined balance in its portfolio that reflects the stock valuations in its index. It does not sell those stocks that are not performing well. The other reason that large funds often index is that it is far less expensive to run an indexed (or majority indexed) fund than a stock picking fund where managers attempt to out perform the market. Thus, indexing (or shadow indexing, a somewhat looser indexation strategy) drives large institutions to use a variety of formal and informal corporate governance mechanisms, short of selling, to influence poorly performing firms.

Thus, owing to their sheer size, and the fact that the largest institutions have portfolios that usually mirror those of other large institutions, most major fiduciary capitalists cannot sell. And if they cannot sell, then they must "care." Caring in this context takes the form of active ownership. Large institutions are locked into the market and into the shares they own on behalf of their beneficiaries and investors. In 1997, institutional investors owned almost 60 percent of the outstanding equity of the largest one thousand U.S. corporations. Not only does this ownership pattern lock them into the market and make selling (doing the "Wall Street Walk") neither wise nor possible; it also creates an added dimension that as yet is neither widely recognized nor appreciated. These institutions are not merely fiduciary owners, but what this book terms universal owners as well.[5]

Universal Owners

A universal owner is a large institutional investor that holds in its portfolio a broad cross section of the economy, holds its shares for the long term, and on the whole does not trade except to maintain its index. As such a universal owner's cumulative long-term return is determined not merely by the performance of each individual firm it owns, but by the performance of the economy as a whole. In short, its total long-term return is greater than the sum of its parts. This logic has a number of potentially important consequences. First, it means that when universal owners evaluate the behavior of the firms they own one significant dimension should be how each firm's activities affect the economy as a whole, and hence the portfolio of the universal owner. For example, the universal owner (like the economy as a whole) can capture positive externalities generated by a firm. An externality as a spillover effect is either a positive or negative effect which falls on a third party not immediately party to the contract.

The spillover effect from the training and education of its workforce by a firm is a classic example of a positive externality. While such training and education is always good for the economy as a whole since it tends to increase productivity (in addition to being of benefit to the individuals educated and trained), firms may not provide the economy-wide optimal education for fear of losing their investment when employees change jobs, or because their competitors may not be incurring the same costs. Firms, therefore, tend to underinvest, and potential gains are not realized. Universal owners are well positioned to encourage and pressure firms to provide the socially optimal degree of education and training since over the long term they can capture the benefits of these gains across their well-diversified portfolios. The case is similar with negative externalities such as environmentally damaging activities. Universal owners' portfolios are negatively impacted by pollution since one firm's waste is another firm's expense. Thus, it is in the economic interest of a universal owner to attempt to minimize the environmental damage of each of its firms since it will capture the long-term and society-wide benefits, although specific firms in its portfolio will bear the costs of cleanup or restructuring to produce in more environmental-friendly modes.

A second consequence of the existence of universal owners is that they come to occupy a quasi-public policy position as having an economic interest in the long-term health and well-being of the whole society. This unusual position suggests that they have an interest not only in standard macroeconomic policy issues, but more specifically in regulatory policy and the provision of public goods such as education and health, tort law, and infrastructure generally, both physical and human. Confronted with this potential many universal owners have moved cautiously, not only for fear of stepping on politically sensitive toes over a variety of immediate "hot button" issues such as health or the environment, but also due to their concern about exercising what has come to be a significant amount of economic power. Public pension fund managers do not generally conceive of themselves as public policy makers, in spite of their growing recognition that they are or may be forced by the logic of economic efficiency to play such a role. This work suggests that as the ultimate beneficiaries come to realize the importance of universal owners acting as such, more fund managers will find the political room to act on the potentials that universal owners possess.

However, while the reconcentration of ownership into the hands of fiduciary institutions has the potential to internalize externalities and to lead to policies enhancing the quality of life and economic security of future generations, concentration also has the potential for abuse. The abuse may take many forms, such as corruption of the political process, monopoly exploitation of customers, unfair business practices, and so on. There is a long history in the United States of the suspicion of abuse of concentrated economic power. It finds its expression in the antitrust laws, among other places, and was responsible for Depression era reforms that, according to Roe, prevented banks and insurance companies from amassing holdings that would have allowed them to act as owners.[6] Whether pension funds and mutual funds might come to be viewed as latter day "trusts," subject to the withering criticism of a modern Louis Brandeis, remains to be seen.[7] There is certainly widespread concern with mergers and acquisitions and with executive compensation, particularly the generous use of stock options, though this hasn't as yet hardened into legislative concern. The main antidote to abuse of power would seem to be those recommended by Brandeis: transparency of the policies of financial institutions, scrutiny by a vigilant press, and accountability of board members. These are reforms that fiduciary institutions should seek to foster.

Most large institutional investors have yet to seriously recognize the multiple implications of their universal owner status, and to then develop programs based on this understanding. One of the purposes of this book is to suggest that universal owners need to confront their status, and that their beneficiaries and investors need also to recognize their potentially important role in pressuring universal owners to analyze and act on their universal owner qualities.

Stockholders and Stakeholders

One way often used to conceive the position of the tens of millions of individuals and families that have concrete interests as beneficiaries and investors in universal owners is through the widely used concept of the stakeholder. Stakeholders are generally considered to be groups in the population who have a legitimate claim on the behavior (and sometimes resources) of the corporation. Examples of stakeholders include employees, communities in which the corporation operates, environmental groups, suppliers, and debt holders. The stakeholder idea is a relatively old one, and for decades many have suggested that firms have a range of responsibilities and obligations to stakeholders, in addition to maximizing financial returns to stockholders.[8]

This book argues that with the huge growth of universal owners in the last few decades, the older divide between both individual and institutional stockholders (interested in maximizing financial return), on the one hand, and stakeholders (interested in a variety of financial and nonfinancial aspects of corporate behavior) on the other is increasingly blurred in fact, and potentially blurred in future actions if and when universal owners (and many of their beneficiaries and "owners/investors") come to realize the potential of their ownership status. Since more than 40 percent of the adult population has direct and indirect (beneficial) claims on fiduciary institutions and direct stock ownership holdings, stockholders are also stakeholders.[9] Universal owners are uniquely positioned to help structure an economy that can create and capture the economic efficiencies of this newly emerging conjuncture of economic interests.

It is argued that universal owners are uniquely positioned to develop and pursue a potentially virtuous efficiency cycle of minimizing negative externalities and encouraging positive ones by the firms in their portfolios. They can do this not merely due to the representative cross section of the economy they own, but also to the huge numbers of citizens they must effectively represent through their fiduciary duties. Universal owners need to begin a process of extending the definition of prudential fiduciary duty to include attention to the universal aspects of their portfolios. This attention should emphasize how the generalized interests are defined and how they should come to be defined, thereby linking the tens of millions of "citizen-stakeholder-stockholders" to whom these institutions are bound. In order to accomplish this fiduciary duty, agents as managers of other people's money, to borrow the phrase that Justice Brandeis used early in the twentieth century, must act, must have incentives to act, and/or be mandated by state and federal regulation to act in the long-term interests of their beneficiaries, which includes their interests as beneficial "owners" of universal investors. Thus, what is often referred to as an "agency chain" (which is discussed in subsequent chapters) exists not only between institutional owners and the firms they own, but equally between the investors and beneficiaries in mutual funds, corporate pension funds, and most especially in public and cooperative pension funds.

This is perhaps the latest qualitatively new twist on the age-old question:

"Who should the corporation serve?" The simple answer provided in the traditional MBA finance class is to repeat the mantra: "The shareholders, by maximizing profits." Yet the emergence of universal owners whose claimants and beneficiaries constitute more than 40 percent of the adult population makes such disarmingly simple formulas particularly unhelpful. Maximizing shareholder wealth (even over the long term) may be quite different for a firm individually than for a diversified universal investor who may find itself weighing, for example, financial gains from investment in tobacco firms against the costs inflicted directly on its members through smoking as well as the costs to the taxpayers (an important consideration if it is a public pension fund) for medical care and health premiums. In this situation, what it means to maximize shareholder return is somewhat problematic, and is a surely complex calculation.

This work suggests that confronting this complexity is the responsibility of universal owners and their members and/or investors. This is a long-term challenge that will involve multiple redefinitions of and debates about what is in the "interests" of the institutions and their owner-members. Yet it is a challenge that if confronted offers the potential for greater economy-wide efficiencies, integration, and the participation of large sections of the population in what has become known as active ownership by fiduciary institutions. The role of owner-beneficiaries in these institutions is an issue that has barely been examined, in part because of the quiescence of the vast majority of the participant-owners themselves. This is the classic problem of who will watch the (fiduciary) watchers? Yet, changing circumstances bring forth not only new questions and sensitivities, but potentially new actions by those affected. In the absence of actions by the tens of millions of those affected having direct financial interests in the actions and activities of their fiduciaries, these developments risk a massive concentration of financial power the like of which has not been seen in the United States since the early twentieth century, if then. Yet the authors of this work hope that this book will contribute through an analysis of these changing conditions and thereby call attention to the importance of increasing consciousness of them.

This book differs from other published work about corporate governance in three primary ways. First, although incorporating the major literature on U.S. corporate governance in its discussion, the book focuses on the rise and activities of fiduciary institutions, as well as on the theories and evidence that attempt to explain their behavior. Second, the book suggests that this rise affects not just the recent corporate governance activities of these large institutional investors, but also offers a significant potential for economy-wide efficiency gains due to their universal investor nature. To the authors' knowledge, aside from the suggestion that universal investors are new, there have not been any studies conducted about them nor has the concept been developed or elaborated. Third, this book presents initial research on the status of U.S. universal investors at the close of the second millennium.

   This book is purposefully limited in scope. It does not make any attempt to examine the increasingly global scope of corporate governance activities in the advanced industrial countries, in the newly developed economies, nor in the economically less developed and developing world. While of great significance, the global aspects of corporate governance are beyond the scope of this work. This limitation is at least twofold. A wealth of important insights can be gained from comparative studies of corporate governance. Additionally, to an important degree, global corporate governance developments are not merely comparatively based, but rather truly global in scope since many of the largest institutional investors have or are developing governance programs that span the globe. CalPERS and CREF, for example, are forceful corporate governance actors in the United Kingdom, France, Germany, and Japan, among other countries. In turn, European institutional investors are active in the United States. What the role of a universal owner could and should be in its transnational aspects will await future work by the authors and others. The authors would note, however, that while U.S. universal owners possess by American historical standards significant equity in U.S. firms, the ownership patterns of some institutional investors in the rest of the world is far, far more concentrated than in the United States. Logically, the implications of universal investors operating in countries other than the United States could be greater abroad because they own more and there are typically far fewer of them.[10]

Chapter 1
The Universal Owner:
Stockholder as Stakeholder

In the United States the growth of institutional investors (public and cooperative pension funds, corporate and union pension funds, and mutual funds and bank trusts) over the past twenty-five years has concentrated a substantial amount of corporate equity into the hands of a relatively small number of fiduciary institutions. This change in the ownership structure from individuals, who held about 80 percent of stock in the early 1970s, to institutional owners, who currently own almost 60 percent of the largest one thousand U.S. firms, reflects the growth of various forms of indirect ownership (e.g., mutual funds) and beneficial claims (e.g., pension funds) in the U.S. economy. It is estimated that 45 to 50 percent of all Americans currently have some form of direct or indirect beneficial ownership or other financial claims linked to institutional stock ownership.[1]

One consequence of this new and relatively widespread form of mostly indirect "ownership" is that institutional owners increasingly act as long-term and permanent holders of a cross section of corporate America. Thus, they find themselves being concerned not only with the long-term performance of individual firms, but also with the performance of the economy as a whole. Increasingly these institutions are called upon by various constituencies ("stakeholders") to vote proxies on a wide assortment of issues, often labeled "social" — for example, issues dealing with diversity, the environment, human rights, plant closings, and executive compensation. (The proxy voting policies of several important institutional investors are examined in the next chapter.)

The claims on the assets of these fiduciary institutions may be characterized as claims of beneficial "ownership." In fact they are a form of indirect or mediated ownership because they represent claims to payments rather than alienable claims to the equity or debt instrument itself. Similarly, mutual funds represent merely a claim on residual gains (or losses), not on the actual stock certificate itself.

Hence, ownership and indeed private property in the corporate form is rapidly being transformed into an institution in which agents represent agents in what can be quite long and complex chains between the firm at one end and the ultimate beneficial "owner" or claimant at the other.[2] Property and ownership have increasingly become bureaucratic and organizational while the rights and responsibilities of operational ownership (that is, investment decisions, proxy voting, and so on) increasingly reside in the hands of professional management teams operating as fiduciary intermediaries.

The concept of "stockholder as stakeholder" questions the received wisdom of much academic and policy discussion on the appropriate role of the owners of corporate equity in the governance of the modern corporation. The traditional approach assumes a clear division between those who own stock — the stockholders — and those who have a variety of "claims" on the corporation — the stakeholders — who are affected in some positive or negative way by the actions of the corporation. Viewing stockholders as stakeholders immediately raises the question of whether public goods (typically in terms of both negative and positive externalities) such as education, the environment, or health have the potential to be conceptualized and treated quite differently in an economy increasingly dominated by universal owners.

The stakeholder tradition implicitly or explicitly begins with a critique of what is typically called the finance or stockholder primacy model of the firm.[3] In their various forms, finance models all begin with the view that the firm exists for only one reason: to maximize shareholder wealth (whether over a longer or shorter time frame). The divorce of ownership from control noted in the 1930s by Adolph Berle and Gardner Means raised the question of whether managers might systematically pursue goals that were counter to the interests of owners.[4] Following this lead, much of the discussion of corporate governance over the past fifty years has primarily concerned itself with the problem of aligning the interests of those agents, principally managers and the board of directors, with those of the owners. This work argues that while principal agent problems are important, they do not begin to capture fully and adequately the complex interests and potential roles of large institutional investors such as pension funds, mutual funds, and others that are what this work calls universal owners. An examination of the interaction between different categories of both stockholders and so-called stakeholders begins to reveal this complexity.

The interests of various stockholder and stakeholder groups are not clear-cut, simple, or unambiguous. Indeed, these "interests" have barely begun to be articulated or conceptually formulated either by ultimate recipients and "owners" or by most senior institutional managers themselves. Most important, demographic, regional, employment, and other factors cause or may cause significant divisions among different classes of shareholders and beneficial claimants. What is interesting is that these divisions cut across both groups, rather than divide them neatly into stockholders and stakeholders.[5]

This will make for interesting corporate governance politics. Indeed, as well illustrated below, it already has begun to do so in the United States.

Striking, therefore, is this historically new basis for a significant, although far from full, convergence between stakeholder (perhaps increasingly defined as "citizen") and shareholder. However, there is much to understand in the complexities of the bureaucratic representations of individual "ownership" as fiduciary, public, union, nonprofit, corporate, and mutual fund institutional investors come to dominate much of the ownership landscape. The political and regulatory implications of these historical shifts are barely discussed in the literature. A discussion is not attempted here, either, although the subject is critical. However, Robert Monks and Nell Minow make a number of important points. First, the federal government has a financial stake in how all pension funds operate since they are (mostly) tax exempt at a tax expense of about $50 billion per year, thereby giving the government the legitimate right to "define broadly how pension fund trustees should function in their capacity as owners of the country's industrial establishment." Second, although universal owners' interests may be "congruent with those of society," they are unlikely by themselves to be able to deal with the collective choice problems in areas such as education, energy conservation, occupational health and safety, and the environment. Monks and Minow conclude, "This is an agenda that can be addressed only by government in *conjunction* with a 'universal shareholder' " (emphasis added). The implications of this for how universal owners might come to confront the tremendous influence of their portfolio's firms, which conduct influential political lobbying against such public goods, may be of the utmost importance.[6]

Universal Owners

A universal owner is an institutional owner whose holdings are highly diversified and, typically, held long term. The holdings of many institutions are a small but significant cross section of publicly traded stock (and debt) in the economy and, therefore, have the characteristic of representing the entire economy.[7] However, because of their large size some institutional owners have the ability to "move markets."[8] To counteract this tendency as well as for sound investment reasons, large universal owners disproportionately follow an index strategy rather than an actively managed strategy for most of their equity investments.[9]

Mutual funds, corporate pension funds, public pension funds, the College Retirement Equities Fund (CREF, the largest fund in the United States), and labor union funds are all examples of universal owners. However, they differ significantly among themselves in investment strategies (portfolio composition, time frame, turnover rates, and so on) and in their recent history of corporate governance activities.

The relationship between corporate governance activism and activities that reveal aspects of universal owner consciousness and behavior is direct. Activism is invariably expressed as a concern at a particular company (say, with director independence), but it is grounded in general principles thought to promote an efficient corporate sector. Furthermore, institutional investors are well aware that their actions at individual companies may have impacts on the entire corporate sector.[10] From this realization it is a relatively short step to the recognition that there may be certain public policy issues — education, training, workplace health and safety standards, and so on — that have similar implications for portfolio returns beyond whatever impact they may happen to have at individual firms.

The portfolio-wide issues confronting universal owners are typically long-term performance ones. Corporate governance is about performance via active ownership that, given a specific risk-return strategy and time frame, can increase performance. A few of the institutions on the leading edge of corporate governance activities have exhibited some characteristics of being conscious of their universal owner status, although this is currently exceptional rather than typical.[11]

Monks and Minow suggest that institutions are rapidly becoming universal owners because

their holdings are so diversified that they have the incentive to represent the ownership sector (and the economy) generally rather than any specific industries or companies. This endows them with a breadth of concern that naturally aligns with the public interest. For example, pension funds can be concerned with vocational education, pollution, and retraining, whereas an owner with a perspective limited to a particular company or industry would consider these to be unacceptable expenses because of competitiveness problems.[12]

They further note:

The goal of corporate governance is to find a way to maximize wealth creation over time, in a manner that does not impose inappropriate costs on third parties or on society as a whole. Wealth creation can be looked at from a macro perspective . . . although doing so requires rigorous and quantitative calculations to prevent vague "stakeholder" claims. Inappropriate costs can include agency costs imposed on investors as reflected, for example, in excessive CEO pay. They also include externalized costs imposed on society at large, like pollution, price fixing, and other criminal behavior. In order to understand what needs to be done, we must first ask what we are trying to achieve, not just in the context of the corporate structure, but in the societal systems that create and surround it. (pp. 262–63)[13]

Thus universal owners may have (and indeed they should have) interests in firm activities that minimize negative externalities (e.g., environmental damage) by taking account of them to a greater degree, thereby internalizing them and reducing social, third-party costs for the portfolio as a whole. Such third-party costs come in a variety of forms, from direct damage to other holdings (e.g., real estate) and indirect costs (e.g., higher tax rates for expensive clean up) that are ultimately levied on the economy as a whole and/or on the tax base of various state localities. Likewise, for positive externalities. Their creation or expansion may be beneficial for universal owners' portfolios, which may have interests in their "externalization" since gains can be captured by the portfolio as a whole. This is the case, for example, with education and training.[14] Universal owners need also to take into account what can be termed second order or broader "citizenship" effects. For example, the conflict between their tobacco investments on the one hand, and the long-term health and quality of life of their beneficiaries on the other, present universal owners with difficult trade-offs.

For a universal owner, and thus for its beneficiaries, the whole may well be greater than the sum of its parts since long-term profit maximization for the portfolio of a universal owner involves enhancing not just return on a firm-by-firm basis, but enhancing productivity in the economy as a whole. This approach to the role and responsibility of universal ownership simply takes two basic ideas, externalities and portfolio theory, the former from economics 101 and the later from finance 101, and combines them.[15]

Universal owners exhibit three fundamental characteristics: size, portfolio composition, and investment strategies. Institutional owners increased their ownership share of the largest one thousand U.S. firms from 46.6 percent of total equity in 1987 to 59.9 percent in 1997. In fact, institutions held more than 50 percent of the equity in 71.3 percent of the largest one thousand corporations and more than 90 percent of the equity in forty of them.[16] The largest institutions also account for a growing fraction of the ownership of the largest corporations. In 1985, the top twenty-five institutions held an average 19.8 percent of the equity of the largest twenty-five companies. Twelve years later their ownership share had risen to 28 percent — an increase of more than 40 percent. This occurred at the same time that the fraction of all institutional shares owned by the largest twenty-five institutions has remained nearly constant at about 55 percent. Clearly, institutional ownership by the largest fiduciary institutions has grown substantially over the last decade and a half and that growth has been particularly concentrated in the largest companies.[17]

While the simple fact that institutions own a large fraction of the equity in the United States is important in itself and goes a long way toward establishing their claim as universal owners, it is equally important to look at the investment strategies adopted by the various institutional owners. This information for 1997 is presented in Table 1.1. In this table investments are categorized by the institutional investor having the responsibility for making the investment decisions. Institutions, particularly public pension funds, often delegate this responsibility for a fraction of their portfolio to one or more money managers. Hence, money managers account for the largest single category — 45.2 percent of total institutional assets — while public pen-

TABLE 1.1: Percentage of Equity Portfolio Value Allocated to Various Investments Strategies, 1997

	Aggressive Growth	Growth	GARP[a]	Balanced	Classic/ value	Value/ Income	Income	Index Only	TOTAL
Corporate Pensions	—[b]	29.7	14.2	4.0	10.5	15.4	13.7	11.2	1.7
Public Pensions	—[b]	13.2	0.5	26.3	11.1	11.7	—[b]	37.1	6.4
Mutual Fund Managers	24.8	8.9	34.6	0.8	0.8	15.9	6.0	8.3	19.0
Money Managers	9.8	22.5	19.0	0.5	13.1	20.4	3.1	11.7	45.2
Insurance Companies	11.8	58.8	15.7	2.1	4.7	2.1	0.5	4.4	7.0
Banks	0.4	30.3	0.8	0.2	10.6	18.8	2.9	36.1	20.7
TOTAL	10.0	23.6	16.7	2.3	19.5	17.3	3.4	17.2	100.00[c]

Source: *Institutional Investment Report*, 2, no. 2, August 1998, table 6, p. 18. Calculated for year ended December 31, 1997.

[a] GARP: Growth at a Reasonable Price
[b] Trading base too small for significant calculation
[c] Detailed portfolio analysis covers about 90% of total institutional equity holdings

sion funds, which account for about 10 percent of U.S. equity ownership, only managed themselves about 6 percent of all institutional assets in 1997. The remaining public pension fund assets appear in the money manager category. The amount of discretion give to money managers varies widely — from a set of general objectives to detailed guidelines as to how proxies are to be voted or which investments are suitable.

What is most striking is the high level of indexation among public funds and banks and, to a smaller degree, corporate funds and money managers.[18] Index funds by definition mirror some market basket such as the S&P 500 and "automatic" trading takes place in order to adjust the portfolio to the changing composition of the index. What is important about indexation is that it is by definition long term and stable and prevents any form of voluntary exit (doing the "Wall Street Walk"). Indexing therefore necessitates various forms of voice or active ownership as the only means for an owner to influence corporate policy and, it is hoped, the return on an investment. The result is that the market is bypassed as a means of expressing either disapproval or satisfaction.

In 1996, the indexed proportion of all institutional investors' portfolios had a turnover rate of only 15.0 percent, compared to an overall average for all institutions of 43.1 percent. This is evidence that their investments are long term and relatively stable in nature. Public pension funds (the prototype of the universal owner) had the lowest turnover rate of all institutions, 20.5 percent in 1996. In that same year, banks had a turnover rate of 28.9 percent, insurance companies 38.6 percent, corporate pension funds 39.4 percent, mutual funds 43.3 percent, and money managers (which also manage many, but not all public funds' actively managed funds) had the highest turnover rate at 53.5 percent.

In terms of the total assets of the largest two hundred defined benefit and defined contribution funds, in the former there has been a steady increase in indexation as a strategy, while in the latter it held steady until the 1996–97 bull market, when it declined markedly. In 1996, 34.6 percent of the total equity owned by the largest two hundred defined benefit plans was indexed, up from 28.2 percent in 1990. For defined contribution plans, indexed equity increased from 26.1 percent in 1990 to 30.0 percent in 1995, dramatically falling off by 1996 to 18.0 percent as individuals more actively managed their funds in an attempt to capture greater returns in the bull markets of these years.[19]

Profile of a Universal Owner

Individually, universal owners own large, diversified portfolios of equity, debt, real estate, and other financial assets. Collectively they own a substantial fraction of the economic wealth in advanced industrial economies. The largest twenty U.S. institutional investors according to *Pensions and Invest-*

TABLE 1.2: Largest U.S. Retirement Funds (in millions of dollars)

Rank	Sponsor	Location	Total Assets	Defined Contribution	Defined Benefit
1	California Public Employees' Retirement System	Sacramento, Calif.	127,656	127,599	57
2	New York State Common Retirement Fund	Albany, N.Y.	95,812	95,812	
3	General Motors Investment Management Corp.	New York, N.Y.	90,600	71,700	18,900
4	California State Teachers' Retirement System	Sacramento, Calif.	78,900	78,900	
5	Florida State Board of Administration	Tallahassee, Fla.	71,940	71,940	
6	New York State Teachers' Retirement System	Albany, N.Y.	68,738	68,738	
7	Texas Teacher Retirement System	Austin, Tex.	64,221	64,221	
8	New Jersey Division of Investment	Trenton, N.J.	59,933	59,109	824
9	General Electric Co.	Stamford, Conn.	56,915	39,000	17,915
10	Federal Retirement Thrift Investment Board	Washington, D.C.	55,491		55,491
11	New York City Retirement Systems	New York, N.Y.	54,712	54,712	
12	IBM Corp.	Stamford, Conn.	53,122	39,151	13,971
13	Wisconsin (State of) Investment Board	Madison, Wis.	50,051	49,394	657
14	Lucent Technologies	Murray Hill, N.J.	48,447	36,009	12,437
15	Ford Motor Co.	Dearborn, Mich.	47,775	35,700	12,075
16	Boeing Co.	Seattle, Wash.	47,200	31,400	15,800
17	Ohio Public Employees Retirement System	Columbus, Ohio	47,077	44,162	2,915
18	Ohio State Teachers Retirement System	Columbus, Ohio	44,055	44,055	
19	Michigan (State of) Department of Treasury	Lansing, Mich.	42,717	40,087	2,630
20	North Carolina Retirement Systems	Raleigh, N.C.	41,500	41,500	
	TOTAL		1,246,862	1,093,189	153,672

Source: *Pensions and Investments*, http://www.pionline.com/research/r100.shtml, November 29, 1998.

ments, a trade journal for the industry, have combined assets of $1.2 trillion, of which all but $154 billion is held in defined benefit programs (Table 1.2).[20] These ten institutions accounted for about 10 percent of the $14.2 trillion in assets held by all U.S. institutional investors combined.[21] Not only are these institutions the largest retirement funds in the United States, they are among the largest retirement funds in the world. U.S. funds account for 80 percent of the assets of the largest twenty retirement funds in the world (Table 1.3).

In fact, Tables 1.2 and 1.3 omit some of the largest institutional investors: mutual funds, insurance companies, and the Teachers Insurance and Annuity Association-College Retirement Equities Fund — better known by the acronym TIAA-CREF. According to *Pensions and Investments*, TIAA-CREF is not categorized as a pension fund but rather as a financial services company. Mutual fund companies are even larger. For example, Fidelity Investment Company manages more than $900 billion in customers' assets. Of that amount, $197 billion are assets in defined contribution accounts.[22]

The Portfolio of a Universal Owner

TIAA-CREF is one of the largest financial service organization in the United States and one of the largest retirement system in the world. Based on total revenue, it ranked thirtieth in *Fortune* magazine's 1997 listing of the largest U.S. companies.[23] A look at its financial structure in general and its equity portfolio in particular provides insight into the nature of the universal owner.

As of September 30, 1998, TIAA-CREF had more than $222 billion under management. Of this total, $100 billion was in the TIAA portion (the annuity association). The bulk of these assets were invested in bonds, commercial mortgages, and real estate. Almost all of the remaining $122 billion was in the CREF portion of the organization. These assets were primarily invested in the equity of domestic and foreign firms. A small fraction of the assets consists of three other TIAA-CREF entities: life insurance, mutual funds, and a trust company (Table 1.4).

CREF assets were invested in sixty-seven industry groups containing 4,669 different equity issues in the middle of 1998 (Table 1.5).[24] At that time the total market value of the common stock positions in the CREF portfolio was more than $111 billion.[25] Investments in most industry groups represent less than two percent of the total portfolio; however, six industry groups accounted for more than 5 percent each and three — Chemicals and Allied Products, Communications, and Depository Institutions — each accounted for more than 10 percent of the total value of the CREF portfolio. Of the total value of the stock account portfolio, most of the equity, 82 percent, was invested in U.S. companies while 18 percent was invested in the common stock of companies in 35 foreign countries. Of the portion of the portfolio

TABLE 1.3: World's Largest Retirement Funds

Rank	Fund	Country	$U.S. Millions
1	California Public Employees' Retirement System	U.S.	127,656[a]
2	Stichting Pensioenfonds ABP	Netherlands	114,324[b]
3	Association of Local Public Service Personnel	Japan	98,986[b]
4	New York State Common Retirement Fund	U.S.	95,812[a]
5	General Motors Investment Management Corp.	U.S.	90,600[a]
6	California State Teachers' Retirement System	U.S.	78,900[a]
7	Allmanna Pensionsfonden (Board 1,2,& 3)	Sweden	76,374[b]
8	National Public Service Personnel (National Government Employees Maa)	Japan	73,895[b]
9	Florida State Board of Administration	U.S.	71,940[a]
10	New York State Teachers' Retirement System	U.S.	68,738[a]
11	Public School Personnel (Public Schools Maa)	Japan	65,527[b]
12	Texas Teacher Retirement System	U.S.	64,221[a]
13	New Jersey Division of Investment	U.S.	59,933[a]
14	General Electric Co.	U.S.	56,915[a]
15	Federal Retirement Thrift Investment Board	U.S.	55,491[a]
16	New York City Retirement Systems	U.S.	54,712[a]
17	IBM Corp.	U.S.	53,122[a]
18	Wisconsin (State of) Investment Board	U.S.	50,051[a]
19	Lucent Technologies	U.S.	48,447[a]
20	Ford Motor Co.	U.S.	47,775[a]
		TOTAL	1,453,419

Source: *Pensions and Investments*, http://www.pionline.com/research/r100.shtml, November 29, 1998.

[a] As of September 30, 1997
[b] As of December 31, 1997

TABLE 1.4: TIAA-CREF Assets Under Management as of September 30, 1998
(in billions of dollars)

TIAA	
General Account[a]	98.63
Stock Index Separate Account	0.62
Real Estate Separate Account	1.05
Total TIAA[b]	100.31

CREF	
Stock Account	97.21
Money Market Account	5.59
Bond Market Account	2.68
Social Choice Account	2.76
Global Equities Account	5.13
Growth Account	5.62
Equity Index Account	2.68
Inflation-Linked Bond Account	0.13
Total CREF	121.80

TIAA-CREF Life	
Total	0.25

TIAA-CREF Mutual Funds	
Growth Equity	0.20
Growth & Income	0.17
International Equity	0.09
Bond Plus	0.13
Money Market	0.18
Managed Allocation	0.13
Total Mutual Funds[c]	0.77

TIAA-CREF Trust Company	
Total	0.07

Total Assets Under Management[d]	222.59

Source: TIAA-CREF web site, http://tiaa.org/assets.html, November 29, 1998.

Note: The sum of the individual accounts may not add up to the totals shown above due to various consolidations, eliminations, and other accounting adjustments.

[a] Estimated
[b] Total TIAA assets reflect statutory accounting adjustments for reporting Separate Account assets
[c] Total mutual fund assets are adjusted to avoid double counting of Managed Allocation Fund investments in other mutual funds
[d] Total assets under management is an estimate based on the estimated total for the TIAA General Account. Totals are adjusted to avoid double counting of: TIAA investments (if any) in CREF, TIAA-CREF Life, TIAA-CREF Mutual Funds and TIAA-CREF Trust Company; TIAA-CREF Trust Company's investments in TIAA-CREF Mutual Funds; and Managed Allocation Fund investments in the other mutual funds.

TABLE 1.5: Common Stock Holdings in CREF's Stock Account, by Industry Group, June 30, 1998

Industry Group	Value (000)	Percentage of Portfolio	Number of Issues
Agricultural production — crops	$ 56,324	0.05	6
Agricultural services	7,522	0.01	3
Amusement and recreation services	252,318	0.23	37
Apparel and accessory stores	531,868	0.48	34
Apparel and other textile products	275,174	0.25	41
Auto repair, services and parking	49,316	0.04	12
Automotive dealers and service stations	107,849	0.10	14
Building materials and garden supplies	572,578	0.52	24
Business services	5,472,672	4.92	370
Chemicals and allied products	13,322,615	11.99	279
Coal mining	7,434	0.01	4
Communications	11,423,115	10.28	165
Depository institutions	11,696,027	10.53	322
Eating and drinking places	686,916	0.62	49
Educational services	36,097	0.03	7
Electric, gas, and sanitary services	4,197,549	3.78	218
Electronic and other equipment	8,168,505	7.35	270
Engineering and management services	350,020	0.31	54
Fabricated metal products	1,263,794	1.14	58
Food and kindred products	5,369,315	4.83	177
Food stores	677,998	0.61	31
Forestry	2,828	0.00	4
Furniture and fixtures	94,467	0.09	13
Furniture and home furnishing	201,858	0.18	24
General building contractors	410,696	0.37	65
General merchandise stores	2,284,349	2.06	86
Health services	806,376	0.73	68
Heavy construction, except building	121,304	0.11	37
Holding and other investment offices	1,374,268	1.24	211
Hotels and other lodging places	321,384	0.29	51
Industrial machinery and equipment	6,179,395	5.56	266
Instruments and related products	2,452,135	2.21	146
Insurance agents, brokers, and service	403,589	0.36	21
Insurance carriers	4,997,800	4.50	166
Leather and leather products	65,501	0.06	8
Legal services	2,058	0.00	1
Local and interurban passenger transit	89,109	0.08	8
Lumber and wood products	332,222	0.30	34
Metal mining	298,397	0.27	72
Miscellaneous manufacturing industries	1,263,526	1.14	34
Miscellaneous retail	1,068,187	0.96	48
Motion pictures	589,538	0.53	11
Nondepository institutions	2,586,572	2.33	57
Nonmetallic minerals	72,079	0.06	7
Oil and gas extraction	4,093,475	3.68	133
Paper and allied products	867,845	0.78	71
Personal services	162,826	0.15	14

TABLE 1.5: *Continued*

Industry Group	Value (000)	Percentage of Portfolio	Number of Issues
Petroleum and coal products	$ 2,510,997	2.26	50
Pipelines, except natural gas	2,027	0.00	1
Primary metal industries	778,667	0.70	100
Printing and publishing	1,412,323	1.27	85
Railroad transportation	530,654	0.48	22
Real estate	303,742	0.27	74
Rubber and miscellaneous plastic products	858,944	0.77	35
Security and commodity brokers	1,328,075	1.20	48
Social services	3,220	0.00	3
Special trade contractors	18,014	0.02	9
Stone, clay, and glass products	463,206	0.42	39
Textile mill products	168,925	0.15	22
Tobacco products	939,365	0.85	15
Transportation by air	727,016	0.65	51
Transportation equipment	4,051,756	3.65	105
Transportation services	144,600	0.13	15
Trucking and warehousing	95,948	0.09	16
Water transportation	125,799	0.11	33
Wholesale trade — durable goods	210,894	0.19	60
Wholesale trade — nondurable goods	781,679	0.70	55
TOTALS	111,122,641	100.00	4,669

Source: *College Retirement Equities Fund Stock Account Financial Statements (Unaudited) Including Statement of Investments, June 30, 1998.*

invested abroad, the largest foreign investments were in the United Kingdom (21 percent), Japan (17 percent), Germany (10 percent), France (9.6 percent), and Switzerland (7.4 percent) (Table 1.6).

Clearly, the CREF Stock Account represents a broad cross section of the industrial and financial wealth in the world. While not exactly a passive index fund in the pure sense, the fund compares its performance to a weighted average of two broad-based market indexes: the Russell 3000, representing the entire U.S. stock market and the Morgan Stanley EAFE and Canada Index, representing foreign stock markets. Thus, as for any universal owner, the performance of the CREF Stock Account depends crucially on the macroeconomic performance of the economies in which it is invested. This dependence is recognized in the discussion of the account's performance in the TIAA-CREF annual report: "The Stock Account's double-digit performance [26.36 percent in 1997] was primarily the result of the strong showing of the U.S. stock market and the European market. Like similar funds, the Stock Account was negatively impacted by the weak performance of many Asian markets during the second half of the year" (p. 20).

TABLE 1.6: Largest Foreign Positions in CREF's Stock Account, June 30, 1998

	Investments in U.S. Dollars (000)	Percentage of Total Portfolio	Percentage of Foreign Common Stock Investments
United Kingdom	4,109,777	3.69	20.78
Japan	3,435,002	3.08	17.37
Germany	2,051,396	1.84	10.37
France	1,892,628	1.70	9.57
Switzerland	1,454,602	1.31	7.36
Italy	1,346,656	1.21	6.81
Netherlands	1,308,282	1.17	6.62
TOTAL	15,598,343	14.01	78.87

Source: *College Retirement Equities Fund Stock Account Financial Statements (Unaudited) Including Statement of Investments, June 30, 1998.*

Fiduciary Ownership of Large Corporations

Not only do universal owners act as professional owners of a very large amount of wealth in absolute terms, but also, as a group, they tend to invest in the same large, liquidity-traded companies.[26] Furthermore, their investments in these companies have tended to increase over time as the institutions themselves have grown in size. In 1985, institutional investors as a group owned on average 36.1 percent of the largest twenty-five U.S. corporations (Table 1.7). By 1997, their share in the twenty-five largest corporations had grown to 48.7 percent.

Institutional ownership varies substantially from one company to another. Table 1.8 shows the fraction of equity held by all institutions and by the top twenty-five institutions at the end of 1997. For all institutions, ownership ranges from a low of 15.7 percent at Berkshire Hathaway to a high of 64.8 percent at Cisco Systems. At three companies, institutional ownership exceeded 60 percent of the equity of the company. At ten companies, it exceeded 50 percent of the equity.

The top twenty-five institutions also control the smallest fraction of stock at Berkshire-Hathaway, 13.5 percent, but their largest position is at Eli Lilly, where they own almost half of the equity. By themselves, this group of twenty-five universal owners controlled more than 30 percent of the equity at eight of the largest twenty-five corporations in the United States.

Table 1.9 displays the largest twenty-five owners of General Electric, the largest company in Table 1.8. The distribution of ownership in this company closely parallels the overall institutional ownership of the twenty-five largest companies. While no institution owns more than 3.5 percent of the common stock of General Electric, the largest ten owners control 16.2 percent of the stock. While not a majority block, it would certainly be considered a controlling block if owned by a single individual or institution.

TABLE 1.7: Concentration of Institutional Investor Holdings by the Largest 25 Institutions in the Largest 25 U.S. Corporations, 1985, 1990, mid-1995, and 1997

	1985		1990		mid-1995		1997	
	Average % Held	% of All Institutional Shares	Average % Held	% of All Institutional Shares	Average % Held	% of All Institutional Shares	Average % Held	% of All Institutional Shares
All institutions	36.1	100.0	45.3	100.0	48.6	100.0	48.7%	100.0%
Top 5 institutions	8.5	23.5	10.6	23.4	10.8	22.2	12.8%	26.3%
Top 10 institutions	12.6	34.9	15.1	33.3	15.1	31.1	18.8%	38.6%
Top 20 institutions	17.9	49.7	20.8	45.9	22.3	45.9	25.7%	52.8%
Top 25 institutions	19.8	54.8	22.9	50.6	24.5	50.4	28.0%	57.5%

Source: *Institutional Investment Report; Patterns of Institutional Investment and Control in the United States*, The Conference Board, 2, no. 2, August 1998, table 19, p. 37.

Note: Data for 1985, 1990, and 1997 are as of December 31; data for 1995 are as of August 1.

TABLE 1.8: Equity Ownership of the Largest 25 Corporations

Rank	Corporation	% of Total Shares Held by All Institutions	% of Total Shares Held by Top 25 Institutions
1	General Electric Co.	48.8	25.4
2	Microsoft Corp.	35.1	20.1
3	Coca-Cola Co.	49.3	34.4
4	Exxon Corp.	41.7	23.3
5	Merck & Co.	52.8	27.3
6	Pfizer Inc.	56.3	29.3
7	Wal-Mart Stores	37.1	23.8
8	Intel Corp.	46.9	23.4
9	Procter & Gamble Co.	46.4	25.2
10	IBM Corp.	49.3	25.6
11	Bristol-Myers Squibb	57.4	30.9
12	AT&T Corp.	45.7	30.0
13	Lucent Technologies Inc.	39.9	22.6
14	Johnson & Johnson	54.5	28.7
15	Philip Morris Cos. Inc.	59.9	33.7
16	Berkshire Hathaway—CLA	15.7	13.5
17	E. I. Du Pont De Nemours	55.6	33.3
18	American International Group	54.6	28.0
19	Cisco Systems Inc.	64.8	36.6
20	Walt Disney Company	49.3	27.7
21	NationsBank Corp	49.7	29.2
22	SBC Communications Inc.	43.6	25.0
23	Bell Atlantic Corp.	39.0	22.2
24	Travelers Group Inc.	63.9	37.5
25	Eli Lilly & Co.	61.3	43.5
	Average Ownership	48.7	28.0

Source: *Institutional Investment Report; Patterns of Institutional Investment and Control in the United States*, The Conference Board, 2, no. 2, August 1998, table 20, p. 38.

Implications

The fact that 16 percent of the stock of General Electric is split among ten institutions makes the monitoring problem of any one institution more difficult. Nevertheless, coordination among ten or so institutional investors is possible, and in specific cases has been done. However, the sheer magnitude of the individual positions is likely to concentrate the minds of the owners on the performance of the company. For example, Fidelity Investments' 3.5 percent stake in GE represented about $8.4 billion at the end of 1997. The top ten owners of GE had a combined investment in the company amounting to about $39 billion, while the combined positions of the twenty-five largest owners came to somewhat more that $60 billion. At these levels of investment, an increase in the price of a share of GE stock of a single

TABLE 1.9: Institutional Ownership at General Electric as of December 1997

Rank	Manager	Percentage Held
1	Fidelity Investments	3.5
2	Barclays Global Investors, N.A.	2.9
3	Bankers Trust Company (New York)	1.8
4	State Street Corporation	1.6
5	Mellon Bank Corporation	1.3
6	College Retirement Equities Fund	1.2
7	Vanguard Group, Inc.	1.1
8	General Electric Investment Corp.	1.0
9	Putnam Investment Management, Inc.	0.9
10	Fayez Sarofim & Co.	0.9
11	Wells Fargo & Company	0.8
12	Northern Trust Corporation	0.8
13	Travelers Group Inc.	0.7
14	Equitable Companies, Inc.	0.7
15	Chase Manhattan Corporation	0.6
16	NationsBank Corporation	0.6
17	PNC Bank Corporation	0.6
18	American Express Financial Corp.	0.6
19	Wellington Management Company, LLP	0.6
20	First Security Corporation	0.5
21	First Union Corporation	0.5
22	California Public Employees' Retirement System	0.5
23	Fleet Financial Group	0.5
24	American Century Investments	0.5
25	United States Trust Company (New York)	0.5
	Total Held by All Institutions	48.8
	Top 5	11.1
	Top 10	16.2
	Top 20	22.9
	Top 25	25.4

Source: *Institutional Investment Report; Patterns of Institutional Investment and Control in the United States*, The Conference Board, 2, no. 2, August 1998, table 21A, p. 39.

Note: Percentages may not add to totals because of rounding.

dollar for a stock priced at about $73 at the time would add over $800 million to the wealth of these twenty-five institutional owners. Likewise, a dollar's decline clips almost a billion dollars off the value of their collective portfolios.

It is little wonder that universal owners are seriously concerned about the performance of the individual firms in their portfolios — the GEs. And that they should be mindful of the impact of macroeconomic issues — particularly, sound fiscal and monetary policy, sensible and effective environmental regulations, and educational and other policies that enhance the long-term economic growth of the economy — on the performance of the economy at large. Effective policies translate directly into higher economic growth and higher economic growth means greater wealth accumulation for the owners of equity. Not only should these institutions be concerned with the performance of the U.S. economy, but they should also be concerned with the performance of the world economy since about 20 percent of the assets of these universal owners are invested in companies outside the United States. Through this wealth creation, the professional "owners" in U.S. fiduciary institutions accumulate the resources necessary to discharge their obligations to approximately one-half of Americans who are in one way or another their beneficiaries.

Ownership has been concentrated in the hands of financial institutions at other times and other places. Notable is the role played by financial institutions in the City of London in the nineteenth and twentieth centuries and by the German banks since World War II. The possibility of creating a "financial Leviathan" is always present, but the situation with institutional investors in the United States at the end of the twentieth century is a bit different. First, these institutions have become universal investors holding portfolios that reflect a broad cross section of the economy. When, in the case of pension funds, especially the noncorporate ones, this is coupled with their fiduciary duty to their beneficiaries to provide benefits over very long time horizons, the result has the potential to be quite different. U.S. fiduciary institutions are not identified with a small set of firms or industries as the individual German banks are, and they aren't primarily suppliers of private capital as the City of London was. However, the current situation in the City is that institutional ownership is highly concentrated, but activism is muted because of an "old boy" culture that far too often substitutes affinity relationships for the actions of "professional" investors.

Fiduciary Duty and the Professionalization of Ownership

Behind the obligations of the professional managers who run these fiduciary institutions (public funds, mutual funds, and bank trust departments and the like) is the common law notion of "fiduciary duty." This duty is codified in the Employees Retirement Income Security Act of 1974 (ERISA). ERISA rules and regulations apply directly to private pension funds. However, most state-run public funds have adopted ERISA standards as their fiduciary guidelines, and in many cases ERISA rules are stipulated by state law or in state constitutions.[27] Consequently, the standards are broadly followed by most public pension plans. In its simplest form a fiduciary is an individual or institution with the legal responsibility to manage economic assets on behalf of one or more beneficiaries. An example would be a bank trust department that manages an inheritance for a minor child.

The concepts of "duty of loyalty" and "duty of care" are central to the notion of fiduciary duty.[28] Duty of loyalty places on the fiduciary the responsibility to act solely in the interests of the beneficiary. This is often expressed as the "exclusive benefit rule," wherein all actions of the fiduciary are judged by the criterion that the action be taken for the exclusive benefit of the beneficiary. Duty of care requires that the fiduciary discharge his or her duty in the manner of a "prudent investor." In pension fund management the prudent investor rule has evolved from choosing investments from an approved list (often limited to aaa-rated bonds) to a modern portfolio theory approach where duty of care is determined by the policies and procedures (due diligence, and so on) that are used to construct a portfolio.

Fiduciaries are "owners" because they exercise almost all of the rights and privileges of ownership. Most fundamentally, they make the investment decision to buy or sell assets. Since the U.S. Department of Labor's famous Avon letter in 1988, ERISA institutions also have had a positive obligation to vote proxies because issues put to a shareholder vote may have a significant impact on the value of assets in their portfolio.[29] The duty of care requires fiduciary owners to exercise their proxy rights. The obligation can be discharged directly by the fund or by adopting a policy with regard to proxy issues and then delegating the responsibility for actually voting the proxies to their money managers. In 1994, this obligation was extended to the overseas holdings of U.S. institutions.

Fiduciaries themselves can make proxy proposals, file suit against companies as owners, and, as some activist institutional investors have done, identify and lobby for change at underperforming companies or companies with particularly egregious corporate governance structures. What sets a fiduciary owner apart from individual owners is that the fiduciary does not have a claim on the stream of returns generated by the investments. Those returns are the exclusive right and are to accrue to the exclusive benefit of the beneficiaries.[30]

As noted above, about 50 percent of the equity of U.S. corporations is owned by fiduciary institutions. In the exercise of their fiduciary duty these institutions have become professional owners in much the same way that firm managers have become professionalized over the last forty or more years. A law degree and/or an MBA with a specialization in finance is an educational qualification for many of the chief investment officers, general counsels, and heads of fiduciary institutions. Professional conduct is governed by rules articulated by codes of good practice, by the rules of individual institutions, by state law, and by ERISA. Furthermore, an entire industry has grown up to help institutions discharge their proxy obligations. Organizations such as the Investor Responsibility Research Center (IRRC) and Institutional Shareholder Services (ISS) provide institutional investors with detailed analyses of proxy proposals and, if they wish, voting recommendations consistent with the guidelines of a particular institution. The Council of Institutional Investors (CII) tracks corporate governance developments and, among other functions, provides a forum for institutional investors to meet, explore, and discuss issues of mutual concern. Currently, the CII has more than one hundred members with combined assets of well more than a trillion dollars.

The frontiers of professional ownership and potentially the definition of the duty of care itself were given a broad interpretation by CalPERS in December 1997. At that time staff announced that its board was considering a policy that "urges trustees to cautiously consider taking public-company board seats when the fund owns enough shares to be seen as a 'controlling shareholder.' "[31] While the policy proposal was ultimately rejected, the proposal itself was a reflection of the professionalization of ownership and the logical result of the ever-growing fraction of the equity owned by fiduciary institutions in general and the large stakes some individual institutions are accumulating in some companies.

Had the proposal actually been carried out, a board seat would certainly have presented some problems since it would have automatically conferred insider status on CalPERS. Thus, the fund would have had to carefully weight the benefits of board representation against the costs—which may include restrictions on their ability to buy and sell the company's stock. However, such a restriction may not be a serious obstacle for an institution like CalPERS that is highly indexed and thus does not follow a trading strategy for most of its assets. With insider information potential antitrust issues may be raised as well since CalPERS owns most major competitors in any given industry group. How, for instance, might it deal with a crisis at a firm that directly competes with another firm on whose board it sits?

What most clearly characterize the professional owners' approach to their responsibilities are the two duties—care and loyalty—mentioned above. Traditionally, these twin duties have tended to tightly focus fiduciaries on the economic performance of their investments. Or, as it was put in an interview with an official of the Minnesota Investment Board, "It's our fiduciary duty to make money for the owners. Period."[32] Board membership may prove to be an effective way to promote these goals, but it must also be reconciled with the concern a universal owner has for the overall performance of its portfolio and not just for the success or failure of any individual investment.

The duty of care is not a historical constant either in law or in fiduciary practice, for it has evolved, albeit slowly, over time. Recent U.S. examples include the already mentioned 1988 Avon letter and the recent mandate to vote overseas proxies. A complete or what might be called a holistic portfolio analysis (for the moment, regardless of what an institution may do with its results) may well be the next logical step in fiduciary duty if it can arguably increase long-term return. Such an analysis would take into account not only return on investment and analysis of firm performance (using a variety of indicators, e.g., stock price, economic value added, benchmarking), but also both positive and negative externalities produced by the firms in its portfolio. On the basis of such an accounting, a cost-benefit analysis could be undertaken, much as CalPERS has done for its own investor activism.[33] For universal owners such an analysis should be seen as part of the duty of care, the first step of which must be information and knowledge. If one must vote, one must be informed. To not undertake a holistic portfolio analysis represents a potentially very large opportunity cost for each universal owner individually and potentially for the whole economy, thus restricting the scope and meaning of duty of care.[34]

Universal Ownership and the Wider Economy

The fundamental characteristic of a universal owner is that it cares not only about the governance and performance of the individual companies that comprise its investment portfolio, but that it cares about the performance of the economy as a whole. Simply put, the universal owner's concern with overall economic performance is the recognition that it "owns" the economy (typically, a highly representative sample of the economy) and, therefore, bears the costs of any shortfall in economic efficiency and reaps the rewards of any improvement.

As has been suggested in the case of CREF, the quintessential universal owners are the largest of the public and private pension funds because they have amassed investment portfolios that naturally comprise a broad cross section of the financial assets available for investment and their objective — to provide pensions — naturally gives them a long-term perspective toward wealth maximization. As a result these fiduciary institutions have a strong incentive to consider economy-wide economic performance when seeking to improve the returns they receive on their investments. If size and/or an indexing strategy prevent them from trading in and out of the market, they must look beyond liquidating a position as a way to meet their obligations.[35] If they cannot sell, they must care.

Indeed, since the mid-1980s, institutional investors have been doing exactly that.[36] Their first and most sustained foray into active ownership has been to direct their attention to traditional corporate governance issues such as poison pills and split voting rights in an attempt to eliminate impediments to the market for corporate control. They also viewed these policies as an attack on the rights and abilities of owners (themselves, as professional representatives of the ultimate beneficiaries) to hold management accountable. By and large, these attacks were directed at individual companies in individual situations, but the general message was clear. The fiduciary institutions were going to protect their rights as owners. Not to do so would be a failure of their duty of care, as came to be recognized and mandated in the Avon letter.

Unfortunately, while good governance campaigns made sense in the abstract, some institutions, notably CalPERS, quickly encountered the problem that most owners were only concerned with the economic performance of their investments and had, at best, a mild interest in the way portfolio companies were governed. Their interest was particularly mild in the case of firms whose market performance was judged to be adequate (or even better than adequate). Also, by the late 1980s, antitakeover statutes and the collapse of the junk bond market had largely put an end to the market for corporate control and the discipline of underperforming management that it provided. As a response, CalPERS, United Shareholders Association (USA), the Council of Institutional Investors (CII), and other shareholder rights groups began to target companies because of their poor economic performance. The same corporate governance issues — augmented with calls to separate the positions of chairman of the board and the chief executive officer and for other boardroom reforms, notably increasing the number of independent directors — were used as points of leverage. However, everyone involved knew that the issue of concern was economic performance, not board room reform. The raw power of institutional investors reached a high water mark when in a short period in the early 1990s the chief executive officers of a number of household-name firms such as General Motors, Westinghouse, and American Express were replaced with the help of institutional pressure.[37]

The activist institutions quickly realized that making an example of a few, select companies would also get the attention of other companies — and that there would be a positive spillover to nontargeted companies in the form of a renewed focus on providing value to the shareholders. For example, CalPERS was clearly aware that by virtue of their status as the owner of a broad cross section of the economy — as a universal owner — they would capture those benefits as well as any benefits generated at targeted firms. As the result of its focused activities at selected companies, the system has also gained the attention of other companies regarding common issues in a peer group and concepts of corporate governance in a general sense. Taking advantage of this phenomenon, CalPERS seeks to "move the herd" rather than follow it, while still retaining the risk-reward reliability of an indexed portfolio.[38]

While there is still a great deal to be done in traditional areas, the time has come for institutional investors to explicitly recognize that economy-wide, macroeconomic issues heavily influence the returns they will earn on their investments. As the above quotation illustrates, some institutional investors already recognize in a general way the impact that broad issues in the economy can have on their portfolio return. This is the beginning of universal owner "consciousness," but there have only been a few tentative steps working out the implications of this for their role as a universal owner. An examination of several specific areas will illustrate the types of issues that universal owners might find fruitful areas of attention.

The Environment

In standard economic theory negative externalities lower the cost of the firm generating the externality by imposing those costs on other firms and on citizens at large. Because of their ownership of the economy as a whole, universal owners end up bearing those costs both as owners of other firms, and in the case of public funds, as involved third parties linked to the tax base. Since the costs are generally larger than the benefits that accrue to the company causing the externality, universal owners experience an overall net loss. Consequently, a universal owner's portfolio returns would be directly enhanced by a proper treatment of the externality in the first place.

Some institutional investors are acutely aware that environmental issues are important economic considerations. For example, Kim Johnson, General Counsel for the Colorado Public Employee Retirement Association (PERA) reports, "You bet that we look at environmental issues very, very closely. We know that aside from the ideal that it is socially desirable to have a healthy and long term stable environment there are also some good economic reasons for our actions. We have suffered the consequences of holding property with environmental problems so we know the costs first hand. But I also think our trustees are aware that in a macro sense this is a good thing to do."[39] The State of Wisconsin Investment Board also considers these issues explicitly. The board's general counsel, Kurt Schaht, says: "We have a rather lengthy discussion of social responsibility issues in our proxy voting guidelines. If something in a company's product or service is inherently bad for the environment or social well-being of the U.S. that is taken into account in the economic analysis because those products or services are going to become less attractive, less competitive over time."[40]

A variation on the textbook example occurred when CalPERS weighed in on the controversy surrounding the Maxxam Corporation and the headwaters forest controversy.[41] CalPERS owned a substantial stake in Maxxam and was deeply interested in the economic implications of any settlement that Maxxam might make. Negative publicity and a disregard for the concerns of an important, organized, and potentially powerful group were economic issues for CalPERS, which considered this a contingent liability.[42] In a similar vein the Colorado PERA focused on what they considered to be the narrow corporate governance issue of how well Maxxam's management was handling this issue.[43] In this way the narrow economic performance of a company merged with the impact of the company's actions on the economy as a whole.

Education and Training

The quality of the skills and education of a labor force are widely recognized as crucial to the long-run economic growth of a country. It has also long been recognized that a company will tend to underinvest in the education and training of its work force because it can't capture all of the benefits that training provides.[44] However, a universal owner *does* capture those benefits because it captures the benefit of enhanced education and training to the economy at large. These returns are likely to be quite substantial since researchers have estimated that the social returns to education are from 1.6 to 1.7 times larger than the private returns.[45] CalPERS and the combined New York City Funds recognize this through their "High Performance Workplace" programs. CalPERS has a "workplace" screen in which it surveys companies about their human resource policies and publishes the results. New York and CalPERS issued studies on workplace practices and economic performance.[46]

In this area, as in many others, the question arises as to whether the policy should be pursued by individual firms or by the society at large. In fact, both avenues are appropriate and universal owners should be concerned with both general educational policy as well as with the human capital investments made by individual portfolio companies.

Research and Development

A telling example of the divergence between firm-specific self-interest and the investment of a universal owner can be drawn from the high tech industry. Research and development activities in this industry are crucial to its success. But some firms might be tempted to underinvest because they cannot capture all of the returns, as the following story told by Gordon Moore, one of the founders of the Intel Corporation, illustrates.

Before forming Intel, Moore and Robert Noyce, the company's other co-founder, started Fairchild Semiconductor. The research and development department at Fairchild was quite successful at identifying a large number of important technical advances, but the company lacked the ability to commercialize many of these discoveries. As a result, Moore reports that numerous ideas that had been developed at Fairchild actually ended up benefiting their competitors. When it came time to found Intel a conscious decision was made by Moore and Noyce to not have a permanent research and development department. Rather, technical teams would be assembled on a project-by-project basis and disbanded when the project was completed. This was an explicit attempt to avoid the spillover benefits that Fairchild had contributed to other companies (and, of course, to the economy as a whole) and to better capture for Intel the benefits of its research and development expenditures.[47]

A universal owner should prefer a Fairchild model to an Intel model since it would almost certainly capture the benefits of any technical advances regardless of the particular company that commercialized the discovery. In any case, while it may not be in the interest of any one company to push forward the frontiers of knowledge unless it can capture a substantial portion of the benefit, it is certainly in the interest of a universal owner — and of society as a whole — to do so. Universal owners may do this either by encouraging individual companies in their research and development efforts, by supporting industry-wide research and development consortiums, or through their political support for publicly funded basic research.

Tobacco

The recent tobacco controversy both highlights the relatively narrow lens through which fiduciary responsibility is currently viewed, and reveals some limited awareness of problems confronted by universal owners. Funds have taken different approaches to this issue, yet all have struggled with the problem of how the macroeconomic effects of smoking (increased healthcare costs and reduced productivity from sickness and premature death) might affect the economy as a whole. In addition, a number of funds provide health care for their retirees and, therefore, have had to face the disquieting possibility that superior returns from tobacco stocks were being directly offset by rising health-care costs. These particular funds faced an expanded form of universal owner responsibility.

President Clinton's September 1997 rejection of the proposed tobacco settlement led to new calls for pension funds to divest tobacco stocks. For example, within one week of the president's rejection, a bill requiring the Massachusetts Pension Reserves Investment Management Board to divest was expected to pass the state senate with the support of the chief administrator of the pension. Similar pressure built in the California assembly while in Pennsylvania, State Treasurer Barbara Hafer sought reconsideration of the tobacco divestment issue.[48] However, to date, divestment of tobacco stocks has made little headway and ultimately no divestment by any public pension fund occurred.

In the spring of 1997, CalPERS officials met with the chair and CEO of Philip Morris to assure him they were not considering selling the company's stock. CalPERS' official position is that smoking is bad for the health of its beneficiaries and, as a provider of health care to its beneficiaries, it has for years has run an aggressive antismoking campaign on the "service" side of their operations. However, on the "fiduciary" side, they see Philip Morris as a good investment, and do not intend to sell nor, in the words of the president of CalPERS, William Crist, "to respond to social pressure."[49]

CalPERS constructs what its general counsel calls a "super fiduciary firewall" between the two sides of its operation and it took both a private and publicly active anti-Joe Camel role in the advertising controversy in 1997.[50] Crist argued this was a "very specific thing, a political risk. It had the real possibility of damaging the value of the asset by hurting the profitability of the company."[51] In theory he agrees that there is a cost to the economy and to their overall portfolio from smoking, but no one knows how to calculate it to their satisfaction. Meanwhile, the investment in tobacco stock has been highly profitable. Similarly, the State of Minnesota's Investment Board voted 2-2, effectively defeating the Secretary of State Joan A. Gowe's proposed freeze on new tobacco stock purchases. She had argued that tobacco stock prices did not accurately capture the economic risk.[52] Nevertheless, the board told its money managers to purchase no more tobacco stock in that part of its portfolio that is actively managed unless it first notified the board and then justified its new purchases.[53]

A similar position was adopted by the New York State Combined Fund. The fund is 75 percent indexed and 25 percent actively managed. Carl McCall, sole fund trustee, announced three actions:

1. The fund would maintain its indexed holdings on the basis that to take tobacco out of the index would destroy the index, and potentially open the door to other exceptions.
2. The fund would instruct its active managers that they could hold what they had, but not buy more tobacco stock. This was defended on the basis that tobacco was highly volatile and the fund did not want to increase its exposure.
3. They would exercise their rights as professional owners and become a more active shareholder. That meant that in 1996, according to Linda Scott, Director for Investment Affairs, "we put forward shareholder resolutions in the four companies we held; two were appealed to S.E.C. and got no action letters and two were kept on the ballot. The resolution called for complying with F.D.A. advertising regulations."[54]

Jon Lukomnik, former deputy comptroller for pensions of the City of New York, reflected on the issue when he said:

The easy answer is that [tobacco] is a social issue, we're here for the exclusive benefit of the beneficiaries, etc. But this misses the real world. In the real world tobacco is a highly political issue. It has major [national and international] political risk as an investment, whether they are seen as legitimate or not. It is very hard to quantify. If we do [political risk analysis on] tobacco we will be accused of having a political agenda. If Fidelity does risk analysis it is seen just as a prudent risk analysis. In the case of divesting from South Africa was "political" but when Goldman Sachs did a risk analysis it was country risk. The answer is that one needs some judgement. It is a very uncomfortable issue to have to look at everything outside the [dominant paradigmatic] box, and is not doable. If you start doing it all [looking at all the issues], the problem is how to prioritize and what is the appropriate level of response. This is very difficult. Pension funds have limits . . . but we cannot and should not run the world . . . there is government, the private sector, charities, etc. How far you go down the slope is a question of judgment.[55]

It is noteworthy that when portfolio-wide universal owner issues arose (most clearly in New York City's and CalPERS' discussions), it was felt that there was a lack of hard data equivalent to financial data, which might justify stronger actions. Stronger action need not mean divestment, but rather active lobbying of firms for particular goals, e.g., the nature of settlement of legal suits and long-term plans to spin-off tobacco units.

Other Examples

A number of other areas should be of concern to universal owners, some of which have received varying degrees of attention. These areas include reducing barriers to international trade, leveling the playing field on health and safety regulations, and the revelation of contingent liabilities through transparency of accounting information and other measures of corporate practice and performance.[56] Areas particularly mentioned in interviews were health care (e.g., Columbia/HCA, Oxford, and the general state of managed care), discrimination, and diversity.[57]

To expand on the first example, it has long been understood that a reduction in protective tariffs and quotas and other barriers to the free flow of goods and services between countries is in the economic interest of the economy as a whole. At the same time, it is also well understood that barriers can confer substantial economic benefits on the individual companies receiving the protection. However, the benefits to individual companies are usually a fraction of the costs imposed on the society as a whole. A universal owner would be able to capture the increased benefits due to freer trade policy even if some individual companies in the institution's portfolio were harmed in the process. Particular concern for the employment impact on communities could be addressed through a variety of innovative projects that some state plans have pursued in other areas, such as so-called economically targeted investments (ETI), and through active campaigning for effective economic development and adjustment programs.[58]

In the health-care arena, CalPERS, while not a contractor with Columbia/HCA on the serviced side of its operation, joined in the New York State Fund's shareholder suit against the company. They did this for the narrow reason of protecting their investment in the company, but also, in Crist's words, because, "we have a responsibility for the credibility of the industry [as a whole]."[59] Considering the "credibility of the industry" is the type of analysis one would expect from a universal owner with stakes in most publicly traded companies in the industry. It is a small step to considering the broader impact of certain company-specific actions on the economy as a whole — and, through the economy, on the overall return on the universal owner's portfolio.

Another important area of concern to fiduciary investors is information transparency and, in particular, contingent liabilities. Examples include an environmental liability or action, a pending legal action, or anything else that might affect the economic performance of a company in the future. These liabilities are contingent because the magnitude of the liability depends on the outcome of some uncertain future event such as a lawsuit. Jon Lukomnik, the former deputy comptroller of the New York City Combined Pension Funds noted that funds "are particularly interested in disclosure issues in these examples (environmental liabilities, discrimination, suits, etc.) and others on the assumption that if you can get management to focus on these issues it will have a long term effect that is positive."[60] Universal owners have a general interest in receiving timely, complete, and relevant information from their portfolio companies because the outcome can have a marked impact on performance over the long run.

Conclusions

The universal owner will recognize that certain public policy issues — health care and the health effects of certain products such as tobacco, education, training, basic research and development efforts, and perhaps even monetary, fiscal, and international trade policy — may have impacts on its portfolio that are more important than the impact of a corporate governance issue at a particular firm. Consequently, the universal owner should examine these issues and, when appropriate, formulate polices and take actions in support of positions promoting the highest overall return to its portfolio. This may well involve accepting lower returns at some portfolio companies, at least in the short and medium term. This might occur, for example, if a portfolio company was forced to internalize a negative externality such as environmentally damaging processes or products. However, the general economic benefit captured as lower costs at other portfolio companies should more than offset the reduction in returns at the former company. These universal investor concerns overlap with the broad interest in good corporate governance, accounting transparency, and other issues that have traditionally occupied the attention of institutional investors.

Universal owners also need to be conscious of the fact that in many cases the welfare of their beneficiaries depends on both the narrow economic return that an institution earns on its investment portfolio and on the quality of life that can be enjoyed by their beneficiaries with that return. That is, that beneficiaries for whose benefit the institutions exist have both stockholder and stakeholder interests in the decisions that universal owners make. In certain cases, this dual perspective makes it appropriate that institutions consider and act upon difficult trade-offs between social issues and more traditionally conceived economic issues. For example, the current high level of concern about the health effects of smoking in the United States brings this type of universal investor issue into sharp focus and has forced many institutional investors to explicitly consider the stakeholder implications of their investments in tobacco stocks on their beneficiaries. Regardless of the outcome, the fact that institutions are considering both the narrow effect on portfolio performance and the possible effects of legal liability on those companies and health effects on beneficiaries, reflects a universal owner's concern with the broader implications of ownership.

In short, universal owners, by virtue of the fact that they are coming to control large blocks of equity, are being forced to consider issues that can be seen as quasi-public policy in nature. They have an inescapable responsibility to discharge that responsibility. However, as always, when acting as universal owners these institutions are bound by their twin fiduciary duties of loyalty and care. Institutions must make a clear distinction between purely "social issues" and issues that affect the *economic* return on a portfolio investment, in spite of the fact that sometimes this is a quite difficult judgement call. As, for example, when concerns about contingent liability arise from what are initially seen as purely "social" issues. Despite the statement quoted earlier that universal owners have "a breadth of concern that naturally aligns with the public interest," universal owners must also focus on their obligation to their beneficiaries and take only those actions that are wealth enhancing. It has been argued here that these actions extend beyond a narrow conception that limits fiduciaries to traditional "corporate governance" issues and that without considering broader, wealth-enhancing, macroeconomic issues these professional owners will be *failing* in their duties of loyalty and care. William Crist, president of CalPERS' board of administration, captured what may be the first steps on the part of some universal owners toward this understanding when he said, "We are cognizant of a deep fiduciary responsibility on both a firm-by-firm and portfolio-wide basis. We have been focused mostly on the former, but the very nature of indexing may drive us towards portfolio-wide fiduciary concern as well."[61]

Chapter 2
Proxy Voting

Among the most important rights of equity ownership are the rights to submit proposals to be included with a company's proxy statement, to vote on proxy proposals, and to vote for or against individuals nominated to the board of directors. Informed proxy voting requires prior monitoring of the firm, which can be costly in time and money. The act of voting for or against a proxy proposal, and the quite expensive undertaking of initiating a proxy, is an attempt to influence the behavior and attitude of incumbent management, and therefore has been recognized in the United States and elsewhere as an asset. Since 1988, the U.S. Department of Labor, in addition to some state laws, recognized that informed proxy voting adds to the value of shareholding, and therefore mandates that proxies be voted.

The right to submit proxy proposals, to vote on them, and to vote for board of director nominees are typically exercised prior to and at the company's annual meeting and provide owners with a formal opportunity to influence management. They are in addition to the opportunities owners have to directly approach management or to conduct other activities such as the "targeting" of companies that CalPERS and the Council of Institutional Investors have used to attempt to influence management at underperforming portfolio companies. Recently, in addition to submitting proxies, some institutions have begun to submit amendments to the corporation's bylaws.[1] The important distinction is that bylaw amendments are binding changes in the constitution of a corporation while proxies are only advisory.

Evaluating proxy proposals written in dense, legalistic prose and developing consistent policies with respect to a number of issues can be a difficult, time-consuming process. It comes as no surprise that the typical individual common stock owner does not have the time, expertise, or inclination to intelligently vote the proxies on the equity he or she owns. This apathy is rational given the tiny fraction of equity held by the typical individual, and, therefore, the insignificant influence voting 100, 500, or 1,000 shares of stock might have on any issue.[2]

Voting proxies for an institutional investor with more than a thousand different companies in its portfolio would seem an impossible task, except for three mitigating factors. First, the payoff to achieving a favorable outcome is directly proportional to the size of an investor's position. An individual holding 100 shares of Archer Daniels Midland may not find it worthwhile to read a proxy statement carefully and to analyze its possible impact on the worth of the firm. However, an institutional investor such as the College Retirement Equities Fund, which at the end of 1997 owned almost 6 million shares of the company, may find it very much in its interest to vote its considerable position in favor of wealth-enhancing proposals and against wealth-destroying ones. Second, there are economies of scale in voting proxies since similar issues — poison pills, classified boards, and so on — often appear at many different companies over a period of several years. This spreads the expense of the original analysis over a number of different decisions. Finally, part of the duty of a fiduciary is to intelligently vote proxies because the outcome of proxy contests can directly affect the value of the assets of the institution. Not only is this part of the duty of loyalty and duty of care that bind fiduciaries, but the Department of Labor in its Avon Letter has explicitly instructed ERISA funds to consider proxies as plan assets, thus placing the funds under a positive injunction to vote their proxies in accordance with the duty of care.[3]

To help professional investors discharge their proxy obligations, an industry has grown up to supply the information needed to identify proposals that may impact the value of specific companies and to identify the appropriate way to vote in each case. Two of the largest proxy advisory services are the previously mentioned Institutional Shareholder Services (ISS) and the Investor Responsibility Research Center (IRRC). Proxy advisors track issues, analyze proposals for their impact on shareholder value, and issue alerts and suggestions. The recommendations of proxy advisory services are very important. Black reports that "Between the shares that ISS votes on behalf of clients, and the shares held by institutions who follow ISS's recommendations, an ISS recommendation can make a 15–20 percent difference in the support that a shareholder proposal receives."[4] As the quotation indicates, if the institution wishes, the services will help with the development of proxy-voting guidelines and, if desired, execute the proxy-voting program as an agent for the institution. Even the largest institutional investors who have sufficient resources to do their own analysis typically subscribe to one or more of the professional proxy advisory services as a source of additional information.

While ERISA rules only apply to private pension funds, they have had a general influence on public pension fund policies, particularly when they defined proxies as plan assets. For example, the State of Wisconsin Investment Board (SWIB) states, "As a fiduciary to plan beneficiaries, SWIB and its staff treat each of its proxy votes as another asset of the fund. Each proxy issue is reviewed and analyzed in accordance with the following guidelines and with the votes then being cast in an efficient and timely manner."[5]

Likewise, in a cover memorandum to its 1997–98 proxy voting report submitted to its investment committee, CalPERS, after considering the results and costs of the program, states that "The cost/benefit ratio notwithstanding, PERS has a fiduciary obligation to vote proxies since the shareholder vote is considered a plan asset. Government Code 6901 requires every state agency to 'vote the proxies of the stock it owns.' "[6]

During 1997–98, CalPERS voted on proxies at more than 1,600 domestic companies and at 740 international companies. During that year, the system submitted shareholder proposals at three companies: Advanced Micro Devices, Electronic Data Systems, and Sybase. The cost of the proxy-voting program came to $350,000. The system concluded that "since proxy voting is a significant component of corporate governance, which has been found to add considerable value to the PERS portfolio, it is to be concluded that the cost/benefit ratio is such that a continuation of the domestic and international proxy voting program appears warranted" (pp. 15-1 to 15-3). Of course, as the above quotation notes, the system is obligated both by its fiduciary duty *and* by the California Government Code to vote its proxies.

Proxy Voting Programs

Developing consistent proxy policies and guidelines, keeping track of the issues submitted to shareholders, and actually casting votes are important characteristics that distinguish professional ownership from typical private ownership. To rationalize this process the largest institutional investors develop in-house programs staffed by professionals to develop and execute their proxy programs. For example, CalPERS "Domestic Proxy Voting Guidelines" runs to 32 single-spaced pages and discusses in detail the system's policy stance on a wide range of corporate governance and social/political issues.[7] On some issues, such as resolutions to create board seats to represent particular constituencies, the system will always cast a "no" vote. On other issues, such as opting out of Delaware's antitakeover law, it will always cast a "yes" vote, while on still other issues, such as changes in a corporation's capital structure, CalPERS will vote on a case-by-case basis after a careful analysis of the impact of the change on shareholder value. When issues are settled, the proxy program amounts to identifying the correct criteria to apply in each case. When a new or a case-by-case issue arises, the process requires additional analysis and, therefore, is more costly.

The combined New York City Funds have developed a "Statement of Procedures and Policies for Voting Proxies" that divides proxy proposals into four broad groups: social issues, financial issues, corporate governance issues, and routine business issues.[8] The comptroller of the fund is directed to vote for or against proposals in a manner "consistent with the resolutions/policies promulgated by the trustees" or consistent "with past votes on issues detailed in the periodic vote reports provided to trustees" (p. 5). The guidelines developed by different institutional investors are broadly similar and often identical on issues such as poison pills, classified boards, and director independence. Sometimes, institutions adopt positions for or against particular proposals submitted by third parties. For example, many institutional investors currently support resolutions asking corporations to adopt the MacBride Principles for Non-Discriminatory Employment in Northern Ireland and the Coalition for Environmentally Responsible Economics Principles (CERES).[9]

As the foregoing examples show, most institutional investors distinguish between "corporate governance issues" and "social issues." The former generally concern board policies (e.g., poison pills) or board structure (e.g., independent directors). The latter cover a broad range of issues from employment in Northern Ireland to various environmental issues to labor conditions in third-world countries. In the corporate governance area institutions generally favor proxies that enhance shareholder rights, improve the board's ability to monitor management, or that allow a company to respond to takeover offers without unduly entrenching current management. The guiding principle here is enhancing shareholder value.

Most sponsors of social issues tend to be either advocacy groups, such as CERES, or religious organizations. The most famous—and most successful—of these social issue campaigns was the antiapartheid Sullivan Principles of the 1970s calling for companies to divest their investments in South Africa. The fiduciary duty of institutional investors requires them to respond to all proxy proposals, including those classified as social. They are also sometimes the object of lobbying campaigns from groups of interested beneficiaries or, in the case of public pension funds, from state legislatures, governors, and other political groups. However, institutional investors usually reject that advice as evidenced by the relatively meager support social-issue proxy proposals receive relative to corporate-governance proxy proposals. It can often be difficult to distinguish between social issues as such and social issues that affect long- or short-term performance, and financial performance in particular. For example, social issues such as racial or gender discrimination can and often do have large financial impacts, as the liability settlements at Texaco, Mitsubishi, and Denny's exemplify.

Corporate Governance Issues

Table 2.1 displays the major governance shareholder resolutions presented at the companies followed by the Investor Responsibility Research Center during 1996, 1997, and 1998.[10] Issues range from resolutions to separate the CEO and the chairman positions to repealing classified boards and redeeming or requiring a vote on poison pills. For 1998, IRRC reported a total of 442 resolutions through June. Many other proxy proposals failed to make it to a vote. Some were rejected by management as inappropriate — often supported by a "no action letter" from the Securities and Exchange Commission.[11] Others are withdrawn or in many cases never formally filed because the issue raised in the proposed proxy was settled through direct negotiation with the company. In fact, threatening to file a proposal is an important tactic institutional investors use to get a company's attention. Many of the withdrawn proposals never come to the attention of the press or the investing public, although information about them may be exchanged informally among institutional investors.

The pole star used by institutional investors to decide most proxy issues in the corporate governance area is the proxy's impact on shareholder value. This perspective flows directly from the institution's fiduciary responsibility to its beneficiaries — the twin duties of loyalty and care — and the imperative toward wealth maximization driven by those duties. Consequently, institutions pay particular attention to issues that either reduce shareholder value directly or that make it more difficult for shareholders to exercise their oversight and monitoring function. Examples of the former include poison pills and excessive compensation schemes. Examples of the latter are the various "independence" resolutions calling for more independent directors on the board or on particular board committees such as the compensation committee.

Table 2.1 shows that during these three proxy seasons most corporate governance issues fail to attract a majority of the votes cast. There are a number of reasons for this. First, a substantial fraction of individual shareholders either fail to vote or uncritically vote with management. Since passage typically requires a majority of the outstanding shares, those shares not voted are effectively "cast" in favor of management's position. Second, important blocks of shares are often in management-friendly hands such as the company pension fund or an Employee Stock Ownership Plan (ESOP), other private pension funds, and at charitable foundations beholden to management. As will be discussed in Chapter 3, these institutions often have commercial or other ties to the corporate community that predispose them to supporting management's position. Third, the voting process is not secret, so management knows how the vote is progressing. It can use this knowledge to solicit favorable votes from shareholders that haven't voted and it can even go to shareholders that have voted and lobby to get them to change their vote — which they can do until the vote is closed at the annual meeting. Finally, unless a company is experiencing severe financial difficulties attributable to current management decisions, most shareholders are either apathetic or supportive of what they view as a "successful" management team. Given the bias against shareholder proposals, a significant minority vote is a clear signal of shareholder displeasure. It is often a signal that

TABLE 2.1: Corporate Governance Voting Results as Tracked by the Investor Responsibility Research Center

Proposal Issue	Average Vote (%)			Total Filed in	
	1996	1997	1998	1997	1998
Redeem/vote on poison pill	53.4	54.9	56.7	33	17
For confidential voting	34.3	45.0	45.2	6	8
Repeal classified board	42.2	43.8	44.5	65	63
Restrict non-employee director pensions	34.2	30.3	30.1	14	7
For cumulative voting	24.0	27.8	26.1	38	40
Vote on future golden parachutes	40.6	34.9	25.6	8	6
Majority of independent directors	13.5	16.9	23.8	15	9
Independent compensation committee	N/A	7.2	21.6	N/A	5
Separate CEO and chairman	12.0	12.5	21.2	9	6
Independent nominating committee	24.8	21.6	19.9	7	7
No re-pricing underwater stock options	N/A	N/A	19.0	N/A	7
Increase board diversity	12.6	11.2	15.1	16	18
Pay directors in stock	13.1	11.7	13.0	25	4
Spin-off/sell company/hire investment bank	19.9	19.0	10.1	46	46
Restrict executive compensation	11.6	12.2	9.5	25	29
Disclose executive compensation	N/A	8.2	5.9	10	9
Link compensation to social hurdle	N/A	6.7	5.1	19	25
Eliminate discretionary voting	19.7	17.9	N/A	5	N/A
Require minimum stock ownership	15.9	9.4	N/A	5	N/A

Sources: 1997 and 1998: *Corporate Governance Bulletin*, 15, no. 2, April–June 1998, Investor Responsibility Research Center, Washington, D.C., p. 3.
1996: *Corporate Governance Bulletin*, 16, no. 2, May–June 1997, Investor Responsibility Research Center, Washington, D.C., p. 3.

Note: IRRC tracked about 1,500 companies in 1996, 1,800 in 1997, and about 2,000 in 1998.

management hears and heeds. This is particularly true if the same proposal is submitted at the same company over a number of years and gains support as time goes by. However, a recalcitrant management can even ignore majority votes because most proxies are advisory in nature only.

During the proxy seasons between 1996 and 1998 the only proposals that received more than 50 percent of the average votes cast were those asking companies to redeem existing poison pills or to submit future poison pills to a shareholder vote (see Table 2.1). Poison pills (also called shareholder rights plans) come in many forms, but the objective of all of them is to make it difficult or impossible for a hostile takeover to take place. Managements generally support poison pills since they insulate companies (and managers) from the harsh discipline of the market for corporate control. They also argue that this insulation is necessary to prevent the company from becoming embroiled in costly, distracting, and time-consuming control contests and to give the company leverage in dealing with prospective buyers. Shareholders recognize that poison pills may have the positive purposes of

TABLE 2.2: Most Successful Shareholder Resolutions in 1998

Company	Resolution	Vote %	Institutional Ownership %
Federated Department Stores	Repeal classified board	84.6	95.2
Venator	Vote on poison pill or let it expire	80.7	84.8
Bristol-Myers Squibb	Repeal classified board	74.3	59.2
Fleming	Repeal classified board	74.3	62.2
Eastman Kodak	Repeal classified board	71.4	55.1
Jostens	Repeal classified board	71.0	78.7

Source: *Corporate Governance Bulletin,* April–June 1998, Investor Responsibility Research Center, p. 6.

Note: The information in this table is drawn from IRRC's universe of about 2,000 companies in 1998.

assuring that management has an adequate amount of time to respond to a hostile takeover attempt and, theoretically, to obtain the best results for shareholders. Consequently, many guidelines suggest a case-by-case approach to shareholder rights plans rather than an outright "no" vote. However, most guidelines view the adoption of a poison pill as an important shareholder matter and, therefore, vote for proposals requiring companies to submit poison pills to a shareholder vote.

Particular issues at particular companies received higher or lower vote totals than the averages in Table 2.1. Table 2.2 shows the shareholder resolutions that received votes of more than 70 percent in 1998. The issue at all but the Venator Group (formerly Woolworth) was the repeal of classified boards.[12] At Venator, the issue was an antipoison-pill resolution. A common characteristic of these successful resolutions is the very high level of institutional ownership at the companies involved. As noted above, one of the central characteristics of a universal owner is that it treats its ownership obligations professionally. Companies with widely dispersed shareholdings tend to get more or less automatic approval for management proposals because individuals typically either do not vote, in which case the uncast proxy is counted as a "for" vote, or they explicitly vote with management with little or no evaluation of the issue or its impact on the company. Consequently, when these issues do get substantial — although not majority — votes, a strong signal is sent to the company. It should also be noted that a number of these companies had turned in very substandard economic performances in previous years. Venator, for example, had five-year returns of −18.9 percent while the return of an average S&P 500 companies over the same period was 151.5 percent. The company was also the target of two groups: UNITE (the Union of Needle Trades and Industrial Textile Employees), the sponsor of the resolution, and Greenway Partners, a limited partnership that targets underperforming companies.

As the forgoing case illustrates, a company with a combination of substantial institutional ownership and persistent subpar economic performance quickly attracts shareholder attention.[13] Furthermore, a number of large institutions — CalPERS, SWIB, CII, TIAA-CREF, the New York Funds, the Teamsters Union, and UNITE, among others — explicitly identify and target underperforming firms. Since their concerns are similar, they often support each other's proxies. Thus, it is no surprise that institutional ownership is highly correlated with the size of the vote a particular proxy receives.

As part of their programs institutions use a number of tools as a means of expressing dissatisfaction with management's performance. These tools include direct communication with management, press conferences, and proxy proposals. The fact that the proposals typically make good corporate governance sense is not entirely beside the point, but for a proposal to attract substantial support from the general shareholder community, additional elements need to be present. The overarching purpose of these campaigns is to improve economic performance at the target company and a large vote on a proxy proposal very effectively validates shareholder concerns. It is also a signal to the financial community at large that the owners are dissatisfied with the performance of their managers.

Unfortunately, in the past most proxy proposals have, in effect, been straw polls of shareholder sentiment because they were not binding proposals that management had to accept. However, this has recently begun to change. In 1997, a decision by a federal district court in Oklahoma allowed the Teamsters Union to go ahead with a proxy proposal at the Fleming Company that, if passed, would be a binding amendment to the company's bylaws. In fact, the proposal was approved by shareholders and in early 1999 the Teamsters won their case in the Oklahoma Supreme Court.[14]

In the 1999 proxy season, there have been at least 30 binding proxy proposals, of which at least 14 were on the subject of poison pills alone by several different sponsors, including State of Wisconsin Investment Board and UNITE. This is up from a total of 22 binding proxy proposals in 1998 and only 7 in 1997. As an article in the Investor Responsibility Research Center's *Corporate Governance Highlights* notes: "The proposals mark a possible sea change in shareholder resolution activity, which has centered in the past on precatory (nonbinding) proposals that request boards to take action. The rise of mandatory proposals is fueled by institutional investor anger over the number of shareholder resolutions that have been approved by a majority of shareholders but ignored by management."[15]

It remains to be seen whether the "sea change" suggested by IRRC really comes to pass or as Patrick McGurn, director of corporate programs at Institutional Shareholder Services has said, "we're going to see binding bylaw resolutions become the weapon of first choice for institutional activists."[16] Still, this is one of the most important recent developments in shareholder activism, and it certainly has the potential to give professional owners a powerful new tool for affecting corporate policy.

Social Issues

In addition to the corporate governance issues discussed above, shareholders are often asked to vote on a broad array of social issues. These range from fairly narrow interest group issues such as prohibiting animal testing or ending the free supplies of infant formula to hospitals and maternity wards to broad environmental principles. These issues present professional owners with a special challenge since they require the balancing of the merits of particular social concerns against the fiduciary responsibility of the institution. CalPERS, for example, tries to square this circle with the following statement from its "board social responsibility criteria":

The Board's stated fiduciary duty is to obtain the highest return for the Fund commensurate with acceptable levels of risk. This implies that nonfinancial considerations cannot take precedence to pure risk/return considerations in the evaluation of investment decisions. However, actions taken by the Fund as a share-owner can be instrumental in encouraging action as a responsible corporate citizen by the companies in which the Fund has invested.[17]

CalPERS' "Domestic Proxy Voting Guidelines" go on to discuss board policies with respect to social issues. The policy distinguishes between two types of requests that are frequently included in social proxy proposals: reports and actions. The fund typically supports proxies that request a report from a company to shareholders on a particular matter. This is generally rationalized as good for shareholders because it provides them with more information. However, it opposes requests that are either burdensome or that appear solely intended to embarrass the corporation. It also generally opposes proactive policies when the activity is sufficiently regulated in the country where the activity occurs or if the proactive policy would "impose a substantial financial burden on the company" (p. 23). For those issues that are to be considered on a case-by-case basis, the presumptive policy is to vote against the proposal. Of the 124 guidelines CalPERS has on specific issues, 84 call for an "against" vote, 16 for a case-by-case vote (presumptively "against") and 1 calls for an abstention. The guidelines for the remaining 24 issues (19 percent) is to vote "for" the issue. The "for" votes are clustered in the areas of equal employment, environmental issues, and tobacco issues.

Table 2.3 displays the voting record on social issues during the proxy seasons in 1996, 1997, and 1998. The issues receiving the highest average vote in 1998 were board diversity (adding minorities and women), Northern Ireland (MacBride Principles), and equal employment. These issues were also among the top vote getters in 1996 and 1997 as well.

In contrast to corporate governance issues, social issues receive considerably less support. This is probably due to the reluctance on the part of many institutional investors to support proxy proposals that are not tightly fo-

TABLE 2.3: Social Issue Voting Results in 1996, 1997, and 1998

Proposal Issue	Number Voted in			Total			Average Vote %		
	1996	1997	1998	1996	1997	1998	1996	1997	1998
Board diversity	6	7	8	26	15	17	12.6	11.2	15.0
Northern Ireland (MacBride)	7	3	5	14	5	10	12.6	12.8	14.8
Equal employment	9	8	4	26	40	22	10.8	8.2	14.4
Military	N/A	7	9	N/A	12	9	N/A	6.4	9.0
Intl. labor standards	6	4	7	12	11	19	6.6	5.6	8.7
Charitable contributions	2	2	4	5	14	28	8.8	3.2	8.7
Endorse / report on CERES	8	10	15	16	41	30	10.5	8.6	8.3
Energy	8	8	9	12	13	9	7.3	5.7	7.2
Political issues	N/A	13	16	N/A	18	23	N/A	6.0	6.7
Political contributions	2	2	N/A	12	10	N/A	4.8	5.0	N/A
Human rights	7	8	11	13	13	13	5.3	5.7	6.2
Tobacco	17	18	12	41	35	21	7.1	6.6	5.1
Executive compensation	3	10	13	7	21	24	6.6	6.8	5.0
Other environmental	5	8	12	15	16	24	6.1	4.6	4.7
Equal credit opportunity	1	2	2	2	6	11	5.3	7.0	1.4
Maquiladoras	6	3	0	11	6	4	7.9	6.9	0.0

Source: 1997 and 1998: *Corporate Social Issues Reporter*, June–July 1998, Investor Responsibility Research Center as reproduced in the Florida State Board of Administration, Annual Report of Corporate Governance, July 1, 1997 to June 30, 1998. p. 6. 1996: *Corporate Social Issues Reporter*, June–July 1997, Investor Responsibility Research Center as reproduced in the Florida State Board of Administration, Annual Report of Corporate Governance, July 1, 1996 to June 30, 1997, p. 5.

cused on traditional corporate governance and performance issues. Large corporate activist institutions vary in how they treat these matters. For example, the CalPERS guidelines discussed above either call for an "against" vote for issues relating to Northern Ireland (for example, to sign the MacBride Principles) or a case-by-case vote. However, those of the Florida State Board of Administration call for a "for" vote on the MacBride Principles.[18] What determines a particular institution's stand on a particular issue is a complicated matter combining local politics, history, and personalities. Little if any research has been done on the economic implications of most of the social issues and, with the possible exception of the Sullivan Principles on apartheid in South Africa, there has been nothing approaching a consensus. This is in contrast to most of the corporate governance issues that have been the subject of academic research and some — allowing shareholders to vote on poison pills, for example — have resulted in generally accepted positions.

However, if one means by "universal owner issues" something that might have a definable economic impact on the returns to an institutions' portfolio beyond a specific company or that might have a definable impact on the welfare of the institutions' beneficiaries, then a number of such issues do appear in some institutions' social issues guidelines. For example, CalPERS' guidelines call for an "against" vote on proposals to "limit corporate contributions only to those that further the interests of the corporation," and a "for" vote on proposals asking a corporation to "report on the creation of a high-performance workplace."[19] Both of these issues, as well as the tobacco issues that call for minimum labeling and marketing standards for sales in third-world countries and against the "Joe Camel" campaign, could be considered broadly favorable to the fund's beneficiaries. However, the fund's guidelines call for "against" votes on all other tobacco proposals — which range from stopping the production and sale of cigarettes and divesting tobacco equities to the adoption of a "smoke-free" restaurant policy. Consequently, it is very difficult to generalize about how individual funds perceive their universal investor status. Indeed, although some funds do not think of themselves as universal investors at all, they still approach certain issues in a way a universal investor might.

Conclusion

Formal, regularized proxy-voting programs are one of the hallmarks of the professional owner. Individual investors tend to either follow the lead of management or to sell their position when they disagree. Professional owners, on the other hand — particularly those with very large and/or indexed portfolios — treat proxies as valuable assets. First, their fiduciary duty, reinforced by ERISA regulations and, in some cases, state laws, requires them to exercise the duty of care with respect to all plan assets. Second, proxies *are* valuable — both with regard to the issues presented and as an important tool for professional owners to use in the exercise of their oversight responsibility. The impact on shareholder value is sometimes as short term and direct as in a takeover fight. Sometimes the impact is medium term, as with a stock-option plan to provide incentives to management. And in the long run, shareholder-friendly proxies contribute to the possibility that a strong, independent board may be able to surface problems more quickly than a weak, management-dominated board. If problems do arise, an effective board representing shareholder interests may be better able to take the difficult actions required to rectify the situation.

The focus on good corporate governance embodied in the proxy guidelines of most professional investors could be considered examples of attempts to articulate and implement universal owner concerns. That is, the concern for good corporate governance goes beyond the performance of any one company and extends to a concern for efficiency across the entire corporate sector. Institutional investors are aware that actions at one firm may positively affect other firms and therefore the overall return on their portfolios. Written guidelines serve notice of the likely reaction from professional owners to companies considering a particular issue and announce policies of powerful institutions that may result in better corporate governance without the particular issue ever reaching the level of proxy submissions.

While Security and Exchange Commission rules and regulations and corporate law as interpreted by various state courts places limits on the types of issues that can be brought before shareholders in the form of proxy resolutions, many issues do make it to a vote. And many other issues, such as proxies calling for the division of the position of CEO and chairman of the board or "just vote no campaigns" in which shares are voted against board candidates, have been used to signal investor dissatisfaction about other aspects of corporate behavior. Of course, professional owners are free to communicate their concerns about any matter directly to management. They can also work together through formal organizations such as the Council of Institutional Investors, the MacBride and CERES Principles, or in informal coalitions formed around specific issues. In short, once articulated there are avenues for expressing universal owner concerns both within the current proxy system and, creatively, outside of it.

Chapter 3
The Rise of Institutional Ownership in the United States

The twentieth century has seen several sea changes in corporate ownership. At the end of the last century and into this century corporations were dominated by "captains of industry," as characterized by supporters, while dubbed "robber barons" by critics. Such wealthy individuals as Morgan, Rockefeller, Carnegie, and du Pont not only owned large blocks of stock in companies such as Standard Oil and United States Steel, but they exercised their rights as owners to control these companies. Typical of this era of ownership was the role Pierre S. du Pont played at General Motors during the 1920s. When the company fell on difficult times he, as the major shareholder, moved into the executive suite and personally guided the company back to financial health.[1]

By the 1930s, the ownership pattern of corporate equity in the United States had changed so much that Adolph Berle and Gardiner Means could conclude in their seminal work on the modern corporation that the trend in corporate ownership had resulted in "the dissolution of the old atom of ownership into its component parts, control and beneficial ownership."[2] This was the age in which effective control over the typical corporation was no longer exercised by the legal owners of equity — the shareholders — but an age in which control of corporate America was exercised by hired, professional managers. U.S. capitalism had become, in Chandler's terms, "managerial capitalism."[3]

The phenomenon that Berle and Means identified in 1932 — the divorce of ownership from control — would come to dominate most thinking about issues of corporate governance for the rest of the twentieth century. It would also come to influence most policy on the federal and state level in this area. In its modern form the ownership-control problem is a prime example of the more general "principal-agent" problem. "Agency problems arise when a principal hires an agent to perform certain tasks, yet the agent does not share the principal's objective. To align the agent's objectives with his own, the principal may use a variety of instruments, including cash bonuses, equity shares, promotions, and dismissals to provide adequate incentives for the agent to act in the principal's best interest. Common examples of principal-agent relations include those between shareholders and CEOs."[4]

As Gilson puts it: "the central corporate governance inquiry in the United States took the form of the academic equivalent of the search for the holy grail—the quest for a technique that minimized agency costs by bridging the separation of ownership and control."[5] In his 1979 book *The Unseen Revolution: How Pension Fund Socialism Came to America*, Peter Drucker argues that forces were underway that would again remake the landscape of corporate ownership. This time the responsibly of ownership was being concentrated in the hands of a relatively small number of institutional investors—primarily public and private pension funds—acting on behalf of a large, almost universal group of individual beneficiaries. Drucker proclaimed, "If 'socialism' is defined as 'ownership of the means of production by the workers'—and this is both the orthodox and the only rigorous definition—then the United States is the first truly 'Socialist' country."[6] While Drucker's point about socialism is primarily a rhetorical one, he does raise important issues about the decline of traditional, personally held private property in equity form and the rise of equity held by fiduciary institutions.

These sea changes in the ownership of corporate America have had profound effects, and hold the future potential to have greater impact. They have influenced politics and government, the business community, the way we, as citizens, conceive of the relationship between corporations and society, and the way shareowners view their rights and responsibilities. The most recent sea change—from individual ownership to ownership by fiduciary institutions—has been underway since at least the 1950s. But only at the end of the century has the shift become so large and so profound that it has the potential to redefine some of the fundamental relationships that traditionally have governed the ownership, control, and use of private property. This reconcentration of ownership in the hands of fiduciary institutions has already reversed the separation of ownership and control at the heart of the Berle and Means' critique.

But a new form of separation of ownership from control appears to be emerging. While corporate managers are far more responsive to shareholders (overwhelmingly to institutional ones) than previously, the ultimate beneficiary or investor is one more step removed, thereby restructuring ownership and control through a long series of organizational agency chains. Before turning to a more detailed examination of the dimensions of this historic shift in ownership, it is appropriate to examine briefly the history of the corporate form of business.

A Brief History of the Corporation

It is not an exaggeration to say that the history of business in the United States is a history of corporate business.[7] There are few exceptions to this statement among large, commercial enterprises. Consequently, the concern with "big business" that has surfaced again and again throughout our history is really a concern with the corporate form because without that form it is unlikely that these organizations could have been established in the first place. Some of the elements of the modern corporate form have been around for a long time and one of the central features of the corporation, limited liability, goes back to at least 2000 B.C. as part of the arrangements merchants made to finance seagoing vessels. These high-risk endeavors prompted the invention of legal ways to limit liability.[8]

But limited liability alone doesn't define a corporation. The corporate charter — the creation of an organization with certain legal rights independent of its membership — was invented in medieval Europe and was for a long time one of the principal grants of authority (or "franchise") that states could confer on a group of individuals. Corporate charters allowed these groups to engage in what we would today consider public or quasi-public purposes such as building a toll road, running a ferry, starting a university, or engaging in a specific commercial enterprise.[9]

The Dutch East India Company, chartered in 1602, is often considered to be the first joint stock company with a permanent fund of capital (p. 59). The Hudson Bay Company, like the Dutch East India Company, is another famous example of an early corporation with exclusive trading rights in a particular area, while the South Sea Company is an equally infamous one. The latter enterprise promised extravagant wealth from exploiting trading rights in Spanish South America (adjacent to the South Seas) that were expected to flow from England's victory in the War of the Spanish Succession. So sure were they of success that the organizers of the South Sea Company offered to pay off a portion of the English national debt incurred during the war.[10] The spectacular collapse of the company in what came to be known as the South Sea Bubble was, in fact, so infamous that it inspired the Bubble Act of 1720. This act required all joint stock companies to have a royal charter and in England, all but put an end to corporate chartering for commercial purposes for the rest of the century.

Through the end of the eighteenth century corporate charters were viewed as contracts between the state and the corporation — negotiated on a case-by-case basis. In the United States, the concept of incorporation found particularly fertile ground. So fertile, in fact, one author called it "as American as apple pie."[11] Incorporating gradually became more widely available for business activities during the first decades of the nineteenth century until in 1837, Connecticut passed the first modern statute allowing incorporation "for any lawful business purpose."[12]

Now, instead of being chartered for a particular purpose such as running a ferry at a particular place or engaging in a particular line of business such as cotton spinning, a corporation could now engage in *any* profit-making endeavor it wished. Incorporation also became much easier and, in the spirit of the new country, more democratic. No longer did the organizers of a corporation need to obtain from a state legislature a specific, uniquely crafted piece of legislation. Now they could avoid the problems of negotiating with politicians, a process that often left the fruits of incorporation to either the aggressive and persistent or to the powerful and the well connected. Instead, anyone could incorporate a business by simply paying a modest fee and filing the appropriate papers with the secretary of state of the state in which they wished to incorporate.[13]

The unique role of the corporation in the American scene received a major boost when the Supreme Court in the 1886 case of *Santa Clara County v. Southern Pacific Railroad* interpreted the Fourteenth Amendment to the U.S. Constitution to mean that a corporation was a "person." Not only was this person now protected by the constitution from restrictions on its free speech and from the taking of its property without compensation, but it also clearly existed independent of the individuals constituting the corporation. In partnerships, each partner is personally liable for the unpaid debts of the partnership. In a corporation, the corporation is liable for its debts, not individual officers, employees, or shareholders. The concept of limited liability first introduced to protect merchant traders was now a central feature of the modern corporation.

Early corporations had many of the attributes of the modern corporation, but they lacked one very important feature. Compared to modern corporations, their stockholder lists were miniscule. Berle and Means cite the Boston Manufacturing Company, organized in 1813, as the first important manufacturing enterprise in the United States formed as a corporation. The original stock of the corporation was held by only 10 shareholders. By 1830, the number had risen to 76 and no individual owned more than 8.5 percent of the total. Even twenty years later the company still had only 123 stockholders. Many legal and financial partnerships today are larger. But by 1850, Berle and Means found the journey toward the divorce of ownership from control was well on its way, since by that time the management of the Boston Manufacturing Company held "only" 11 percent of the stock outstanding.[14]

The great railroad building boom of the latter half of the nineteenth century created the first of the modern corporations — very large business organizations with many employees and many shareholders. In 1853, the New York Central Railroad was created by combining the assets of ten small railroads operating between Albany and Buffalo with a total of 2,445 investors. For its day, it was a large business organization with relatively dispersed ownership, but by 1900, the U.S. Steel Corporation had almost 55,000 stockholders while the Pennsylvania Railroad had about 51,000.

The Separation of Ownership from Control

For the first half of the twentieth century, most research conducted on the question of equity ownership focused on individual firms or on a small sample of firms. Little was known about the overall characteristics of equity owners and few researchers attempted to estimate the total number of stockholders in the country. Fewer still tried to investigate the size of individual holdings or to relate them to the characteristics of their owners. Reflecting the minor role institutional investors — university endowments, pension funds, and so on — played in the equity markets early in the century, only a few studies tried to break down the total number of equity owners into various types. However, holdings by some financial institutions on behalf of individuals — bank trust holdings and holdings of stock for individuals by brokerage houses and by nominees — were important and drew the attention of the early scholars.[15]

After a careful analysis of the studies conducted by various researchers between 1900 and 1960, Edwin Cox, in a book on the trends in the distribution of stock ownership, reached the following conclusions. Even though the data before 1927 is very thin, it appears that at the turn of the century there were about 1 million stockholders in the United States. This would be about one out of forty adults over the age of twenty-one living in the country at that time. This number rose to 5 million by 1927 and in the next three years — despite the stock-market crash in 1929 — doubled so that by 1930, there were, according to Cox, 10 million stockholders in the United States.[16] Thus, the first three decades of the twentieth century saw a tenfold explosion in the number of individuals owning stock. However, some observers saw the increase in the number of stockholders of record after 1929 not as an increase in the absolute numbers as much as the result of a shift in investor preference away from holding securities in street name to holding securities in the name of the individual owner.[17]

By 1930, a high-water mark in the dispersal of equity ownership was set that wouldn't be reached again until the late 1950s. In between, the ranks of the equity-owning public declined over the decades of the 1930s and 1940s so that by 1950, the number stood at 5 million, roughly the number of stockholders that Cox found in 1927.[18] However, the fraction of the adult population that were stockholders fell from about 14 percent in 1930 to about 5 percent in 1950. But the 1950s, like the 1920s, were a good time for equity ownership. The long downward trend was reversed so that by the end of the decade, the number of stockholders stood at 12.5 million. Cox concluded that "If the size of the adult population is considered, the prevalence of stockownership among the population in 1959 was approximately the same as in 1929, one adult in eight" (p. 198).

Cox also reviewed studies that examined the relationship between equity ownership and income class, extending such research through the 1950s.

This work is largely based on dividend income reported on individual tax returns. Cox reaches the following conclusions: "We have seen that a substantial decline has occurred in the share of dividend income received by the top percentile of all income receivers. The decline extended from 1926 to the early 1940s and may have been a reduction in the percentage share of the top percentile of as much as 40 percent" (p. 144). Thus, from dividend records Cox concludes that over time equity ownership had become less concentrated in the very highest income classes. This conclusion, however, has been hotly contested by a number of authors.

For example, in *Changes in the Share of Wealth Held by Top Wealth-Holders, 1922–1956*, Robert Lampman concludes "that of total corporate stock held by individuals, the wealthiest 1 per cent of adults held 61.5 per cent in 1922, 65.6 per cent in 1929, 69.0 per cent in 1939, 61.7 per cent in 1945, 64.9 per cent in 1949, and 76.0 per cent in 1953."[19] This directly contradicts Cox's conclusions, and in an appendix he attempts to reconcile the two estimates by pointing out some technical differences in the two approaches. Most likely to account for the difference is the fact that Cox is looking at the distribution of ownership by income class, while Lampman is looking at distribution of ownership by wealth class — and the wealth distribution is more heavily skewed than the income distribution.

In any case, Cox notes that "The emphasis which has been placed upon the long-term decline in the share of individual income received by the top 1 per cent of the population and by the top 1 per cent of persons benefiting from dividend income has perhaps obscured the fact that there remains a very high degree of concentration in both distributions" (p. 144). Share ownership may or may not have become less concentrated among the very highest income classes or among the very wealthiest during the period of Cox's study — but it is only a matter of degree and does not indicate any significant democratization of wealth over the first six decades of the twentieth century.

Much of the work on equity ownership covered by Cox is concerned with enumerating the number of individual equity holders. This is understandable since the overwhelming majority of equity was owned by individual shareholders and there was little systematic information about just how numerous this group was in the population at large. However, Cox does present some information by type of shareholder — including institutional shareholders — for a few selected years.

Based on table 4 from *Trends in the Distribution of Stock Ownership* (p. 52), Table 3.1 presents data on the type of holder for one year before midcentury, 1922, and for 1952, 1956, and 1959.[20] The 1922 data was published in *National Wealth and Income* and comes from a sample of more than 4,000 companies surveyed by the Federal Trade Commission.[21] The original population was a random sample of 10,000 corporations filing federal income tax returns. Cox notes that the respondents represented 1.2 percent of all cor-

Table 3.1: Percentage Distribution of Record Shareholdings and Value or Number of Shares, by Type of Shareholder

	1922		1952		1956		1959	
Type of Holder	Shareholdings	Shares (by value)	Shareholdings	Shares (by number)	Shareholdings	Shares (by number)	Shareholdings	Shares (by number)
Common								
Individuals	92.2%	64.9%	92.1%	57.6%	91.8%	57.4%	91.7%	53.3%
Fiduciaries	3.4	10.4	4.5	6.9	4.6	7.4	4.4	7.2
Brokers and dealers	1.7	11.9	1.1	10.4	1.1	9.4	1.1	8.5
Nominees	NA	NA	0.6	9.9	0.8	9.9	0.8	12.6
Others	2.9	12.7	1.7	15.2	1.7	15.9	1.8	18.3
Preferred								
Individuals	91.0%	67.8%	85.0%	45.7%	84.7%	39.8%	84.5%	34.9%
Fiduciaries	3.5	9.9	8.2	7.4	7.7	8.1	7.0	6.8
Brokers and dealers	1.4	8.7	1.6	8.0	1.4	6.4	1.5	6.8
Nominees	NA	NA	1.5	15.6	2.1	17.1	2.5	23.6
Others	4.1	13.6	3.7	23.3	4.1	28.6	4.5	27.8

Note: Data in 1922 presents the distribution of shareholdings as "shares by value" while in 1952–1959, the corresponding distribution is "shares by number."
Sources: 1922: Federal Trade Commission, *National Wealth and Income* (1926); 1952: Lewis H. Kimmel, *Share Ownership in the U.S.* (Washington, D.C.: Brookings Institution, 1952); 1956: *Who Owns American Business? 1956 Census of Shareowners* (New York: New York Stock Exchange, 1956); and 1959: *Share Ownership in America: 1959* (New York: New York Stock Exchange, 1959).

TABLE 3.2: Beneficial Versus Record Holdings of Common and Preferred Stock, 1952

Type of Holder	Common Stock			Preferred		
	Record Holdings	Beneficial Holdings	% Diff.	Record Holdings	Beneficial Holdings	% Diff.
Individuals	57.6%	67.6%	17%	45.5%	54.9%	21%
Fiduciaries	6.9	12.3	78%	7.4	15.7	112%
Institutions and foundations	1.8	2.8	56%	3.2	4.6	44%
Brokers and dealers	10.4	0.7	−93%	8.0	0.6	−93%
Nominees	9.9	0.0	−100%	15.6	0.0	−100%
Others	13.3	16.5	24%	20.0	24.2	21%

Note: Holdings are measured as a percentage of shares held in the 3,954 issues in Kimmel's data set.
Source: Lewis H. Kimmel, *Share Ownership in the U.S.* (Washington, D.C.: Brookings Institution, 1952), pp. 15, 17, 64, and 66.

porations and 11.9 percent of outstanding common stock. He recognized that this was not a random sample and, therefore, the study may be subject to selection bias. The data for 1952 through 1956 come from studies either commissioned by or performed by the New York Stock Exchange.

While in Table 3.1 individuals were the most important owners of equity, fiduciaries, nominees, and, especially, brokers and dealers were also important owners during this period.[22] Individuals held approximately 65 percent of the common stock by value in 1922 and about 53 percent of the common shares by number in 1959. In charting the rise of professional ownership, the important question is the extent to which these owners of record exercised the prerogatives of ownership such as voting proxies, making the decision to buy or sell stock, communicating with management, and so on. It is likely that fiduciaries did exercise these responsibilities since this category includes bank trust departments and other trustees whose job was to administer investments on behalf of minor children, the insane or incompetent, and other individuals legally or mentally incapable of managing their finances. The other two categories, nominees and broker-dealers, were typically record owners of convenience and may have passed on all or almost all of the rights and responsibilities of share ownership to the beneficial owners.

The distinction between record owner and beneficial owner is an important one. To shed some light on the degree of beneficial ownership in late 1951 and early 1952, Kimmel used a sample of financial institutions to determine the actual beneficial ownership of 20 issues that he then used to assign beneficial ownership to the shares owned by trustees, broker/dealers, and nominees.[23] As might be expected, when holdings of record are assigned to their ultimate beneficiaries, the largest absolute increase in ownership occurs among individuals. The simple reason is that in 1952, individuals, as a group, owned more equity that all of the other groups combined and much of the equity held in street name by brokerage houses and by nominees was beneficially owned by individuals. The decline in common stock ownership of record by broker/dealers and nominees amounted 19.6 percentage points. Ten of these percentage points were redistributed to individuals. As a result, their ownership increased from 57.6 to 67.6 percent.

However, the reassignment of ownership from record owners to beneficial owners had a proportionally larger impact on fiduciaries, institutions and foundations, and the other category. These categories are made up of organizations that are professionally run and therefore may have been more comfortable holding investments in street name at broker/dealers or with nominees. Also, since they are professional owners, they might find it more convenient to decline to take delivery of equities and thereby to become owners of record. When positions are assigned to beneficial owners, fiduciaries see their holdings of common stock increase by 78 percent—from 6.9 to 12.3 percent—while their ownership of preferred stock more than doubles from 7.4 to 15.9 percent. Institutions and foundations and the other category also experience large proportional gains in their shares in the ownership of both common and preferred stock when ownership is assigned to beneficiaries. Taken together, these three categories see their fraction of overall common equity ownership rise from a record ownership of 22 percent to a beneficial ownership of 31.6 percent. Likewise, when ownership is assigned from record owners to beneficial owners for preferred stock, ownership by these three categories of institutional owners rises from 30.6 to 44.5 percent.

With respect to preferred shares, individuals owned a somewhat larger fraction and fiduciaries and broker-dealers a somewhat smaller fraction of the shares outstanding in 1922. However, by the 1950s, individual ownership of preferred shares seems to have diminished markedly. In 1922, individuals were record owners of almost 68 percent of the preferred shares by value. By 1952, this fraction had dropped to about 46 percent of the number of shares outstanding. Caution must be used since one figure is for the value of the shares and the other is for the number of shares. However, for the three observations in the 1950s, which are all in number of shares, individual ownership of record also declined from 45.7 percent of preferred shares outstanding in 1952 to 34.9 percent in 1959. Much of this might be due to the substantial rise in nominee holdings from 15.6 to 23.6 percent over the same period. But even if this entire 8-point rise in nominee holdings is reassigned to individuals, individuals holdings would still have fallen by almost 3 percentage points over this seven-year period.

In Tables 3.1 and 3.2, the most interesting institutional owners for our purposes — public and private pension funds, open- and closed-end mutual funds — are buried in the others category. This reflects the relative lack of importance of institutional ownership at the time. To the extent that earlier research included institutional owners, they tended to focus on those institutions — fiduciaries, broker-dealers, and nominees — that were, in effect, stand-in owners for individuals. However, as the others category in Table 3.1 clearly indicates, this was about to change. The fraction of shares of common stock of record owned by the members of the others category accounted for 15.2 percent of the shares outstanding in 1952. By 1959, this fraction had grown to 18.3 percent.

The others category already represented a substantial fraction of the ownership of preferred stock in 1922 (by value) and an even larger fraction in the 1950s (by number). In the later period owners classified as others held a relatively larger fraction of the preferred shares outstanding than of the common stock outstanding. The preponderance of preferred shares in the others category was probably due to a preference on the part of many institutions for these somewhat more conservative, bond-like investments. By 1959, owners in the others category accounted for almost as large a fraction of shares outstanding as did individuals, 27.8 percent versus 34.9 percent. Nominee holdings, however, also increased greatly over this period, from 15.6 percent of shares outstanding in 1952 to 23.6 percent in 1959. Given the pattern in Table 3.2, most of this increase was probably owned beneficially by individuals, since the redistribution of shares to beneficial owners raises individual holdings by 9.4 percentage points and that of the others category by 4.2 points.

Nonetheless, ownership by public and private pension funds and by mutual funds was ready to explode. While it isn't possible to extract accurate information on the trends in ownership by these holders from the data published by either Cox or Kimmel, Cox does make the following relevant comments:

Since 1922 there has been a shift in shareholdings and shares in common and preferred issues alike from individuals, fiduciaries, and brokers to nominees and institutions (the largest factor in the "others" category). The decline in relative holdings of individuals, fiduciaries, and brokers reflects the rising importance of institutional investors and investment companies.[24]

In conclusion, during the first six decades of the twentieth century ownership of corporate equity was highly concentrated in the hands of individuals, either as owners of record or as beneficial owners. Within this owning group or class, concentration was highly skewed to the top 1.0 percent or even top 0.5 percent. According to Cox, the high-water mark for equity ownership during this period, reached in both 1929 and 1959, was about 12.5 percent of the adult population, or about one in eight adults. Thus, during the first half of the century almost 90 percent of the adult population did not own equity and, therefore, had no ownership stake in corporate America. Few Americans were stockholders, while most Americans were stakeholders. As is explored in the next section, this is in quite sharp contrast to the spread of equity ownership — largely due to the indirect ownership of beneficiaries — that has been achieved by the end of the century.

The Rise of Institutional Ownership

The Investment Company Act of 1940 allowed the formation of open-end mutual funds and wartime employment practices led to a substantial expansion of pension benefits granted by private sector employers. State and local public employee pension programs also started to grow during this period, along with growing employment in this sector. However, it wasn't until the 1970s that state pension funds began to shift a substantial fraction of their assets out of conservative investments such as U.S. government bonds and into corporate equities. For example, only after a 1996 referendum changed the state constitution was the Indiana Public Employees' Retirement Fund able to invest any of its assets in corporate equity. Until then, the "new" constitution adopted in 1841 barred the state from owning stock in any company. The prohibition had resulted from the near bankruptcy of the state after its investments in canal company stocks and bonds were made nearly worthless by the rise of the railroads.[25]

Table 3.3 and Figure 3.1 display the percentage of corporate equity owned by the household sector (including equity held in bank personal trusts and estates) and by financial institutions (pension funds, mutual funds, and life insurance companies). While roughly comparable with the data presented in Tables 3.1 and 3.2, the data in this table comes from different sources and therefore the categories are subject to slightly different definitions. Most importantly, the institutions collected in the others category in Tables 3.1 and 3.2 — insurance companies and investment companies, among others — emerge here as independent line items. The trend in equity ownership since 1945 has been clear and dramatic. In 1945, the market value of corporate equity was slightly less that $120 billion and more than 90 percent of that was owned by individuals either directly or through bank-managed personal trusts. In that year institutions owned only 4.2 percent of corporate equity. By 1998, the market value of corporate equity exceeded $15 trillion and the ownership share going to individuals had fallen by half — to only 44 percent of outstanding equity. At the same time, equity ownership by financial institutions on behalf of various beneficiaries had risen from $4.9 billion in 1945 to more than $7.4 trillion in 1998. By then institutions owned 48 percent of the total equity outstanding, or more than $500 billion more than individuals owned in that year.[26]

In 1945, institutional ownership was concentrated in mutual funds and insurance companies, as Table 3.4 indicates. Together these two types of institutions owned 94 percent of the equity owned by all institutions while pension funds owned most of the remaining 6 percent — but total institutional ownership only accounted for only 4.2 percent of corporate equity outstanding. Fifty years later, the most important institutional owners are the pension funds, which now own 52 percent of the equity owned by institutions. Strikingly, pension funds now own 25 percent of total equity — more

TABLE 3.3: The Ownership of Corporate Equity in the United States, 1945–1998

Billions of Dollars

Type of Owner	1945	1950	1955	1960	1965	1970	1975
Household sector[a]	109.5	128.7	248.2	359.8	616.1	660.4	590.9
Mutual funds[b]	1.8	4.5	9.7	19.8	36.5	44.0	39.5
Private pension funds	0.3	1.1	6.1	16.5	40.8	67.1	108.0
State and local gov. retirement funds	–	–	0.2	0.6	2.5	10.1	24.3
Rest of the world	2.7	2.9	6.6	9.3	14.6	27.2	33.4
Insurance companies	2.8	4.7	9.0	12.5	21.0	27.8	41.7
Other[c]	0.8	0.7	1.9	1.8	3.5	4.9	8.0
Holdings at Market Value	117.9	142.6	281.7	420.3	735.0	841.5	845.8

Percentage Distribution

Type of Owner	1945	1950	1955	1960	1965	1970	1975
Household sector[a]	92.9%	90.3%	88.1%	85.6%	83.8%	78.5%	69.9%
Mutual funds[b]	1.5%	3.2%	3.4%	4.7%	5.0%	5.2%	4.7%
Private pension funds	0.3%	0.8%	2.2%	3.9%	5.6%	8.0%	12.8%
State and local gov. retirement funds	0.0%	0.0%	0.1%	0.1%	0.3%	1.2%	2.9%
Rest of the world	2.3%	2.0%	2.3%	2.2%	2.0%	3.2%	3.9%
Insurance companies	2.4%	3.3%	3.2%	3.0%	2.9%	3.3%	4.9%
Other[c]	0.7%	0.5%	0.7%	0.4%	0.5%	0.6%	0.9%
Holdings at Market Value	100.0%	100.0%	100.0%	100.0%	100.0%	100.0%	100.0%

Source: Federal Reserve System, *Flow of Funds Accounts of the United States: Annual Flows and Outstandings,* (Washington, D.C.: General Printing Office, 1999), Series L.213 Corporate Equities. Available at the Federal Reserve Board of Governors web site: http://www.bog.frb.fed.us/releases/Z1/data.htm, accessed May 13, 1999.
Notes: Details may not add to totals because of rounding.
[a] Includes bank personal trusts and estates not shown separately in the flow of funds until 1969
[b] Includes both open-end and closed-end mutual funds
[c] Includes state and local governments, brokers and dealers, savings institutions, and commercial banking

TABLE 3;3: (Continued)

Billions of Dollars

Type of Owner	1980	1985	1990	1995	1996	1997	1998
Household sector[a]	1,037.9	1,298.9	2,001.4	4,219.7	4,777.3	5,734.2	6,817.4
Mutual funds[b]	47.3	117.9	249.4	1,062.9	1,513.6	2,068.9	2576.1
Private pension funds	223.5	494.9	561.9	1,238.4	1,490.9	1,863.9	2,232.3
State and local gov. retirement funds	44.3	120.1	293.0	753.5	955.7	1,305.8	1,592.8
Rest of the world	74.7	136.8	243.8	527.6	656.8	915.9	1,110.3
Insurance companies	78.6	131.0	161.8	449.6	558.8	746.5	950.1
Other[c]	7.6	19.4	25.4	79.7	109.3	140.8	158.7
Holdings at Market Value	1,513.9	2,319.0	3,536.7	8,331.4	10,062.4	12,776.1	15,437.7

Percentage Distribution

Type of Owner	1980	1985	1990	1995	1996	1997	1998
Household sector[a]	68.6%	56.0%	56.6%	50.6%	47.5%	44.9%	44.2%
Mutual funds[b]	3.1%	5.1%	7.1%	12.8%	15.0%	16.2%	16.7%
Private pension funds	14.8%	21.3%	15.9%	14.9%	14.8%	14.6%	14.5%
State and local gov. retirement funds	2.9%	5.2%	8.3%	9.0%	9.5%	10.2%	10.3%
Rest of the world	4.9%	5.9%	6.9%	6.3%	6.5%	7.2%	7.2%
Insurance companies	5.2%	5.6%	4.6%	5.4%	5.5%	5.8%	6.2%
Other[c]	0.5%	0.8%	0.7%	1.0%	1.1%	1.1%	1.0%
Holdings at Market Value	100.0%	100.0%	100.0%	100.0%	100.0%	100.0%	100.0%

Source: Federal Reserve System, *Flow of Funds Accounts of the United States: Annual Flows and Outstandings*, (Washington, D.C.: General Printing Office, 1999), Series L.213 Corporate Equities. Available at the Federal Reserve Board of Governors web site: http://www.bog.frb.us/releases/Z1/data.htm, accessed May 13, 1999.

Notes: Details may not add to totals because of rounding.

[a] Includes bank personal trusts and estates not shown separately in the flow of funds until 1969

[b] Includes both open-end and closed-end mutual funds

[c] Includes state and local governments, brokers and dealers, savings institutions, and commercial banking

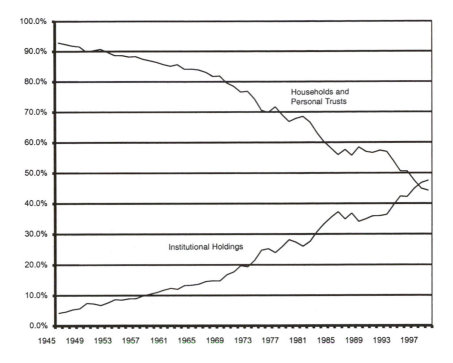

Figure 3.1: Ownership of Corporate Equity by Households and Institutions, 1945–1998

than six times the ownership share of *all* institutions in 1947. At the same time, mutual funds now own about 17 percent of total equity and 35 percent of the equity owned by institutions. Pension funds first surpassed mutual funds as equity owners in the early 1960s. Insurance companies, while owning about a billion dollars worth of equity in 1997, still own only about 13 percent of the equity owned by institutions, down from the 57 percent they owned in 1945. Who are these institutions? What implications do they have for the possible reunification of ownership with control and what are their significance for the economy at large?

U.S. Financial Institutions

The U.S. financial institutions that play a major role in the ownership of equity capital are bank trust departments; private pension plans, including multiemployer labor union pension plans; public employee pension plans; not-for-profit/cooperative pension funds (mainly CREF); mutual funds; and insurance companies. These institutions own equity on behalf of individuals — retirees, potential retirees, insurance policy holders, and purchas-

TABLE 3.4: Institutional Ownership of U. S. Equity, 1945–1998

Institutional Ownership: Billions of Dollars

	1945	1950	1955	1960	1965	1970	1975
Mutual funds[a]	1.8	4.5	9.7	19.8	36.5	44.0	39.5
Private pension funds	0.3	1.1	6.1	16.5	40.8	67.1	108.0
State and local gov. retirement funds	–	–	0.2	0.6	2.5	10.1	24.3
Insurance companies	2.8	4.7	9.0	12.5	21.0	27.8	41.7
Total Institutional Ownership	4.9	10.3	25.0	49.4	100.8	149.0	213.5

Institutional Ownership: Percentage Distribution

	1945	1950	1955	1960	1965	1970	1975
Mutual funds[a]	36.7%	43.7%	38.8%	40.1%	36.2%	29.5%	18.5%
Private pension funds	6.1%	10.7%	24.4%	33.4%	40.5%	45.0%	50.6%
State and local gov. retirement funds	0.0%	0.0%	0.8%	1.2%	2.5%	6.8%	11.4%
Insurance companies	57.1%	45.6%	36.0%	25.3%	20.8%	18.7%	19.5%
Total Institutional Ownership	100.0%	100.0%	100.0%	100.0%	100.0%	100.0%	100.0%
Institutional Ownership as a Percentage of Total Equity	4.2%	7.2%	8.9%	11.8%	13.7%	17.7%	25.2%

Institutional Ownership: Billions of Dollars

	1980	1985	1990	1995	1996	1997	1998
Mutual funds[a]	47.3	117.9	249.4	1,062.9	1,513.6	2,068.9	2,576.1
Private pension funds	223.5	494.9	561.9	1,238.4	1,490.9	1,863.9	2,232.3
State and local gov. retirement funds	44.3	120.1	293.0	753.5	955.7	1,305.8	1592.8
Insurance companies	78.6	131.0	161.8	449.6	558.8	746.5	950.1
Total Institutional Ownership	393.7	863.9	1,266.1	3,504.4	4,519.0	5,985.1	7,351.3

Institutional Ownership: Percentage Distribution

	1980	1985	1990	1995	1996	1997	1998
Mutual funds[a]	12.0%	13.6%	19.7%	30.3%	33.5%	34.6%	35.0%
Private pension funds	56.8%	57.3%	44.4%	35.3%	33.0%	31.1%	30.4%
State and local gov. retirement funds	11.3%	13.9%	23.1%	21.5%	21.1%	21.8%	21.7%
Insurance companies	20.0%	15.2%	12.8%	12.8%	12.4%	12.5%	12.9%
Total Institutional Ownership	100.0%	100.0%	100.0%	100.0%	100.0%	100.0%	100.0%
Institutional Ownership as a Percentage of Total Equity	26.0%	37.3%	35.8%	42.1%	44.9%	46.8%	47.6%

Source: Federal Reserve System, *Flow of Funds Accounts of the United States: Annual Flows and Outstandings*, (Washington, D.C.: General Printing Office, 1999). Series L.213 Corporate Equities. Available at the Federal Reserve Board of Governors web site: http://www.bog.frb.fed.us/releases/Z1/data.htm, accessed May 13, 1999.
[a] Includes both open-end and closed-end mutual funds

ers of mutual fund shares. Only the investors in mutual funds and possibly those with bank-managed trusts wish to be exposed to the risks and rewards of the financial markets. Equity ownership on behalf of other groups is a by-product of the institution's mission as a provider of pension benefits or insurance. Each of these institutions — as the stewards of other people's money — is subject to the highest standard of care and prudence the U.S. legal system has developed, the fiduciary standard. This standard requires, among other things, that the fiduciary take only those actions a "prudent person" would take with respect to the management of the resources entrusted to the fiduciary. In discharging their fiduciary duty, these institutions buy and sell equities and vote proxies. In effect, they exercise ownership rights on behalf of their beneficiaries.

Earlier in this chapter it was noted that Drucker called this reconcentration of ownership "pension fund socialism." However, the label "fiduciary capitalism" better fits the evolution of equity ownership in the United States. Fiduciary capitalism emphasizes the fact that the reconcentration of ownership has moved into the hands of financial institutions with a fiduciary duty to beneficiaries — policyholders, pensioners, and mutual-fund investors. With this development, a new layer of agents now further removes the ultimate owners from the corporations they own. Other than being bound by the fiduciary standard, these institutions are quite different in their composition, the political, social, and economic influences they are subject to, and, consequently, the roles they play or may potentially come to play in a system of fiduciary capitalism.

Bank Trust Departments

Bank trust departments, typically managers of personal trusts for wealthy individuals and estates, are an important category of institutional investors. In their fiduciary capacity they act as professional owners by making investments and by voting proxies on the equity they hold in trust.[27] In the work by Cox and Kimmel, bank trust departments were classified as "fiduciaries," where they accounted for about 7.5 percent of the shares outstanding early in the century. The data from the Federal Reserve's *Flow of Funds Accounts* summarized in Table 3.3 doesn't break out bank personal trusts and estates as a separate category until 1969.[28] In that year, they accounted for $89 billion in equity ownership out of a total market value of about $850 billion, or about 10.5 percent of the total equity outstanding. Their share held steady at about this level through the late 1970s, at which time the fraction of equity owned by bank trust departments began to decline. By 1998, the latest year for which data is available, bank trust departments accounted for only about 3.5 percent of the ownership of total corporate equity outstanding.

Because of the banking industry's important commercial relationship to corporate clients, bank trust departments are generally considered to be conservative in nature and promanagement in outlook.[29] Consequently, they are unlikely to take or support corporate governance positions that might have the potential to antagonize important clients, even if indirectly. When an issue of concern to shareholders arises in a portfolio company, bank trust departments are most likely to accept management's recommendations. In any case, their importance as institutional investors has diminished greatly over the years.

Insurance Companies

Early in the century life and casualty insurance companies were important institutional owners of corporate equity. While they only accounted for 2.4 percent of equity ownership in 1945, they were still the second most important category of equity owners behind the mammoth household sector (see Table 3.3). In 1945, in fact, insurance companies owned more equity than mutual funds, private pension funds, and state and local government retirement funds combined. The fraction of corporate equity owned by insurance companies has grown slowly but steadily over the decades from the 2.4 percent of all equity in 1945 to 6.1 percent in 1998. Early in the period, insurance companies other than life insurance companies (primarily various types of property and casualty companies) held about two-thirds of the industry's investments in corporate equity. However, since the early 1970s the fraction held by life insurance companies has grown more rapidly so that by 1998, almost 80 percent of the equity held by insurance companies was held by life insurance companies. Part of this growth can be attributed to the development of life insurance products such as universal variable life insurance and tax-deferred annuities that act very much like tax-deferred equity mutual funds. Because most insurance companies, like banks, have parallel commercial relationships with corporations, most observers consider their vigorous exercise of ownership rights problematic.

Mutual Funds

Modern mutual funds—pooled assets invested by a professional money manger where individuals own shares in the fund and not directly in the investments owned by the fund—were authorized by the Investment Act of 1940. However, mutual funds don't begin to account for a substantial fraction of equity ownership until the end of the 1980s.[30] At the beginning of that decade mutual funds accounted for only 3.1 percent of the ownership of corporate equity, down from a high of 5.4 percent in 1971. The bear market of the early 1970s, accompanied by high nominal interest rates, not only depressed equity prices in general, but also discouraged individuals from investing in equity mutual funds. Interest in equity mutual funds as a substitute for direct equity ownership revived in the mid-1980s and was particularly strong during the 1990s. By 1997, the fraction of equity owned by mutual funds had more than doubled from 7.1 percent of all corporate equity in 1990 to 16.3 percent in 1998. In fact, a substantial amount, although not all, of the decline in direct equity ownership by households over this period is probably attributable to the rise in indirect ownership through holdings of mutual fund shares with their promise of superior convenience, diversification, and professional management.

The fact that investors can take money out of an open-end mutual fund at any time dramatically separates these funds from other institutional investors. The need to guard against a general liquidation of a fund's shares is generally thought to impel mutual fund managers to maximize short-term returns at the expense of any longer-term responsibilities of ownership.[31] During the takeover boom of the 1980s, this generally meant tendering shares whenever an offer was made at a premium to the current market price. However, this commitment to liquidity may be illusory since it may aggravate fluctuations in the stock market where redemption orders get quickly translated into sell orders. Friedman attributes some of the excess market volatility in the 1987 stock market crash to this source and worries that the illusion of liquidity may, in certain circumstances, have a destabilizing effect on financial markets.[32]

Although the majority of the pension fund assets are accounted for by the next two categories, a growing fraction of mutual fund assets are, in fact, in individual retirement accounts (IRAs), 401(k), 403(b), KEOGH, and other Internal Revenue Service–sanctioned tax-deferred retirement plans.[33] In these cases, the mutual fund offering the account acts much like a money manager acts vis à vis a public or private pension-fund administrator.[34] By their nature and because of substantial tax penalties for early withdrawals, these funds are invested for long periods of time and the high liquidity preference attributed to other mutual fund investments is reduced.[35] While mutual funds have not been publicly active as "shareholder activists," recently they have been increasingly active informally, working with the more public activists as well as on their own.[36] This is reinforced for large fund families such as Fidelity Investments, where their holdings across all of their funds represent a de facto index of the equity market as a whole. For these funds, anything that enhances the general return to equity investment will benefit their fund family. As a consequence, large fund families have developed their own corporate governance and proxy-voting guidelines that typically take a dim view of corporate policies such as poison pills that destroy shareholder value.

Private Pension Funds

Private pension funds are currently the second largest category of institutional investors. However, as Table 3.4 shows, they were the largest institutional investors between 1965 and 1995, and as recently as 1985, private pension funds held four times the equity of mutual funds. Private pension plans are subject to ERISA rules, and their growth has been driven by a number of factors.[37] Among the most important are the favorable tax treatment of compensation given in the form of pension benefits, demographic and work preference trends, and the growth in the stock market. As Roe summarizes:

> The rise of huge stock-owning pensions was not primarily due to corporate governance issues or public choice decisions. Pension funds became important because of changing social circumstances: Employees' life spans lengthened, their wealth rose and they took some of it in earlier retirement. Public choice plays a background role: private pensions became important because America has just about the lowest publicly-funded old age pensions . . . in the industrialized world . . . once American politics took out the big institutional players — banks and insurers — from playing an active boardroom role or from even owning stock, pensions were the only players left.[38]

Table 3.3 shows that in the 1980s, private pension funds' share of equity ownership was more than 20 percent, but since then it has declined so that by 1998, this category of institutional investor accounted for 14.5 percent of all equity ownership in the United States. The relative decline in private pension funds is due to the general shift from defined-benefit plans to defined-contribution plans and corporate restructuring over this period. Both of these factors led to a smaller growth in private pension-fund assets — particularly when compared with either mutual funds or with another category, state and local pension funds.[39]

A defined-benefit plan (the "traditional" pension plan) provides a pension benefit of a specified amount based on employment characteristics such as years of service, ending salary, age of retirement, or some combination of these factors. The plan sponsor has an obligation to pay the pension. This is usually achieved by making contributions to the pension fund and then having the pension fund administrator make the investments to earn the return necessary to discharge the liability.

A defined-contribution plan does not obligate the employer to pay any particular pension benefit. Instead the employer and/or the employee make periodic contributions to the plan. Almost all defined contribution plans let the employee choose from a menu (sometimes a very large menu) of potential investments. Thus, the pension benefit depends on choices the employee makes and on how well those choices turn out. The contribution is defined; the benefit is not. A defined-benefit plan generates future liabilities for a company. A defined-contribution plan ends the company's obligation with the initial company contribution. Defined-contribution plans are also "immediately vested" and "portable." This means that the assets in the retirement plan are the property of the employee as soon as they are contributed and that the employee can take the plan with him or her when

TABLE 3.5: Assets in Defined-Benefit and Defined-Contribution Pension Plans,
1985–1996

	Total Assets (in billions of dollars)	Defined Benefit Assets	Percentage of Total	Defined Contribution Assets	Percentage of Total
1985	$1,157	$ 763.6	66.0%	$ 393.4	34.0%
1990	$1,668	$ 964.1	57.8%	$ 703.9	42.2%
1991	$1,934	$1,104.3	57.1%	$ 829.7	42.9%
1992	$2,053	$1,123.0	54.7%	$ 930.0	45.3%
1993	$2,277	$1,241.0	54.5%	$1,036.0	45.5%
1994	$2,294	$1,188.3	51.8%	$1,105.7	48.2%
1995	$2,700	$1,414.8	52.4%	$1,285.2	47.6%
1996	$3,031	$1,603.4	52.9%	$1,427.6	47.1%

Source: Employee Benefit Research Institute, reproduced in Conference Board *Institutional Investment Report* 2, no. 1 (June 1998), 41.

moving to a new employer. Defined-benefit plans typical don't provide a pension benefit until some years of employment have been accrued (often as long as 20 years of service) and they are typically not transferable from employer to employer.[40] As Table 3.5 shows, assets in defined benefit plans declined steadily from 1985 to 1996. Over the same period, assets in defined contribution plans rose from 34 to 47 percent of total assets. Most experts expect this trend away from defined-benefit plans and toward defined-contribution plans to continue.[41]

Many observers have noted that individuals tend to make more conservative investments than institutional money managers, partly because they may be less astute at choosing long-term investments and partly because individuals may be justifiably more risk adverse than a manager of a larger, pooled fund. As Margaret Blair notes, "Most individuals with assets in 401(k) plans make conservative investments in, for example, high-grade bonds or mutual funds. The latter, of course, face the same impediments to shareholder activism that mutual funds face."[42]

Private pension funds are further divided into employer-sponsored (company) pension plans and Taft-Hartley funds. The former are closely aligned with their sponsoring corporation that acts as the plan fiduciary or that delegates this responsibility to pension-fund administrators appointed by corporate management. The latter are labor-union pension funds covering workers in a given industry (teamsters, carpenters, service employees, and the like) who typically work for many different employers. Because of the nature of the incentive systems surrounding employer-sponsored plans, they are thought to be particularly passive and particularly inclined to side with management whenever circumstances or policy forces them to act.[43] However, since 1988 the Department of Labor, which administers ERISA and therefore has substantial influence over what constitutes prudent behavior for these fiduciaries, has made rulings that are seen as requiring more aggressive action to discharge their prudent person responsibilities.[44]

Taft-Hartley funds, on the other hand, have recently been among the most active and effective of the institutional investors. However, their motives are sometimes viewed with suspicion by management and by other institutional investors who feel they may mix pure ownership issues with labor's narrower agenda. Labor sometimes has difficulty reconciling its role as a representative of labor and as an owner of equity capital.[45] However, a coalition can be built when labor uses traditional corporate governance issues to take on a corporation at which it also has labor issues. Labor's long running battle with Fleming Companies is an example. The company has seriously underperformed economically, has poor corporate governance policies, and has antagonized its union. In both 1997 and 1998, The International Brotherhood of Teamsters Union sponsored proxy proposals — to redeem or vote on a poison pill and to repeal a classified board — that achieved majority votes. Both proposals — mainline corporate governance reforms — were supported by most institutions and were among the most successful of their proxy season. In fact, the 1997 proposal was a binding bylaw amendment prompted by Fleming's refusal to redeem its poison pill despite a 65 percent antipill vote the previous year.[46]

Public Employee Pension Funds

The final category of institutional owners is the pension funds of the public employees of state and local governments. As Table 3.6 shows, through the 1970s employment growth at the state and local level considerably outpaced employment growth at the federal level. Until 1970, total government employment grew considerably faster than the civilian labor force. After that, both federal and state/local employment grew at about the same rate as the labor force as a whole so that by 1994, all government employment accounted for 14.8 percent of the civilian labor force. Of this, about 85 percent of total government employment was at the state and local level.

The growth of local public employee pension fund assets — and particularly equity assets — has been equally dramatic. As Table 3.4 shows, it wasn't until 1969 that state and local pension fund ownership of corporate equity amounted to more than 1 percent of equity outstanding. Before then these institutions followed very conservative investment policies and invested almost all of their assets in bonds. Beginning in the 1980s, and particularly in the 1990s, these funds turned increasingly to the equity markets so that by 1998, their share of corporate equity had climbed tenfold to 10.32 percent.

Table 3.7 shows the holdings of state and local retirement funds for the fiscal year 1996–1997. These funds held about $1.5 trillion dollars in assets

TABLE 3.6: Civilian Employment by Level of Government, 1940–1995

	As Percentage of All Government Employment			As a Percentage of Civilian Labor Force		
	All Government Employees	Federal (Civilian)	State and Local	All Government Employees	Federal (Civilian)	State and Local
1995	100.0%	14.8%	85.2%	NA	NA	NA
1994	100.0%	15.2%	84.8%	14.8%	2.3%	12.6%
1993	100.0%	15.9%	84.1%	14.7%	2.3%	12.4%
1992	100.0%	16.3%	83.7%	14.8%	2.4%	12.4%
1991	100.0%	16.7%	83.3%	14.8%	2.5%	12.3%
1990	100.0%	16.9%	83.1%	14.7%	2.5%	12.2%
1980	100.0%	17.9%	82.1%	15.2%	2.7%	12.5%
1970	100.0%	22.1%	77.9%	15.7%	3.5%	12.3%
1960	100.0%	27.5%	72.5%	12.7%	3.5%	9.2%
1950	100.0%	33.1%	66.9%	10.3%	3.4%	6.9%
1940	100.0%	25.2%	74.8%	NA	NA	NA

Sources: 1980–1995: U. S. Bureau of the Census, *Statistical Abstract of the United States, 1998* (118th edition) Washington, D.C., 1998, Table 530.
1940–1970: U.S. Bureau of the Census, *Historical Statistics of the United States, Colonial Times to 1970,* Bicentennial Edition, Part 1, Washington, D.C., 1975.
1950–1994 Civilian labor force: U.S. Bureau of the Census, *Statistical Abstract of the United States, 1998* (118th edition) Washington, D.C., 1998, Table 644.

at that time. The bulk of the funds, 82.7 percent, were held by state funds. Of the total, $528 billion, or about 35 percent, represented equity holdings by the retirement funds.

Unlike other institutional owners, public pension funds do not have close commercial ties with the business community, and hence they are freer of the potential conflict of interest that limit the actions of other institutional investors. At least partly for this reason, many of the largest of these institutions have been among the most active institutions in the area of corporate governance. According to former New York State Comptroller Edward Regan, "In fact if you took the CalPERS and the New York City pension fund and TIAA-CREF out of the equation along with our fund [New York State] and Wisconsin, Pennsylvania and to some extent Florida, you might have very little activism at all."[47]

While public pension funds are independent of direct pressure from the business community, they often function in a political atmosphere that makes them particularly susceptible to pressure to make certain types of investments to aid the local or state economy. These are called "economically targeted investments" or ETIs.[48] The funds also face pressure to refrain from making some specific investments such as, in the 1980s, investments in companies doing business in South Africa. Currently many funds

TABLE 3.7: Cash and Investment Holdings of State and Local Government Employee Retirement Systems for Fiscal Year 1996–97 (in millions of dollars)

Asset Class	Total	State	Local	Percentage Distribution		
				Total	State	Local
Cash and demand deposits	$ 75,589	$ 57,623	$ 17,966	5.1%	4.7%	7.1%
Governmental debt	$ 270,441	$ 222,405	$ 48,036	18.3%	18.2%	18.9%
Corporate bonds	$ 217,784	$ 185,237	$ 32,547	14.8%	15.2%	12.8%
Corporate equity	$ 528,695	$ 428,429	$100,265	35.8%	35.0%	39.5%
Mortgages, trusts and other investments	$ 383,705	$ 328,658	$ 55,047	26.0%	26.9%	21.7%
Total	$1,476,213	$1,222,351	$253,862	100.0%	100.0%	100.0%

Source: U. S. Bureau of the Census, http://www.census.gov/govs/per/ret97t4.txt, accessed January 2, 1999.

have felt some pressure to either reduce their holdings of tobacco stocks or to avoid further investments in this industry. Nonetheless, as the quotation indicates, public pension funds have been notable for their leadership on issues of corporate governance. And in many cases the names CalPERS, CalSTRS, the New York City Combined Funds, and SWIB are synonymous with institutional investor activism.[49]

In addition to the state and local employees' pension funds, the Federal Employment Retirement System Act of 1986 (FERSA) established what is in effect 401(k) plans for federal employees. By 1998, FERSA had accumulated more than $55 billion in assets and was ranked by *Pension and Investments* magazine as the tenth largest pension fund in the country. Over time this fund is expected to become the largest institutional investor in the world.[50] However, in order to avoid what was characterized during congressional hearings as "back door socialism," FERSA placed severe restrictions on the types of investments the fund could make. In fact, it is limited to investing in an index fund representing the S&P 500 stock index. The enabling legislation also stripped FERSA's board of trustees of most of its ownership rights by providing that the voting rights — the very exercise of ownership rights — were to be delegated by law to the administrator appointed by the trustees of the fund.[51] This is ironic in light of the 1988 Department of Labor's Avon letter, which mandated proxy voting on the part of ERISA funds.

Black concludes that among all institutional investors there are various types of conflicts of interests such that "no institution is completely beholden to corporate managers; no institution is conflict-free." However, public pension funds have weaker pro-manager conflicts than other types of institutions. "All major institutions have significant conflicts of interests; all but public pension funds have incentives to keep corporate managers happy . . . only public pension funds, and perhaps mutual funds, are potential shareholder proponents."[52]

While pension funds may be relatively free of the kinds of financial entanglements that limit the actions of other institutional investors, banks, and insurance companies in particular, they are still not entirely independent of the web of influence that might constrain their actions. As Romano has pointed out, public pension funds are subject to political constraints that may limit their ability to act as a universal owner.[53] Furthermore, the current debate over rapidly rising CEO compensation and the role that stock options play raises significant questions as to whether professional owners can be effective monitors.[54] After all, many of the trustees of public pension funds are rank-and-file employees elected by their peers and may be over matched when it comes to locking horns with CEOs or financial heavyweights such as Kohlberg Kravis Roberts. Still, the public pension funds have the greatest potential for independent action, although the potential for co-optation is always present.

Conclusions

As the American economy entered the twentieth century, the economies of scale of the modern enterprise were vast and the capital needed to finance these ventures was equally large. The solution provided by the modern corporate form was a ready and efficient vehicle for aggregating the assets of millions of small investors into the mountain of finance capital required by modern manufacturing processes. The result in the first half of the twentieth century was that the equity in most corporations was owned by a very large number of individuals, each of whom owned an infinitesimal fraction of the firm's equity and therefore exercised an infinitesimal fraction of the ownership responsibility of the firm. Collective-action problems prevented the owners from effectively acting as a group — an observation that led Berle and Means to the conclusion that ownership had been divorced from control and that the rights and responsibilities of owners had effectively passed to managers.

Beginning around the middle of the century — but not becoming a pronounced trend until the 1970s and 1980s — the center of gravity of the ownership of corporate equity in the United States began to shift dramatically. Individual ownership declined and institutional ownership rose until by the late 1990s, institutional ownership accounted for a larger fraction of equity ownership, 47.6 percent, than household ownership, 44.2 percent.[55] Individuals are still the beneficial "owners" of most of the corporate equity in the country, but they are no longer the owner of record of much of it. The owners of record are now the mutual funds, insurance companies, and the various pension plans. Individuals do enjoy the rights to the increase or decrease in value of mutual-fund shares, and as beneficiaries they do receive the protection of the insurance policies and the payouts of the pension programs. But where at one time they exercised the (diluted) rights and responsibilities of equity ownership described by Berle and Means with regard to 90 percent of corporate equity, they have since relinquished those rights to a growing fraction of the nation's wealth.

Instead, those rights — to buy and sell stock, to propose and vote proxies, to monitor and communicate with management, and to exercise the other rights of ownership — are now the responsibility of the institutional investors. In short, by virtue of their relatively small number and because of their growing size and importance in financial markets, these fiduciary institutions have become the real, effective owners — professional owners — of corporate America. Because of their professionalism and because of their fiduciary duty to their beneficiaries, some have begun to flex their new-found muscles as institutional investor activists. Since the 1980s they have asked firms to adopt corporate governance rules and regulations respectful of the rights of shareholders and they have held management accountable for the long-term success of their companies. When shareholder value is destroyed through incompetence or opportunism, these new owners are quick to call management to account for their actions and, if necessary, to lobby for new corporate leadership.

The important point is that these new fiduciary owners are relatively small in number and, because of the nature of their fiduciary duties, they take their ownership responsibilities seriously. Their small numbers don't eliminate all of the barriers to collective action, but it significantly reduces them. Furthermore, for large, universal investors, the raw dollar amounts involved provide a powerful incentive to overcoming collective action problems. To discharge their duty of care and duty of loyalty responsibilities to their beneficiaries, fiduciary institutions *must* be vigilant monitors of the companies they invest in and they must carefully discharge their other obligations of ownership as well. Their fiduciary duty is part of English common law, has been codified in the ERISA statutes that govern private pension plans, and informs the rules governing most of the public pension plans as well. The logic of these rules is that institutions must take their ownership responsibilities seriously. For some this means being active investors vigorously pressing the responsibilities of ownership. For all fiduciary institutions it means that they have a duty to carefully consider the choices they make when voting proxies and the support they give to or withhold from the more visible and aggressive actions of other owners. These are among the requirements of professional ownership and they are some of the implications of the reconcentration of wealth into the hands of fiduciary institutions.

Chapter 4
The Finance Model and Its Implications for Corporate Governance

---

There are many views on why corporations exist, how best to understand the choices they make, how to analyze the relationship between the various suppliers of inputs, and how to distribute the wealth they create. The prevailing academic model, the one that informs the behavior of most if not all institutional investors, has been characterized as the "finance model."[1] In simple terms, the finance model views the corporation as an organization bringing together various inputs to produce goods and services for sale in the marketplace. Inputs consist of different kinds of raw materials, labor, physical capital, and financial capital in the form of debt and equity. Contracts, mostly explicit but often containing implicit elements, are used to determine the payments and other terms of the relationship between the corporation and most suppliers. The specific payment to be made to holders of equity capital, however, is not specified by a contract. Instead, holders of equity, the shareholders, have a contract with the firm to receive whatever remains *after* the corporation meets its obligations to the other factors of production. Thus, shareholders are often referred to as "residual" claimants since they receive the "residual" after all other factors of production have been paid.[2]

The standard microeconomic assumption about firm behavior is that firms exist to maximize profits. From this perspective, the firm is a black box—reacting to input and product markets in ways necessary to achieve the goal of profit maximization. Traditional theory says little or nothing about how this is achieved on a level internal to the firm. This is particularly unsatisfactory because it fails to take account of the substantial conflict of interest that exists between shareholders—those paid the residual—and managers—those charged with making the day-to-day decisions resulting in the residual.

To correct this shortcoming, the finance model adds to the traditional theory of the firm an investigation of what is inside the box and how it works.[3] For example, in a classic article Jensen and Meckling formally model agency cost and relate it to ownership structure. They begin with an owner-managed firm and then modify their assumptions to investigate the economic implications of the separation of ownership from control.[4] The authors then investigate the economic implications of the techniques owners should apply when trying to monitor managers and the implications these would have for agency cost.

In the finance model, shareholders are the "owners" of the firm.[5] Ownership has two aspects. The first is to "appropriate the firm's net earnings." The second is the right to "control" the firm.[6] The former is the residual payment referred to above. The latter is generally interpreted as the means by which shareholders assure themselves that the firm is run so as to generate the largest amount of "net earnings" and that those earnings will, in fact, accrue to the owners. This, of course, is one of the primary problems corporate governance is intended to solve.

The Implications of the Finance Model for Corporate Governance

While obviously important to the governance of the modern corporation and identified above as a central concern in the finance model, the observation that managers may not be as careful with shareholder's investment as they themselves would be is at least as old as modern economics. As in so many areas, Adam Smith summed up what today would be called the principal-agent problem between owners and managers when he wrote:

The directors of such companies [joint stock companies] however, being the managers rather of people's money than of their own, it cannot well be expected that they should watch over it with the same anxious vigilance with which the partners in a private copartnery [partnership] frequently watch over their own. Like the stewards of a rich man, they are apt to consider attention to small matters as not for their master's honor, and very easily give themselves a dispensation from having it. Negligence and profusion, therefore, must always prevail, more or less, in the management of the affairs of such a company.[7]

In this context corporate governance seeks to solve two kinds of principal-agent problems that arise when ownership is divorced from control. The first is managerial slack and the second is managerial malfeasance. The solution to these problems can be provided by mechanisms internal or external to the firm. Internal control mechanisms center on the board of directors and are treated in this section. External control mechanisms, primarily the market for corporate control, are treated below.

Slack arises because managers derive satisfaction from both the salaries they earn and from their working conditions on the job. The simplest form of managerial slack occurs when a CEO increases his or her compensation beyond the "market rate." Of course, it is difficult to tell what a CEO's compensation should be. However, the fact that some CEOs dominate their boards and its compensation committee opens the possibility for overpayment. Other possibilities abound for a CEO intent on increasing his or her *effective* salary. An office and the appropriate staff are necessary to do the job. But are lavish expense accounts, a corporate jet waiting on the tarmac, a suite of offices overlooking Park Avenue or a sky box at the Super Bowl also necessary for a manager to do his or her best work?[8] All of these items and many like them could greatly increase managerial satisfaction while adding little or nothing to managerial effectiveness. They would, therefore, come almost entirely at the expense of the residual profits of the shareholders.

A more subtle form of managerial slack occurs when a manager does less than his or her best job. Slacking, in this sense, takes the form of providing less effort to the firm than shareholders expect to receive for the salary paid. This type of slack may occur either in terms of time (e.g., leaving work early, playing golf on company time) or effort (not providing the best effort the person is capable of) or in a combination of the two. It is particularly hard to detect slack of this type since only the manager is likely to know at a given moment whether he or she is performing up to capacity or taking an excessive amount of "on-the-job leisure." However, there can be serious losses to the business in the form of missed opportunities because managers don't pursue them vigorously either for a lack of time or for a lack of interest. Likewise, a slacking manager may not put his or her best effort into important decisions, with possibly expensive consequences.

As important as greed and sloth may be in some situations, firms typically develop motivation and evaluation systems that eliminate the most serious abuses. With regard to top managers, the monitoring and evaluating functions of corporate governance are aimed at minimizing these types of agency problems. As representatives of the owners, the board typically discharges its duty to monitor and its duty to evaluate top management through its audit and compensation committees. However, some boards are so dominated by a CEO with a desire for expensive personal projects that a substantial misdirection of corporate resources can take place. Monks and Minow report an extreme example in their chapter, "Case Studies: Corporations in Crisis." "In 1989, the proxy statement of the Occidental Petroleum Company informed shareholders that the company intended to spend tens of millions of corporate dollars to build a museum to house the art collection of Occidental's founder, CEO and chairman, Dr. Armand Hammer. Furthermore, a much smaller sum would be spent on a book detailing two years in the life of Armand Hammer. The story provides an excellent study of boardroom neglect in the face of a powerful and domineering chief executive."[9] At least in theory, corporate governance is again the finance model's answer to this type of malfeasance. Here the mechanism is for the shareholders to replace the "lapdog" directors with "watchdog" directors.

The board is also charged with putting into place appropriate incentive systems to align the actions of managers with the interests of the owners. One way to give managers an incentive to maximize the value of a company's stock is to pay part of the manager's salary in stock options so that good stock-market performance translates directly into higher compensation.[10] Other compensation schemes can be devised to tie pay to performance, such as bonuses that depend on meeting predetermined financial targets. In any case, the finance model views as a crucial responsibility of the board of directors the hiring, monitoring, compensating, and if necessary, firing of top management.

Except in the most extreme cases, given normal board controls, the amount of money that might be wasted at a large corporation by the types of managerial slack discussed above, is not likely to greatly effect shareholders' returns. However, managers may have important incentives to act contrary to the interests of owners in ways that are more complicated than simple greed or sloth. For example, owners can diversify their personal risk by buying stock in several firms in several different industries either directly or indirectly through investments in mutual funds. On the other hand, managers, whose income and professional reputation depends heavily on the performance of a specific firm in a specific industry and who have a great deal of the human capital tied up in their present position can not so easily diversify their risk.[11] This may provide some managers with a motive to follow a strategy of conglomerate merger in which the company acquires a portfolio of businesses in unrelated fields.[12]

By following this strategy, the manager is in effect doing with the firm what an investor can do with a stock portfolio. He or she is mitigating risk through diversification. For example, in the 1960s Westinghouse began an aggressive diversification strategy to expand from its traditional electrical and broadcasting business to activities as diverse as watchmaking and low-income housing. By the early 1980s, it had become the classic conglomerate complete with its own financial services division, Westinghouse Credit Corporation. Its 135 divisions had little in common, aside from the nominal strategy of focusing on "local monopolies" and avoiding mass markets. When the company fell on hard times in the early 1990s, this corporate strategy almost bankrupted Westinghouse.[13] Obviously, excessive diversification can be more costly to shareholders than a few inflated salaries.

Furthermore, managers typically accumulate a great deal of firm-specific knowledge — knowledge that would be worth much less at another company. Consequently, they may adopt a number of techniques to ensure their continued employment at the firm where this knowledge is most useful and, therefore, most highly compensated. Expansions or investments that make use of the CEO's particular knowledge further entrench management by both enhancing that knowledge and by increasing the firm's reliance on it.[14] The board may be reluctant to replace a CEO spearheading an expansion campaign like that described at Westinghouse compared to one engaged in the day-to-day running of the existing business. That is, as long as returns to shareholders are not reduced too severely.

However, if the returns do suffer because of this or any other form of managerial slack, the finance model sees it as the corporate governance responsibility of the board of directors to discipline wayward management. If the board of directors fail in their responsibility, then the next line of defense is for the shareholders to replace the directors with more aggressive and vigilant ones.

The Value of Separating Ownership from Control

The problems discussed in the previous section arise because of the divorce of ownership from control, and the various corporate governance solutions designed to ameliorate agency costs flowing from that separation. While these costs may be substantial, the same separation has certain important economic benefits. It should not be forgotten that despite the widespread divorce of ownership from control, the American economy performed extremely well in many important ways during the postwar period and provided the highest levels of incomes and wealth the world had ever seen up to that time. As Blair put it, "the possibility that separating equity holding from control would lead to poor business performance seemed largely academic."[15] Following Blair, there are at least three reasons why shareholders invest in companies that require them to delegate control over their investments to others.

First, the atomizing of equity claims into small, affordable units makes possible the mobilization of substantial amounts of capital from a multitude of small shareholders. No longer is a corporate enterprise forced to find a wealthy individual or a small group of wealthy individuals to fund every venture. The small size of the investment alone, while making it available to many, would not have been sufficient motivation to mobilize large amounts of capital without the additional feature of limited liability. Each investor in a corporation knows with certainty that his potential loss is limited to the amount of his investment, and that he is shielded from any additional liability no matter what stupid or illegal thing the company might do. Without limited liability, large corporations with many investors would have been impossible to create.

Second, by separating ownership from control the corporate form greatly increased the pool of potential managers. In a world of sole proprietorships and partnerships, potential managers had to be drawn from the ranks of potential owners. That is, from the group of individuals with enough personal wealth (or closely related to those with such wealth) to become controlling owners.[16] This, of course, eliminated the principle-agent problem, but left a "competency" problem since there is nothing to suggest that the wealthy have any particularly monopoly on the skills necessary to effectively manage a large enterprise, or more to the point, on the ability to obtain the skills through education and experience. By separating owners from managers, the corporate form promoted professional competence over family connections. This expansion of the pool of potential managers (augmented by the rise of professional training taking place at the same time) produced a substantial increase in the average ability of those who rise to the top level of large corporations.

However, while the separation of ownership from control probably led to a general improvement in the quality of managers, management remained, and remains to this day, the bastion of white, Protestant males.[17] While there are undeniably substantial social as well as efficiency benefits to the creation of a class of professional managers, much remains to be done to open up opportunities to all qualified individuals on the basis of merit.

Finally, the corporate form with its multitude of shareholders fostered the rise of liquid capital markets to serve one of the primary attractions of share ownership, the ability to quickly and easily convert an investment in one company into cash or into an investment in another company. If things went badly at a company, a shareholder wasn't joined to it by a complicated partnership agreement. Instead, she or he could sell the shares and quickly redeploy the capital in another direction. Reinforcing the liquidity motive is the fact noted above that investors can easily diversify risk by holding small stakes in many different companies. For these two reasons, the result is a capital market in which investors require lower risk premiums for any particular investment. The great benefit to the economy at large is that firms can then raise capital on the most favorable terms possible.

The first and third factors imply a more efficient capital market in which large amounts of capital can be raised at the lowest possible risk premium. The second factor improves the efficiency of the market for managers by mobilizing a pool of talent regardless of personal wealth or family connections. Taken together, these are formidable benefits. In fact, for at least the middle decades of the twentieth century, casual observation based on the performance of American industry indicates the benefits considerably outweighed any costs associated with the separation of ownership from control.

The Efficient Market Hypothesis and the Market for Corporate Control

The view that efficiency inherent in professional management—monitored by the internal control mechanism provided by the board of directors—would outweigh agency costs began to erode in the 1970s and early 1980s when management "by the numbers" was carried to its logical conclusion in the conglomerate merger movement.[18] By then, concern that managers would be inattentive to their duties or would appropriate part of the income of the enterprise gave way to a concern than that managers would work energetically to make *strategic* decisions to build conglomerate empires at the expense of profitability.

Some of the motive for empire building may have come from the above-mentioned desire to diversify personal managerial risk or to entrench management in lucrative positions. However, a good deal of the conglomerate merge movement may simply have been driven by CEO egos that found satisfaction in empire building or from the increased salary that inevitably was given to a CEO who headed a larger company.[19] By the late 1970s, these acquisition strategies were beginning to look particularly suspect. The finance model's first line of defense is for the board of directors to evaluate the expansion program, and if found wanting, to impose the necessary change of strategic direction on the company. Unfortunately, many boards were captured by their CEOs or were willing participants in the acquisition programs, perhaps because of an excess of free cash flow with which to pursue acquisitions, and were, therefore, unable or unwilling to make the necessary changes.[20] In cases where internal control mechanisms failed to protect the interests of shareholders, the finance models turned to a powerful external corporate governance mechanism, the market for corporate control.[21]

The market for corporate control has been heralded not only as one of the most effective corporate governance mechanisms available to shareholders, but as a major contributor to economic efficiency in the corporate sector.[22] It has also been subject to withering criticism. To understand the appeal of the market for corporate control, it is necessary to understand the efficient market hypothesis. This hypothesis proposes that in an "efficient market" current equity prices accurately reflect all currently known public information about a company and its economic prospects.[23] From this perspective, equity prices are the ultimate summary statistic putting a precise economic value on a publicly traded company. It is as if equity markets were large machines for gathering, processing, and translating information into a price that faithfully reflects underlying economic values. According to the efficient market hypotheses, any change in a company's future prospects — such as that which might come about because of management inefficiency, management shirking, or other forms of malfeasance — will result in a lower stock price, one that accurately reflects the underlying inefficiency.

The logic of the market for corporate control was straightforward. Ill-founded empire building or other value-reducing actions by management would quickly be reflected as a reduction in company's stock price. There would then be a divergence between the public value of the company as given by the financial markets and the private or "intrinsic" value of the company's assets. An astute investor willing to correct managerial mistakes — perhaps by dismantling the company and selling the pieces, certainly by firing the misbehaving managers—could buy the firm at a sufficient premium over the current market price to induce enough shareholders to tender their shares to make the deal happen. The new owners could then install new management charged with correcting previous managerial mistakes (perhaps with the added incentive of equity participation) and in the end come out ahead—sometimes far ahead.[24]

According to the finance model, this was good not only for the shareholders of acquired companies who would receive something closer to the real value of their investment, but it was also good for society at large. Efficiency would not only improve at targeted firms but at other firms as well, as managers redirected their efforts toward creating "shareholder value" in order to avoid the sting of the market for corporate control. Resources locked into inefficient investments would be freed to be used in their highest and best uses.[25]

In a study of mergers in the 1960s and 1970s, Jensen and Ruback found average returns of 30 percent for tender offers, 20 percent for mergers, and 8 percent for proxy contests.[26] In another study that focused on tender offers, Jarrell and Pulson found that returns varied by decade: 19 percent in the 1960s, 35 percent in the 1970s, and 30 percent in the early 1980s.[27] These large gaps between the market value and what a bidder was willing to pay were assumed by the finance model to represent a lower bound on an estimate of the economic inefficiency of target companies.

In the 1980s, securities markets—augmented by the recently invented junk-bond financing—became a powerful tool of external corporate governance, effectively augmenting the more traditional tools of internal control available to owners through the board of directors.[28] If management failed to realize "shareholder value," the market for corporate control stood ready to provide the necessary discipline. As Blair remarked, the phrase "finance model" had now come to refer to "the theoretical underpinnings for the arguments that have been used to defend takeovers and that are now used to advocate enhanced rights for shareholders in corporate governance."[29]

The Waning of the Market for Corporate Control

It is not surprising that the market for corporate control evoked a storm of criticism. Some of it was aimed at whether or not the market for corporate control would always achieve social efficiency, even on its own terms. For example, Grossman and Hart point out a potential free-rider problem in which small shareholders who think whether they tender or not will have little effect on the outcome refrain from tendering their shares in the expectation of postmerger gains.[30] If there are enough small shareholders, it is possible that, from the finance model's point of view, socially desirable mergers may fail to take place. A similar prisoner's dilemma-like problem may occur where shareholders fail to reach an agreement with acquirers to divide the difference between the public and the private values.[31]

Others pointed to what they considered overall weaknesses in the market for corporate control as a disciplining mechanism for underperforming management. To begin with, the gap between a company's private value and its market value had to be 30 or 40 percent or more to attract a takeover bid. This represents a very substantial degree of economic inefficiency—and an equally large failure of corporate governance. Without such a gap, potential bidders would not find the company attractive because of the expenses of making a bid and the real possibility that the company might successfully repel a hostile offer. This limited the disciplining effects of the market for corporate control to the really egregious cases. At less poorly managed companies, the takeover market failed to function as a substitute for more conventional forms of corporate governance unless the managers responded to a "demonstration effect" and took hostile takeovers at other companies as a spur to redirecting their own efforts.[32] Furthermore, companies with large blocks of shares in friendly hands—management, a founding family, or a management-friendly retirement fund, for example—usually did not attract takeover bids even if a large disparity existed between public and private values.

Thus takeovers tend to be a fairly blunt ex post tool for resolving what are typically the most serious governance and performance failures. They have no ability to find and confront a problem in the making before it is out of control; they have no ex ante use, unlike a variety of other "nonmarket" governance mechanisms that are discussed in later chapters. Many have also criticized takeovers and the methods used to accomplish them—primarily the issuance of junk bonds and the increased debt load that results—as promoting a short-term mentality. Some observers argued that managers, preoccupied with increasing the market value of their companies to fend off potential bidders, were adopting policies favoring short-term profits over long-term investments.[33] Successful bidders were accused of holding "fire sales" of corporate assets in order to raise the funds required to pay down the mountain of debt incurred when acquiring the company. This "hollowing out" of companies was viewed as socially inefficient. Others, particularly in the affected communities, were appalled by the factory closings and workforce "downsizing" that often accompanied corporate takeovers.

Others came to question the link between the market for corporate control and the efficient market hypotheses. The link, as discussed above, attributes the difference between the private value and the market-determined public value to be a measure of the value of the company's managerial inefficiency. However, some critics viewed the difference as representing the value of broken implicit contracts between labor and the firm or short-term profit realized by selling assets or by raiding pension funds. If these were the sources of gains from takeovers, they didn't represent an efficiency gain; rather, they represented a transfer of wealth from one group (workers, pensioners, and so on) to another — acquirers. For example, in an analysis of the takeover of TWA by Carl Icahn, Shleifer and Summers estimate that 150 percent of the takeover premium (the supposed gain in economic efficiency) came from the lost wages of three of the company's unions.[34] Thus, wealth was only being redistributed, not created by the market for corporate control.

That markets always price companies correctly is also called into question by a number of anomalies such as the 1987 stock-market crash, where on a Monday the market fell between 20 and 25 percent after a weekend during which there was relatively little negative business news to account for such a drastic reevaluation of value. As Ross, Westerfield, and Jaffe comment, "A drop of this magnitude for no apparent reason is not consistent with market efficiency."[35] Likewise, bubbles in the Japanese stock market in the late 1980s and, possibly, in internet stocks in the United States in the late 1990s — not to mention tulips in eighteenth-century Holland and shares of the South Sea Company in England in the early 1700s — raise questions about the efficiency with which markets evaluate shares.[36] Finally, the widespread use of passive investment strategies by institutional investors in which positions are driven by an abstract investment rule (e.g., invest so as to mirror the S&P 500 index) also calls into question market efficiency. Here, the buying and selling that the efficient market hypothesis requires to adjust share value to new information may occur in thinner and thinner markets as more and more equity is held in the hands of passive investors. By 1997, 17.2 percent of the equity investments of all institutional investors were in indexed portfolios. The amount of indexing was much higher for public pension funds, 37.1 percent, and banks, 36.1 percent.[37]

Managers, of course, were outraged that someone outside "their" company — even an "owner" would second guess their strategic decisions. This reinforced the understandable concern managers had for their personal financial future, should a corporate raider be successful. Labor protested that pension funds were being depleted to pay the debt incurred during some takeovers and that the new owners were tearing up implicit contracts surrounding wages, working conditions, and security of employment — such as at TWA.

Institutional investors, originally quite pleased with the market for corporate control as a robust corporate governance mechanism — and one which quickly returned to them a substantial premium over the previous market value of their investment in a target firm — began to have second thoughts. For one thing, some firms were beginning to pay "greenmail" — that is, buying out the position of a corporate raider at a premium to the current market price. In exchange, the company usually got a "standstill" agreement in which the raider promised not to try to acquire the company for a certain period of time. Greenmail used corporate resources, but only to the benefit of the raider and corporate management. Shareholders were paying the *entire* bill to prevent a hostile takeover. Also, the mountain of low-quality debt used to finance many takeovers had the effect of lowering the overall credit quality of acquired companies. In effect, institutional investors were replacing equity with junk bonds in their portfolios.

Some of the takeovers practiced in the 1980s—the management buy-out where current management acquires the firm—were particularly problematic for investors and finance-model advocates alike. The problem here is that current management is particularly well placed to appreciate the private value of a company since it has access to internal information that must often be estimated by an external bidder. Furthermore, as the acquirer of the company, management has an incentive to engage in practices intended to further reduce the public value of the company in order to reduce the ultimate purchase price.

Toward the end of the 1980s, management and its allies mounted an effective counterattack against hostile takeovers. First, many got their boards to adopt a number antitakeover measures such as poison pills, classified boards, and dual-class stock.[38] Second, a large number of state legislatures passed laws that made takeovers more difficult, laws that were subsequently upheld by state and federal courts.[39] Chief among these was Pennsylvania, which passed a law placing such severe restrictions on takeover bids that major institutional investors strongly pressured portfolio companies to reincorporate in another state. Third, the Delaware chancellery court issued a number of rulings giving the board substantial power to resist unwanted takeover bids.[40] Finally, the Manhattan U.S. Attorney brought indictments in 1989 against Michael Milken and Drexel, Burnham Lambert for various securities' law violations. Milken and Drexel had been a major force in the junk-bond market that had provided crucial financing for many takeover offers.[41] With the collapse of the market for corporate control (in part related to the collapse of the savings and loan industry, and the consequent drying up of liquidity), the end of the hostile-takeover era arrived.

By the early 1990s, proponents of the finance model began to focus on reforms to give more power to owners in an attempt to strengthen the traditional, internal tools of corporate governance. Changes in the legal and social environment meant that takeovers, particularly hostile ones, might have become so expensive to execute that the market for corporate control had truly become an external control mechanism of last resort—one that operated weakly to discipline all but the most inefficient management team. The finance model urged reforms—of communication, board structure, and incentive compensation—that would strengthen internal control mechanisms.[42] Others reformers, although not finance-model enthusiasts, urged the development of long-term relationships between large institutional investors and companies that could then be used to minimize the principal-agent problem.

Conclusions

The finance model with its grounding in traditional economic theory provides a powerful framework for analyzing the principal-agent problem and for investigating the internal and external corporate governance tools available to solve it. Proponents of the model tend to promote any internal reforms to the board of directors or to the rights and responsibilities of shareholders that strengthens the ability of owners to monitor managers. In particular, many institutional investors have found a justification for their activism in the broad outlines and general precepts of the finance model. Commentators grounded in the finance model also usually see the market for corporate control as the ultimate corporate governance tool.

Criticisms of the finance model have most often focused on its emphasis on the narrowly conceived goal of maximizing shareholder value as being synonomous with maximizing the share price of the firm. The next chapter develops this critique by examining a number of criticisms of the finance model, both from within a finance model perspective and from other perspectives about how firms operate.

Critics of the market for corporate control as a useful external corporate governance device typically focus on the blunt nature of the ex post process, the disruption and distraction it causes to ongoing enterprises, the emphasis placed on short-term over long-term actions, and the fact that the size of the required premium means that it is only available to correct truly egregious lapses. In addition, some have questioned whether the takeover premium at the center of the market for corporate control might really represent wealth transfers from employees, suppliers, and the public treasury rather than the efficiency gains claimed by supports.

Regardless of one's view of the market for corporate control, its most direct application, the hostile takeover, has largely been neutralized in the United States by a number of events. By the early 1990s, management was broadly effective at getting state legislatures to enact antitakeover statutes that strengthened the defenses firms could use to fend off an unwanted suitor. A number of court decisions, particularly in the important Delaware courts, validated a number of important elements of these statutes. Furthermore, changes in regulation following the collapse of the junk-bond market and the credit crunch at the end of the 1980s meant the drying up of the most important form of financing used in hostile takeovers. It had also been suggested by some that the hostile-takeover boom of the 1980s both corrected the serious cases of mismanagement and refocused management's attention on creating shareholder value. If true, both of these developments would have removed major reasons for takeovers in the first place. However, this is a less than convincing argument in light of the early 1990s successful "corporate coups" initiated by corporate governance activists against giants such as GM, IBM, Westinghouse, and Sears.

In sum, the financial model offers too narrow a focus to provide an adequate perspective for the universal owner, which holds a diverse and large portfolio that reflects a cross section of the entire economy. From a financial model perspective, such a universal owner is not equipped to either conceptualize nor confront an array of relatively new issues and possibilities opened by these recent developments. The financial-model perspective is not only a stockholder perspective; it is a narrow stockholder perspective that sees each firm as a free-standing institution to be analyzed singularly and in isolation from all other firms in a portfolio. Since the financial model is not concerned with the consequences of the distribution of shareholding that creates fiduciary capitalist institutional investors, it has not (and perhaps cannot from within its conceptual frame) concern itself with the broader agenda that this book argues should confront fiduciary capitalist institutions as universal owners.

Chapter 5
Critiques of the Finance Model: Implications for Corporate Governance

In its simplest form, the finance model described in Chapter 4 asserts two propositions: first, that firms exist for the exclusive benefit of their owners; and second, that in a world of dispersed ownership, the only goal that firms should have is to maximize the return (dividends and capital gains) to its shareholders.[1] This simple idea has evolved into the dominant view of corporations and its relationship to its shareholders as *the* owners of the corporation. However, it is also possible to view the stockholders as only nominal owners or as residual claimants. From this point of view, they are seen more as suppliers of capital, much like the suppliers of other raw materials, rather than owners in any classical sense. They are effectively disenfranchised from the election of directors and, therefore, from exercising little more than a symbolic role in owning the company. This view is rooted in the Berle and Means critique of the separation of ownership from control in the modern corporation and as corporate equity as a form of nontraditional "private" property.

At the time Berle and Means wrote they were understandably concerned with individuals since they owned either directly or through broker/dealers or nominees more than 90 percent of the common equity.[2] But a simple model in which managers are the hired agents of the owners, the "direct-agent" model, meant little to stockholders who were effectively disenfranchised. Instead, as Walter Lippmann wrote in 1914, almost twenty years before Berle and Means' book: "The real news about business is that it is being administered by men who are not profiteers. The managers are on salary, divorced from ownership and from bargaining."[3] What has changed since the middle of the century is that with the growth of large institutional investors a new owner, a professional owner, has arisen. A reconcentration of ownership has occurred, but not of the personal, classical, private-property type envisioned by Adam Smith or Milton Friedman. These new owners, who control large equity portfolios that represent a broad cross section of the economy as a whole, are fiduciaries. They are legally and ethically beholden to their beneficiaries and they are run by professional managers. A new type of property has emerged, one this work characterizes as fiduciary capitalism.

While at first glance the finance model appears to offer a clear-cut view of both the firm and its relation with its owners, or at least its stock*holders* (that is, with those holding stock, which may well not suggest owning the firm), on closer examination the finance model has faced significant conceptual and practical challenges from academics and practitioners alike. These perspectives have come from both those sharing many assumptions of finance-model theorists and from those contesting its core assumptions. They are both normative and descriptive. This chapter discusses three critiques of the financial model: stakeholder theory (in some of its variants), a critique from within the nexus of contracts perspective itself, which otherwise is typically seen as a statement of the finance model; and the transaction-cost economics perspective. It then presents an alternative to the finance model. The aim is not to explore these various and often very elaborate traditions in detail, but rather to draw from them ways to view what none of them have to date adequately considered: that the growth of institutional shareholding may render moot many assumptions and assertions of these often conflicting traditions.

Stakeholder Perspectives

Perhaps the most politically prominent and academically influential argument in opposition to the finance model is the stakeholder view. Numerous stakeholder perspectives exist, but they all share the assertion that there are other legitimate claimants to the resources of a firm aside from its stockholders. These claimants, it is argued, have a right to some form of voice in the firm's decision-making process. Groups commonly identified as stakeholders are the employees, suppliers, and customers of a firm. More broadly, neighborhoods of the firm who might be affected by firm actions in the environmental arena or through its impact on the local transportation system, housing market, and so on are seen as stakeholders. From the broadest perspective, all citizens are stakeholders in every firm in the economy, because each firm has an impact on everyone's economic and social well-being.

In the case of environmental damage caused by a particular firm, for example, a stakeholder might claim some form of mitigation — compensation, pollution control, or the like — that is a direct claim on the firm's resources. This, however, is distinctly different from a shareholder's claim on a firm's residual resources, although mitigating such a stakeholder claim may affect the amount of the residual. Donaldson and Preston, for example, argue that stakeholders, "are identified through the actual or potential harms and benefits that [stakeholders] . . . experience or anticipate experiencing as a result of the firm's actions or inactions."[4] Thus, environmental damage, discrimination, or health issues can be stakeholder issues, and these issue constituencies are consequently stakeholders by virtue of the fact, in the broadest terms, that they have a claim on the firm and/or a desire to influence its activities.

One concrete manifestation of the logic of stakeholder perspectives is the corporate constituency laws passed by state legislatures in more than thirty states as a reaction to the takeover, merger, and acquisition wave of the 1980s. These laws typically require firms to consider, in Blair's words, "the best interest of the corporation as a whole and/or specific stakeholders" — that is, employees, creditors, suppliers, and community in general — when making decisions, especially about takeovers and mergers. Blair concludes that, "While there have not been tests of these general laws to see their extent or degree of sanction, their existence provides some legal form to stakeholder claims."[5] In fact, Delaware court decisions have upheld such claims in a takeover situation based on stakeholder-type factors affecting a "reasonable" threat of a takeover. Outside of the United States, stakeholder constituencies are explicitly represented as in Germany's long history of co-determination, in the recently developed European Union harmonization laws permitting firms to take account of stakeholders, and of course in Japan where such traditions run deep in the very notion of the firm.[6]

Smith and Dyer, writing on the recent history of the corporation, provide a historical context for the stakeholder view. They suggest that in the 1980s and 1990s, a period characterized by significant corporate restructuring and a growing inequality of wages, salaries, and income distribution, a growing reality of unmet "stakeholder" claims paralleled the claims of owners. Owners' claims typically took the form of leveraged buyouts (LBOs) in the late 1980s and early 1990s, while in the 1990s such claims were mainly of those made by various types of institutional owners focused on governance reform and firm-level economic performance per se.[7] Stakeholder claims in the areas of employment, workplace safety, consumer protection, and environmental standards grew at the same time that institutional investors were demanding, and getting, significant corporate governance reforms that they hoped would lead in the longer run to increased firm-level economic performance.

It was also during this period that U.S. firms were coming to depend to a far greater extent than previously on the quality of human resources, rather than on either natural resource endowments or financial capital. Thus, stakeholders' demands, employees' human-capital development, and economic and governance reforms advocated by institutional investors coincided.[8] Can there be a relation among these three historical developments, various models of the firm, and the main thesis of this work: that institutional investors as fiduciary agents, which are also universal owners, have the potential to bridge what at first glance may appear to be a quite divergent set of demands on the corporation?

On its face, stakeholder claims directly challenge the finance model's assertion that shareholders are the only or primary claimants on the firm's residual profits and those with ultimate control authority. For example, in its broadest form a stakeholder perspective takes what can be characterized as the "social debt" of the corporation perspective. This perspective argues that because of its inherent legally "privileged" position (its limited liability status as a legal person with immortality, a privilege granted to it by state legislatures), a corporation owes a social debt, which is necessary to serve a larger social good. The corporation is thus seen as a creature of public policy rather than of the market, and a social price for such privileged creation is seen as a legitimate quid pro quo.[9] In short, the whole society as represented by the government has a stake in the corporation by virtue of the valuable economic privilege bestowed upon it through the political process of incorporation.

Such a quid pro quo was long ago recognized by Berle and Means as a logical concomitant of the separation of ownership from control. Passive owners (that is, shareholders) "have surrendered the right that the corporation should be operated in their sole interest — they have released the community from the obligation to protect them to the full extent implied in the doctrine of strict property rights. . . . The [new controlling groups, the managers] . . . have, rather, cleared the way for the claims of a group far wider than either the owners or the control[ling group]. They have placed the community in a position to demand that the modern corporation serve not alone the owners or the control [group] but all society."[10]

For Berle and Means the divorce of ownership and control justified greater social regulation of the firm, modifying to a significant degree previously unfettered rights of property. Berle and Means' critique of the modern firm led directly to advocacy of and support for New Deal regulatory reforms such as the establishment of the Security and Exchange Commission and the Federal Trade Commission. However, an implicit, yet critical point was their assumption that those passive owners had interests, in their majority, different from and perhaps opposed to "all of society."[11] In the 1930s, this assumption was correct given the tiny proportion of institutionally held equity, and the ownership patterns of highly concentrated ownership in the wealthiest income brackets.

Evan and Freeman reflect a more contemporary view of the stakeholder perspective. They suggest that "managerial capitalism" remains both viable and desirable if and when the purely property rights conception of management having only a duty to stockholders is replaced by a Kantian notion of a respect for persons. Through this line of reasoning, managers come to have a fiduciary relation to both stockholders and stakeholders.[12]

Keasey suggests that because of its sweeping claims against the firm and its rejection of wealth maximization for shareholders, the stakeholder perspectives are "the most fundamental challenge to the principal-agent approach" since the essence of the principal-agent perspective attempts to minimize managerial opportunism in favor of shareholders, even at the expense of all other potentially interested parties.[13] Boatright notes that "The key normative idea in stakeholder theory is that many persons and groups besides shareholders have a legitimate claim or stake in the corporation and that the rights and interests of all stakeholders ought to be respected in some way."[14]

Keasey cites two principal ways in which a stakeholder approach might increase wealth. The first suggests that a socially ethical firm can build trust relations that support profitable investment and mutually beneficial exchanges between stakeholders due to lower long-term (iterative) transaction costs, citing Japan as a primary example. This means that a system of trust is most efficient at reducing transaction costs in those situations requiring widespread iterative, implicit, and highly flexible contracts, recognizing that stakeholder claims in this situation are seen as a means to greater efficiency. This argument is at once normative, descriptive, and prescriptive.

A second situation Keasey cites in which a stakeholder approach might be beneficial to wealth maximization is Margaret Blair's idea of cospecialized (or firm- and industry-specific) human capital assets. This approach gives employees stakeholder claims based on their human capital contributions as residual holders and risktakers. It is parallel in form and content to stockholder-investors as risktakers and residual holders or claimants.[15] This is especially the case when such asset-specific human capital investments are linked to firm profitability through performance pay, bonuses tied to firm profitability and, of course, stock options. The claim of stakeholders in this formulation lies not in a firm's sui generis "legal debt" to society at large nor in ethical prescriptions, but rather they reside in a firms' employees, who are generators and repositories of critical specific human capital and the impact this might have on firm performance.

Blair develops this line of reasoning extensively in her book *Ownership and Control: Rethinking Corporate Governance for the Twenty-First Century,* where she argues that highly skilled labor has made important firm-specific investments in human capital that are analogous to the capital equity owners have invested. The capital labor has contributed to the firm deserves—for reasons of *efficiency* as well as equity—to be represented on the board of directors. Blair views the simple finance view, which identifies the firm with equity owners and views the problem of corporate performance as one of maximizing shareholder wealth, as too narrow. She stresses "that the goals of directors and management should be maximizing total wealth creation by the firm. The key to achieving this is to enhance the voice of and provide ownership-like incentives to those participants in the firm who contribute or control critical, specialized inputs (firm-specific human capital) and to align the interests of these critical stakeholders with the interests of outside, passive shareholders."[16]

Blair's argument is about efficiency and equity, but it is also partially a fiduciary one: if, for example, bondholders and other creditors of a firm in fact share residual risk with shareholders, then employees who may be paid an incentive wage or who share profits as incentive schemes are also residual holders. Indeed, as suggested previously, regardless of debt-holder and creditor status, employees — particularly those with firm-specific investments in human capital — may be residual riskholders as well. Stockholders bear residual risk since, short of selling, they cannot contract out of risk. To the degree that profit-sharing among employees or widespread stock option schemes or incentive wages represent a significant proportion of total compensation, Blair argues that such employees are de facto shareholders — and residual riskbearers — insofar as their compensation comes to depend on firm performance rather than contractual wage or salary payments. The widespread bonus system in Japanese firms in which employees may receive more than one-half of their total compensation in lump-sum bonuses based on firm-level performance comes to mind as an important example of such quasi-residual riskbearer status. This may account for the generally high level of consideration that Japanese firms have historically given to employees as stakeholders.

Blair concludes that "it is possible to reject the simplistic finance model . . . to the extent that it implies that directors' only duty is to maximize values for shareholders, and still retain the compelling logic [that] the private control of private property leads to the most efficient use of society's resources" (pp. 231–32).[17] Her views can be characterized as advocating that employee stakeholders be recognized and rewarded in proportion to their investment in firm-specific human capital, that is, skills and individual and organizational knowledge that is specifically rooted in a particular firm and that would be worth less outside of it. In short, stakeholding employees share with stockholders some degree of business risk and from this, deserve a share in the governance of the corporation (pp. 238–39, 257).[18]

The point of Blair's thesis is that corporate governance should maximize the wealth-creating potential of the corporation as a whole, rather than just maximize shareholder wealth. She notes that, "Most discussions of corporate governance tacitly assume that these two goals are the same, but . . . that is not likely in the modern corporation" (p. 275). Maximizing shareholder wealth, especially in the short term, may be done at the expense of the long-run competitive position of the firm since such return to shareholders could deplete adequate investment in technology, human resources, and the like or could reflect pure opportunism on the part of shareholders.[19]

While the stakeholder approach correctly critiques the finance model as too narrowly focused on shareholders as owners, the concept of fiduciary capitalism suggests a perspective that is different from any of the traditional stakeholder approaches. Although Blair's argument, far more than most other stakeholder theorists, is rooted in an empirically verifiable "stake," she (along with most stakeholder theorists and almost all finance-model theorists) assume that stockholders are typically, if not always, *separable* from stakeholders. The essence of the idea of fiduciary capitalism is that this is increasingly not the case. Rather than begin with either posited lower transaction costs based on trust systems of widespread implicit contracting or what this work sees as an almost total lack of standards for adjudicating stakeholder claims writ large (particularly by nonemployees), this book takes a more institutional and empirical perspective. Simply put, the interests of diverse shareholders have come to represent a broad cross section of at least 45–50 percent of the U.S. population so that conceptual and empirical distinctions between shareholder and stakeholder have begun to blend into each other as a matter of economic interest.

It is not argued here that the interests of various stockholder and stakeholder groups are clear cut, simple, or unambiguous. Indeed, the argument is that these interests have barely begun to be articulated or conceptually formulated by either the ultimate recipients and owners (e.g., pensioners) or by most senior managers of fiduciary institutions. In particular, demographic, regional, class, employment, and other factors cause, or in the future may case, significant divisions among classes of shareholders and beneficial claimants, and between various groups of what we might call "stockholder-stakeholders." What is interesting and important is that these divisions cut across both stockholders and stakeholders rather than divide them. This will make for interesting corporate governance politics.

Striking, therefore, is this historically new basis for a significant, although far from full, convergence between stakeholders (even broadly defined as "citizen-beneficial owner") and shareholders. There is much yet to be understood in the complexities of the bureaucratic representations of individual ownership as fiduciary, public, trade union, nonprofit, corporate, mutual fund, and institutional investors come to dominate the ownership landscape.

The political and regulatory implications of these historical shifts are barely discussed in the literature. Nor does this work attempt to discuss them, although the subject is critical. Again, Monks and Minow make a number of important points. First, the federal government has a financial stake in how all pension funds operate since they are (mostly) tax exempt at a tax expense of about $50 billion per year. This gives the government the legitimate right to "define broadly how pension fund trustees should function in their capacity as owners of the country's industrial establishment." Second, although universal owners' interests may be congruent with those of society, they are unlikely by themselves to be able to deal with the collective choice problems of competing interests in areas such as education, energy conservation, occupational health and safety, and the environment. They conclude, "This is an agenda that can be addressed only by government in conjunction with a 'universal shareholder.'" The implications of this for how universal owners might come to confront the tremendous influence of their portfolio firms, which conduct influential political lobbying against such public goods, may be of the utmost importance.[20]

The Nexus of Contracts Perspective as Stakeholder Theory?

While the stakeholder theory criticizes the finance model for not taking into proper consideration certain constituencies, the nexus of contracts perspective, often seen as synonymous with the finance model, can also be taken as a basis for a critique of that model. The problem the nexus of contracts approach tries to solve is the binding together the various contributors to a firm — labor, raw material and intermediate product suppliers, capital, managerial skill, and the like — toward the end of wealth creation. From this point of view, each contributor's risks and rewards are determined by explicit and implicit contracts. The nexus of contracts terminology is most developed by and is typically associated with the finance model of the firm, and has been overwhelmingly focused on ex ante incentive alignment between principals and agents. (This is discussed in greater detail in the following section.)

However, critics of both the traditional finance model and of stakeholder theory have seen in the nexus of contracts perspective a number of analytical potentials that result in a radical modification of the finance model itself. Blair and Stout, for example, use the nexus formulation to redefine the relation between the board of directors, shareholders, and employee stakeholders. They suggest that rather than seeing the firm as a nexus of contracts (including explicit and implicit, and complete and incomplete contracting), the firm should best be taken as a "nexus of firm specific investments" made by "several groups who each contribute unique and essential resources . . . and who each find it difficult to protect their contribution through explicit contracts."[21] For Blair and Stout this means that while U.S. corporate law views the board of directors as shareholders' agents, in fact they should be seen as "independent hierarchies who are charged not with serving shareholders' interests alone, but with serving the interests of the fictional entity known as the 'corporation.'" Since Blair and Stout argue that the corporation should be understood as a "joint welfare function of *all* the individuals who make firm specific investments," the board of directors is responsible to them as well. Thus, board members are less agents of the shareholders per se than fiduciaries responsible to a number of core value-creating constituencies including, but not limited to, shareholders (pp. 32–33). This follows the central argument Blair makes that if employees are stakeholders who "have substantial firm-specific investments at risk," then they should be included in all aspects of governance.[22]

Blair and Stout make use of the nexus concept to argue for the central role of employee stakeholders—really an extension of the stakeholder critique discussed above. However, they do not follow up on the implications that a nexus of contracts approach to the firm may well undercut the absolute primacy of shareholders themselves by virtue of questioning the primacy of what Berle and Means noted was the end of the corporation as classical private property. Presenting such a radical critique of the finance model from within a nexus of contracts perspective, Boatright is highly critical of most stakeholder perspectives as failing to adequately describe how stakeholder claims can be verified and adjudicated one against another. (Blair's perspective is a partial exception, yet for Boatright it is too limited as it only applies to employees with firm-specific human capital investments.)

Boatright argues that a "plausible" case can be made that the nexus of contracts—what he calls contractual theory—is able to incorporate "the rights and interests of all corporate constituencies."[23] Thus, various interest groups would negotiate actual contracts with firms in order to cement their relationship in existing law, much as a labor union negotiates a contract with an employer. Whether such groups (e.g., an environmental group) would in fact be identical with stakeholder groups is difficult to determine, but in principle they could be.

Boatright's case rests on Berle and Means' argument that the modern corporation, by effectively sundering ownership from control, has simultaneously transformed private property, at least in terms of the firm's relation to its shareholders. Shareholders are, therefore, no longer a privileged group, but rather a group—contracted to supply capital services—on par with other groups that contract with the firm. Thus, one must distinguish between wealth maximization of the firm on the one hand, and the wealth maximization of the shareholders on the other. Boatright cites Berle and Means' statement that "Shareholders of the modern corporation have ceased to be owners and have become merely the 'recipient of the wages of capital' . . . The owners of passive property . . . have surrendered the right that the corporation should be operated in their sole interest,—they have released the community from the obligation to protect them to the full extent implied in the doctrine of strict property rights."[24]

If shareholders are not protected by "strict property rights," how are they protected? Boatright's answer is that they are protected through the strict, legally defined fiduciary obligations of managers to them, especially since neither shareholder interests nor corporate operation can possibly be met by explicit contracting between managers and shareholders. Boatright argues that the nexus of contracts approach can be extended to certain groups of stakeholders on the basis of fiduciary obligation, as specified by regulatory mandates and/or as negotiated between the firm and interest groups. For example, in terms of regulation ERISA mandates that corporate managers must protect employees' pension plans as a fiduciary duty, while

OSHA mandates employee health and safety standards. The first is a fiduciary relationship with stakeholders and the second is a regulatory one. In terms of negotiated contracts between a firm and an interest group, various agreements from the 1960s civil rights era also come to mind. For example, agreements between civil rights groups and employers (and unions) to hire and train minorities or to conform to certain marketing standards. In short, Boatright draws out and extends Berle and Means' original justification for government regulation by placing it in a framework of contractual theory (pp. 7–13).

The Transaction Cost Perspective: Firms as Governance Structures

Boatright and others use the idea of nexus of contracts to critique the finance model by arguing that a nexus of contracts approach can provide stakeholders a means to protect their interests, and thereby can provide for both a more just and more efficient corporate sector. The transaction-cost perspective challenges both the finance model with its simple principal-agent approach and the nexus of contracts approach with its emphasis on ex post contracts as a way to bind the firm together and to protect its various stakeholders. The transaction-cost economics perspective of the finance model attempts to redefine the nature of the firm itself as a form of governance per se. Oliver Williamson, the leading developer of this perspective, uses as a starting point a cross-disciplinary approach, drawn from economics (especially of the institutional variety), law, and organizational sociology.[25]

Williamson's perspective on transaction-cost economics as it relates to corporate governance, specifically as a critique of the finance model and the nexus of contracts variant of the finance model, is important for a number of related reasons. First, the transaction-cost perspective is broader than both the finance model and the nexus of contracts perspective. Its purpose is to join a discussion of corporate governance and the roots of economic productivity in a way the finance model does not and likely cannot. A Williamsonian transaction-cost perspective attempts to search for the link between economic efficiencies and what one could call the deep structure of the firm, rather than the superficial structure in (mostly) managerial incentive alignment that is the core of the finance model and nexus of contracts perspective. Second, Williamson thereby questions the simple shareholder primacy model and the related injunction to "maximize profits" as the purpose of the firm as a meaningful framework. Third, Williamson also challenges the implicit assumption of the nexus perspective that managerial contracts are neutral and without what Williamson sees as significant managerial privilege. Fourth, Williamson explicitly brings politics and institutions onto center stage, in ways that some stakeholder models do, but in an analytically sharper manner, redefining efficiency in terms of what historically "is." Finally, Williamson (and others) look to what Kester has called contractual governance, parallel to and supportive of other aspects of corporate governance. For these reasons, a more detailed examination of Williamson's treatment of corporate governance and his critique of the finance model is warranted.

Rather than view the firm as a neoclassical production function, a transaction-cost approach sees the firm as a "governance structure" (p. 13). It takes bureaucracy as a fact of modernity (an "irremediable" fact) and views it (much as Max Weber did) as rational, both in process and, for Williamson, in outcome as well. That is, from the transaction-cost perspective, hierarchy can serve efficiency purposes. Such a set of organizational assumptions stands in contrast to the finance model rooted in the neoclassical economics tradition, or the nexus of contract (agency theory) perspective, which focuses primarily on financial transactions and residual risk whose unit of analysis is the individual actor. Williamson writes that the transaction-cost economics approach "to economic organization examines the contractual relation between the firm and each of its constituencies (labor, intermediate product, customers, etc.) mainly with reference to transaction cost economizing."[26] Its agenda is therefore far broader than the nexus of contracts approach, and its starting point is not the individual, but the organization.

For transaction-cost economics, institutional, political, and organizational arrangements and structures both matter and are in part nonmarket driven in their process dynamics. They intersect with markets, are affected by and in turn affect them, but fundamentally they are not markets. Institutions, in short, matter as institutions. Williamson credits the institutional economist John R. Commons with the insight that transaction costs should be the basic unit of economic analysis. Both Commons and Williamson are interested in those arrangements which often have "the purpose of harmonizing relations between parties who are otherwise in actual or potential conflict . . . economic organization has the purpose of promoting the continuity of relationships by devising specialized governance structures, rather than permitting relationships to fracture under the hammer of unassisted market contracting."[27]

Transaction-cost economics takes organization as governance as the starting point of its analysis rather than either as its conclusion or its subject. Williamson and Bercovitz write: "Transaction cost economics . . . [analyzes] the firm-as-governance structure (which is an organizational construction)."[28] In other words, economic organization is cast as a problem of contracting both ex post and ex ante. Ex ante contracting must be incomplete since no contract can foresee all future possibilities. Ex post contracting is formal governance. For example, all organizational activities involve ex ante, implicit and informal contracting or understandings of how things will be done and who will do them. These may be temporary and very flexible, or deeply embedded in a social and organizational culture. Ex post contracting tends to be formal and in writing, and concerns the general areas that the nexus of contracts perspective addresses. Because market mechanisms are limited, the goal of transaction-cost economics is to accomplish the often-conflicting purposes of the contracting parties through various typically nonmarket arrangements.[29] This is illustrated, for example, by the many informal "workouts" of employment contracts between unions and employers. This leads to a radical redefinition of efficiency from an abstract deductive category in traditional neoclassical economics to an empirically based inductive one in transaction-cost economics.

Williamson and various coauthors assume that all real-world organizations are characterized not by maximizing profits (or, in terms of the finance model, shareholder wealth), but rather, citing Herbert Simon's work, by "bounded rationality" and opportunism. Bounded rationality observes that human decision makers simply can't process all of the information available to them. Opportunism arises when one party exploits its advantage — perhaps arising from the nature of the situation or from information one party has that the other doesn't.[30] Thus, while human agents ("homoeconomicus") may intend actions to maximize profit, they typically "lack the wits to maximize." Bounded rationality for Williamson, citing Simon, is "Intendedly rational, but only limitedly so."[31] For transaction-cost economics the "organizational imperative" is to "organize transactions so as to economize on bounded rationality while simultaneously safeguarding them against the hazards of opportunism." Williamson posits this broader conception of "the economic problem" in contrast to the finance model's "imperative: 'Maximize profits!' "[32] Indeed, as Alchian points out, profit maximization under conditions of uncertainty is "*meaningless* as a guide to specifiable action."[33]

In all economic organizations, "complex contracts will be unavoidably incomplete. . . . All of the relevant contracting action cannot therefore be concentrated in the *ex ante* incentive alignment, but some spills over into *ex post* governance."[34] That is, what Williamson calls the "institutions of private ordering," which are by definition not legally centralized, dominate ex ante contracting.[35] Such inevitably incomplete contracting, when combined with bounded rationality and opportunism, leads Williamson to focus on what he calls "remediableness," that is, the degree to which a particular "inefficiency" is remediable. If it is not remediable, then one must begin not with the neoclassical assumption that it is "inefficient," but rather start an analysis with "what is." Thus, Williamson and Bercovitz write: "claims of inefficiency due to path dependency [that is, not being able to turn back without extremely high costs] frequently turn out to be irremediable — hence not inefficient at all." Put differently, they take as efficient that which is due to bounded rationality, opportunity, or information asymmetries, "outcomes for which no feasible superior alternative can be described and implemented with net gains [that] are presumed to be efficient."[36]

The implications of this are profound as a critique of the finance model of the firm since "history matters and politics trumps economics, rather than the reverse; efficiency [therefore] sometimes takes convoluted forms." As applied to the division of ownership from control in the corporation and the "distortions" and "inefficiencies" that result, these may be "irremediable," which they define in these circumstances as "impossible to implement a superior organization alternative and realize net gains" (p. 334).

If the firm as structured is basically "irremediably" efficient, then various types of contracting, along with its limited liability and existence in perpetuity are not (as Berle and Means suggest) political favors or grants of social privilege, but rather "an efficiency response to underlying societal/organizational needs" (p. 335). Therefore, "Managerial discretion . . . should surprise no one. It is the *predictable* result of large size (bureaucracy) and is compounded by the separation of ownership from control" (pp. 336–37; emphasis in original). Of course, such irremediably efficient organizations in general do not in the least preclude increasing efficiency through changes in technology, organizational structure and processes, and markets. One obvious example Williamson cites are those employees, especially with specialized skills, who are typically not party to explicit governance roles. Such representation of these interests would in part offset the "tilt" to managerial discretion and the privileged nature of managerial contracting at a potential cost to maximizing firm-level productivity or what is too often a mutually supporting network of managerial opportunism.

Williamson and Bercovitz write, "Thus, although it is useful to view the firms as a 'nexus of contracts' . . . that nexus is not entirely neutral: The management—because it contracts with everyone, including itself—is a privileged constituency." Williamson posits that management distinguishes itself from all other constituencies since it is strategically situated and "is able to present (screen, digest, distort, manipulate) information in ways which favor its own agenda."[37] Thus, to a degree a transaction-cost approach implies a certain degree of explicit pluralist (that is, interest-group) contracting in terms of representational organization structures. On the whole Williamson restricts such explicit representation to those with immediate financial stakes (although he does not use that term) making specific economic contributions to the enterprise.[38]

However, Williamson and Bercovitz open the door, if not to recognition of stakeholder interests directly (e.g., on what they call a "board of supervisors" of a corporation), then to their indirect recognition. Following the logic from their statement that politics trumps economics, "then even if interest group politics lead to what appear to be large inefficiency loses (as revealed by applying standard deadweight loss calculus), those losses may be irremediable" (p. 349). In short, while such interest groups have no place on corporate boards or in official places in the organization, reckoning with them and their politically imposed inefficiencies may be necessary and, if the resulting losses are irremediable, then they may not be a deadweight loss. Indeed, some groups may arguably play a role in limiting managerial discretion and privilege. Such reasoning could, for example, argue for a universal investor to want to minimize negative externalities in specific firms or industries for the benefit of its larger portfolio. Such minimization could limit managerial discretion (and rewards), yet be perfectly efficient from a transaction-cost economics point of view.

Williamson argues against nonowners of capital normally being accorded a place on the board of directors since the role of the board is primarily to safeguard the governance relations between owners of equity and management. Nevertheless, he also suggests that the secondary role of a board is to "safeguard the contractual relation between the firm [and its constituents, e.g., capital, labor, suppliers, customers, the community] and its management."[39] Like most other commentators on governance, Williamson does not question what widespread fiduciary forms of equity (and debt) ownership might imply from a transaction-cost economics and contracting perspective. He does argue that under certain circumstances labor's inclusion on the board (whether in the German co-determination form or some other) can be extremely beneficial, especially if labor with firm-specific assets is represented (pp. 240–47; 304).

In conclusion, what does transaction-cost economics bring to the critique of the financial model? Williamson compares the similarities and differences between that part of transaction-cost economics concerned with governance and that part of agency theory concerned with what Jensen calls the "positive theory of agency." That is, "the technology of monitoring and bonding on the forms of . . . contracts and organizations."[40] The intellectual origin of each approach explain some of the differences. The origins of the transaction-cost approach lies in the "Coase Problem" of firm boundaries, that is, how to explain why vertical integration (hierarchy) rather than markets characterize the corporation.[41] The origins of agency theory is, on the other hand, in the Berle and Means problem of the separation of ownership from control in the corporation. Both conceptions take issue with the neoclassical theory of the firm as a production function to which a profit maximization objective has been ascribed. Agency theory sees the firm, as discussed previously, as a nexus of contracts while a transaction-cost approach views the firm as a governance structure. A transaction-cost approach places greater emphasis than a nexus of contracts approach on bounded rationality and opportunism. Williamson writes that "Incomplete contracting is a consequence of the first of these. Added contractual hazards result from the second." The essence of economic organization is thus to "craft governance structures that economize on bounded rationality while simultaneously safeguarding the transactions in questions against the hazards of opportunism. . . . Crafting 'credible commitments' is . . . the message."[42] Similar approaches are taken by agency theory, although it uses the language of moral hazard and agency costs while typically minimizing discussion of bounded rationality.

Similarly, both the agency theory and the transaction-cost approaches are concerned with contracting. The former emphasizes ex ante incentive alignment while the latter focuses on ex post governance structures to ensure, as Williamson argues, the integrity of the (typically incomplete) contract. The theories also share a similar view of the role of the board of directors that "arises endogenously as a control instrument" and that should be aligned with and serve as an instrument of the residual claimants. Transaction-cost approaches link the board to "safeguarding equity finance, and link equity finance to the characteristics of the assets," as discussed above concerning labor's role as a firm-specific asset, for example (pp. 7–8). A firm-specific asset is similar to (indeed, perhaps identical with) a sunk cost, but "the organizational ramifications become evident only in an intertemporal, incomplete contracting context" (pp. 8–9). This is important since there comes to be a mutual dependency when asset specificity and incomplete contracting intersect. Thus, a transaction-cost approach joins the issue of governance at the board of director level (as well as elsewhere) with the issue of the very nature of firm productivity and human-capital investment. It is possible to extend this logic to the governance relations between universal investors and firms if it can be shown that universal investors' portfolios lead them to be concerned with factors that affect economy-wide performance — for example, externalities.

For Williamson, transaction-cost economics' "focal cost concern" is with what he calls "maladaption." This contrasts dramatically with the dominant nexus of contracts approach, which is overwhelmingly concerned with ex ante contracting and financial alignment of top managers with stockholders and which has as its focal cost concern residual loss (p. 15). Residual loss is of concern to shareholders specifically, while maladaption is concerned with both micro-, and arguable, macroeconomic efficiency—for example, productivity.

Fiduciary Capitalism's Alternative to the Finance Model

Chapter 4 laid out the broad outlines of the finance model, the body of theory and practice that currently informs the ideas and actions of most institutional investors. The essence of that model is that firms exist for the sole and exclusive benefit of their owners. In the corporate form, the owners are the equity shareholders of the firm. The finance model then assumes that what owners want from their firms is to maximize shareholder value. Thus, for the finance model the central problem of corporate governance becomes the construction of rules, regulations, and institutions that will align the actions of managers with the desires of owners, that is, to solve the principal-agent problem inherent in the divorce of ownership from control. For institutional investors, the great attraction of the finance model is that it provides a seemingly clear, single-valued goal — maximize shareholder wealth — one that is consistent with a narrow interpretation of the institutions' fiduciary duty to its beneficiaries.

This chapter has briefly reviewed a number of important critiques of the financial model in order to shed light on the appropriate actions fiduciary institutions may take in relation to the firms they own. The stakeholder model asserts that there are other groups related to the firm besides equity owners and that these stakeholders have a legitimate voice in the way the corporation is run. These groups typically include employees, but are often extended to groups without a contractual relationship to the firm such as communities, interest groups, and, in the most general sense, to the society at large. From this perspective, the corporate governance problem becomes one of identifying and balancing competing stakeholder claims.

The next model, the nexus of contracts model, although traditionally identified with the finance model may, in fact, be thought of as a variant of the stakeholder model. This model characterizes the firm as an interlocking set of contracts — mostly explicit, but possibly containing implicit elements. From this point of view, equity owners are just another group contracting with the firm. History has given them a privileged position, although, conceptually, they are on a more or less equal footing with other groups that contract with the firm. Those stakeholders who can contract with the firm (employees, for example) have a vehicle through which their interests can potentially be protected. Alternatively, stakeholders without contracts with the firm can seek governmental action in the form of legislation and regulation such as antidiscrimination statutes, environmental regulations, and so on to protect their claims. What sets the nexus of contracts perspective off from the stakeholder perspective is the proposition that the only stakeholder claims that the firm need recognize are those that arise from contracts with the firm (such as the employment contract) or that are established by governments. The central corporate governance problem for the nexus of contracts model is the management of the various explicit and implicit contracts that define the firm.

Finally, the transaction-cost model critiques the finance model by pointing out that bounded rationality and opportunism raise severe barriers to the achievement of the finance model's goal of maximizing shareholder value. The transaction-cost model replaces the injunction to maximize profit with the goal of minimizing (transaction) cost. To achieve this, the firm (usually through the board of directors) needs to balance many competing claims on the resources of the firm. Overall wealth maximization becomes the goal of the firm rather than only shareholder wealth maximization. The corporate governance implication is that the firm — not just the board of directors — becomes a governance structure. Its goal is to attempt to mediate the competing pressures on the organization — always keeping in mind that decision makers possess only bounded rationality and that transactions may have varying degrees of opportunism embedded in them.

Despite their various perspectives, each of these critiques share with the finance model a focus on individual firms as the appropriate unit of analysis. Thus, they miss two salient facts that have come to characterize the U.S. economy at the end of the twentieth century. The first is that modern institutional owners own *portfolios* of equity and not individual firms. The second is that by drawing a sharp distinction between shareholders and stakeholders, they miss the fact that this distinction is becoming increasingly blurred as beneficial ownership spreads and the power of fiduciary institutions becomes more concentrated. By recognizing the fact that institutional investors are rapidly becoming universal owners, fiduciary capitalism suggests that it is the duty of institutions to monitor the portfolio-wide effects on them of at least two kinds of firm-by-firm actions. The first are actions taken by individual portfolio firms that might generate either positive or negative externalities. While these externalities are external to the firm that creates them, they are internalized by the economy-wide nature of the portfolio of a universal owner. By focusing on the behavior of individual firms, the finance model would find the generation of negative externalities and the suppression of activities producing positive externalities consistent with firm-level wealth maximization. However, a universal owner would experience the full impact of these actions on its portfolio and, therefore, has a responsibility — derived from the duty of care — to oppose policies that create negative externalities and to support policies that produce positive externalities. In the former category are various actions that degrade the environment; in the latter are programs that enhance productivity such as research and development projects and education and training programs.

The second class of actions universal owners need to monitor and, perhaps, try to influence are collective actions that may affect the performance of the economy at large. Deregulation initiatives and public health programs would certainly fall into this category, as might investments in basic infrastructure such as the communications network that supports the internet. Appropriate and effective public policy in these areas can certainly lead to improved firm performance just as poorly conceived or ineffectively implemented policies can degrade individual firm performance. General issues that would not be undertaken by individual firms, such as improving the general skills of the labor force because they would be unable to capture the benefits, should be of particular concern to universal owners because they would capture the benefits through their ownership of the economy at large.

In addition to failing to provide a proper focus on portfolio-wide returns and despite their various perspectives each of the critiques discussed in this chapter share with the finance model, a sharp division of the world into the owners of corporate equity—shareholders—and other groups that are affected by the corporation but who do not have legal ownership claims—stockholders. But this clear distinction between stockholders and stakeholders is being blurred—and will perhaps come to be erased—by the rise in equity ownership by fiduciary institutions that in turn represent millions of beneficial owners. Increasingly, stakeholders are becoming stockholders and stockholders are coming to have stakeholder-like interests in the firms their fiduciary institutions invest in. This is particularly true for the public employee retirement pension funds. Here, the cost of a narrow focus on profit maximization may not only reduce long-term portfolio returns, but may affect beneficiaries as citizens either directly as a result of the action or indirectly through its effect on their tax bill. For example, investments in tobacco companies have been quite profitable on a company-by-company basis, so beneficiaries as shareholders have done well. However, beneficiaries as citizens in general have had to pay higher taxes and higher health-care premiums in order to cover the cost of treating smoking-related illnesses, to say nothing of the health impacts on those beneficiaries who are also smokers. Clearly, stockholders also have stakeholder-like positions vis-à-vis the tobacco companies.

The corporate governance problem for a universal owner includes those that are of concern to the finance model, that is, to focus the attention of management on the bright, clear goal of maximizing shareholder value. To achieve this, universal owners need to use their power and position as large, patient holders of equity to both assert their rights as owners and to lobby portfolio companies in favor of those corporate governance reforms that will better align the actions of managers with the interests of owners. However, this isn't enough. Universal owners have a broader and more complex governance task. They must monitor their entire portfolios as well as the individual firms that make up the portfolio. In this monitoring they need to be attuned not only to actions that are narrowly beneficial, but also those that have wider impacts for both good and ill, such as the case of tobacco discussed above. Universal owners need to be aware that the size and breath of their portfolio exposes them to economy-wide risks as well as positions them to receive economy-wide rewards. Consequently, they need to develop policies that support public and private programs that affect long-term growth and economic efficiency.

Conclusion

This chapter has briefly reviewed a number of important critiques of the financial model in order to raise questions about the actions of fiduciary institutions in relation to the firms they own. Each of these alternative perspectives — the stakeholder, nexus of contracts, and transaction-cost perspectives — challenges in one way or another the core thesis of the financial model: that firms exist for the exclusive benefit of their owners, and that the only goal that a firm should pursue is to maximize shareholder return (dividends and capital gains).

The previous section presented the universal owners' alternative to the finance model. This alternative starts with a recognition of the power of the finance model to mobilize corporations in order to increase shareholder value. However, it then calls for the finance model to be augmented by a portfolio-wide analysis that recognizes the fact that universal owners essentially own the economy as a whole and, therefore, have a compelling interest in interactions that occur between firms but that are ignored by the finance model and its critics.

The need for this analysis, and for the supporting analysis of regulation and public policy, is driven by the fiduciary institution's duty to their beneficiaries. To maximize wealth is to maximize the value of the universal owner's portfolio, not just to maximize the return on the individual elements of the portfolio. Furthermore, universal owners need to recognize that in many important ways their beneficiary shareholders are also stakeholders with an interest in the quality of life they lead and the quality of the society in which they lead it. This recognition should result in public policy–like positions on such fundamental issues to economic growth as research and development spending, education, training, and environmental quality.

To achieve these goals, universal owners need to monitor their portfolios and the firms that make them up. Their ability to act as effective owners is constrained by existing corporate governance structures and by their ability to influence the behavior of portfolio companies. The next chapter reviews the tools and techniques institutional investors have used to try to influence portfolio companies as they discharge their duty to monitor, and evaluates the body of research investigating their effectiveness.

Chapter 6
Does Ownership Matter?
The Link Between Active Ownership
and Corporate Performance

The dramatic changes in corporate equity ownership that have been responsible for the emergence of universal owners have required institutions that wish to fully exercise their fiduciary duties to engage in a variety of forms of voice. This has been particularly true of institutions that because of strategy or size find it difficult to sell. Active ownership has taken a variety of forms, from making use of the news media (what has been called "corporate governance by public embarrassment"), to formal proxy and bylaw activities, to informal meetings with management. The professional "owners" who run large financial institutions have increasingly come to understand that their fiduciary obligations require that action must be taken whenever a firm is not performing adequately. During the 1980s, such action typically meant relying on the market for corporate control as a monitoring and disciplining mechanism. In the 1990s, however, because of the proliferation of takeover defenses, the drying up of the junk-bond market as a means to finance takeovers, and, perhaps, fewer egregious cases of mismanagement, this route has been traveled less often. In its place has arisen various forms of active ownership. Important questions confronting the active owners, more passive ones, and observers and analysts generally are: Has activism mattered? Has it improved or affected performance, and how can one measure this? This chapter seeks to address these questions.

When commentators speak of "corporate governance" they often mean two interrelated and overlapping things. Some speak of corporate governance in micro terms, that is, in terms of the firm level as defined by state incorporation statutes and other legislation, company bylaws, and court interpretations. For example, in their book *Corporate Governance*, Robert Monks and Nell Minow define corporate governance as "the relationship among various participants in determining the direction and performance of corporations. The primary participants are (1) the shareholders, (2) the management (led by the chief executive officer) and (3) the board of directors."[1] From this perspective, corporate governance issues internal to the firm such as the independence of board members from comprising ties to the corporation, the separation of the positions of chairman and chief executive officer, and the compensation of board members and sometimes top management are of paramount importance.

Other commentators view corporate governance from a more macro perspective. For example, Keasey and Wright define corporate governance to include "the structures, process, cultures and systems that engender the successful operation of the organizations."[2] From this point of view corporate governance is the constellation of financial and legal institutions in which the corporation is embedded. These would include the elements identified by Monks and Minow, but would tend to emphasize corporate governance mechanisms external to the firm. These mechanisms include, among other institutions, the debt and equity markets, the market for corporate control, the managerial labor market, and more recently nonmanagerial employees' relation to the firm, the goods and services markets in which the corporation sells its products, and the legal and social environment that constrains firm behavior. This approach is broadly reflected in the series of country reports on corporate governance prepared by the Organization for Economic Co-operation and Development (OECD) as part of their annual reviews of the major industrial economies. For example, the 1996 U.S. volume of the OECD *Economic Surveys* contains a chapter titled "Corporate Governance: The Market as Monitor."[3] From this point of view, "The characteristic of the U.S. system of corporate governance which sets it apart most clearly from others is the reliance on the market for corporate control as one of the primary disciplinary devices to force managers to seek good corporate performance" (p. 142).

Many commentators emphasize that an important goal of corporate governance is to increase shareholder wealth. However, one can also conceive of linkages between corporate governance — however viewed — and corporate performance that might affect a wide range of social, political, and economic issues beyond the narrow issue of shareholder wealth. For example, corporate governance could be evaluated for its impact on the cost of funds (efficiency in the financial markets) or the role of labor in management (up to and including majority labor-owned firms such as United Airlines or Avis). It could also be evaluated for the role that corporations play in education and training (efficiency in the labor market) or the contribution corporations make to research and development (efficiency in the knowledge market).

Corporate governance could also be judged by its impact on a country's ability to compete successfully in international markets. In fact, one important source of the increased concern with corporate governance in the United States in the late 1980s was the perception that Japan and Europe had better economic performance *because* they had better corporate governance structures. Of course, by the mid-1990s, the analysis tended to reverse. Now many commentators assert that U.S. corporations performed better because of superior corporate governance and now Japan and continental Europe lag behind because of their inferior corporate governance systems.[4]

However, when institutional owners in the United States come to justify their concern with corporate governance, most adopt a narrow view and echo Dale Hanson's remark as CalPERS' CEO when he said an institutional investor has only "one overriding objective: the maximization of long-term investment returns."[5] This position is aligned with the CalPERS' "Global Principles for Corporate Governance," which answers the rhetorical question "Is corporate governance really just somebody's social agenda?" with the statement: "At CalPERS, corporate governance is about making money, not changing the political or social environment."[6] It is clear that the institutions that bear a fiduciary duty to their beneficiaries see enhancing shareholder wealth as the primary, if not the *only*, appropriate goal for the corporation — and, hence, for corporate governance reform. Consequently, the literature investigating the link between governance and performance has been heavily weighted toward evaluating the wealth-enhancing effects of various corporate governance measures and has had little to say about their social consequences.

For much of this century there has been a tension between the narrow and broad views of corporate performance. However, when investigators try to establish a link between corporate governance and corporate performance — however these two concepts are defined — they are implicitly accepting something like the following model. First and foremost, management actions matter to performance.[7] Corporate governance then sets the framework in which management acts. "Good" corporate governance provides the incentives and the monitoring required to align management actions with the goals and desires of owners. It also provides the mechanisms necessary to evaluate and replace poorly performing managers. Since owners desire the "maximization of long-term investment returns," the goal is improved economic performance for individual firms and their shareholders and through its general effects on the corporate sector, for the economy as a whole.[8]

Without "good" corporate governance to oversee, monitor, and evaluate management, the principal-agent problem embedded in the corporate form suggests that management will pursue its own goals (power- and prestige-enhancing acquisitions, large salaries, perquisites such as company jets, and so on) to the detriment of the owners' interests in wealth maximization. The consequence, of course, is poor economic performance and lower long-term investment returns. It may also result in higher production costs, inferior products, lower wages, a declining standard of living, and a generally deteriorating competitive position in international markets.

The literature on the macro and micro points of view of corporate governance and their relationship to corporate performance is large and rapidly growing. Consequently, the following is not intended as a comprehensive review of this literature, but rather as a discussion of the major issues raised by various perspectives.

Corporate Governance and the Market for Corporate Control

The macro point of view of corporate governance encompasses, among other elements external to the firm, the goods and services market, the market for managerial services, and the debt and equity markets. However, the central external control mechanism is the market for corporate control. The market for goods and services tests the ultimate justification for a company's existence, but many poorly performing firms can limp by for years or even decades without falling into bankruptcy. Both internal and external managerial labor markets are important constraints on managerial opportunism, but individuals often avoid responsibility for the collective decisions of "management." Debt and equity markets place effective limits on companies, particularly ones that need to raise substantial amounts of capital, but are of little use in disciplining companies that generate adequate funds internally or that have marketable assets that can be used as collateral. However, the market for corporate control — the buying and selling of companies — can, at least theoretically, work as a kind of super-governance mechanism to discipline companies and their management that underperform on any dimension, including those mentioned above.

From a macro point of view, the proposition that governance matters — and that in the United States governance was sorely in need of improvement — was strongly reinforced by the takeover boom of the 1980s. A number of explanations for corporate takeovers in general and this flurry of takeovers in particular have been advanced. They include, among others, economies of scale, a quest for the spoils of monopoly power, the tax advantages of debt financing, the gains from breaking implicit contracts, and the egos of the officers of the acquiring firms.[9] They also included the corporate governance rationale. Following Manne's original analysis, this rationale applies in hostile takeover situations that result from a new management team's perception that existing management is failing to maximize the value of the assets under its control. Other motives may explain many takeovers, but only those that correct managerial misconduct act as a corporate governance tool.

In the 1980s, some observers came to regard the market for corporate control as the most important external corporate governance tool for correcting the inefficiencies that had been introduced into the American economy by managers over the preceding forty years.[10] However, other observers came to a decidedly less favored view of the market for corporate control. For example, O'Sullivan writes, "the available empirical evidence concerning takeover gains is unclear, and at the very least only provides equivocal support for the governance role of corporate takeovers."[11]

However, by the end of the 1980s, the market for corporate control—as typified by the hostile takeover—had cooled considerably.[12] The continuing high level of merger and acquisition activity in the 1990s is not driven by corporate governance reasons; rather, it is driven by strategic considerations in certain industries (particularly finance, automobiles, and technology, and the like) and to globalization pressures that seem to favor large, multinational firms. Nonetheless, because the market for corporate control is such a potentially powerful governance tool for disciplining misbehaving management, one at the center of the finance model, it is important to examine the empirical evidence surrounding the 1980s hostile merger movement.

There are four questions to ask when evaluating takeovers for their corporate governance implications. First, is there evidence that targeted firms actually suffered from some form of corporate governance failure? Second, did the market react to tender offers in ways that are consistent with the efficient market hypothesis? Third, is there evidence of improved managerial efficiency after the takeover? And, fourth, can the gains to target shareholders, if there are gains, be attributed to improved corporate governance?

Do Targeted Firms Suffer from Corporate Governance Failure?

The evidence on the first question is somewhat ambiguous. Asquith finds large, negative, abnormal returns in the premerger period for the firms in his sample, but the sample period is before the hostile takeovers that typified the market for corporate control really got under way.[13] When Franks and Mayer looked at hostile takeovers, they found no significant difference in the preacquisition share price performance between hostile and friendly takeover targets.[14] The authors conclude that takeovers are not motivated by managerial failures, but by ex ante valuation differences among firms. Finally, Morck and coauthors, in a study that uses accounting data, found that hostile takeovers are more likely to be associated with inferior preacquisition levels of performance compared to firms acquired in friendly takeovers, but the difference is not significant.[15]

Are Stock Price Reactions to Takeover Bids Consistent with the Efficient Market Hypothesis?

Evidence on the next question is quite unambiguous. The stock price reaction of hostile takeover targets is broadly consistent with the proposition that an efficient market values the expected changes in corporate governance and hence in managerial efficiency. Virtually all studies show positive stock price reactions to the announcement of takeover interest, particularly in the form of a hostile offer, and along with Jarrell and coauthors conclude that "Shareholders of targeted firms clearly benefit from takeovers."[16] For example, Limmack reports an overall gain of 37 percent for the completed bids at the 462 companies he studied during the period of 1977–1986. This finding is reinforced by studies that look at the stock price performance of potential takeover candidates before there is a takeover announcement.[17] Mikkelson and Ruback look at 13D filings, which are required when more than 5 percent of a company's stock is acquired by a single individual or institution. They found a positive stock market reaction to the filings, particularly when the purchase is perceived to be leading to a future bid.[18] In a similar study, Holderness and Sheehan find a significantly higher stock price reaction to filings by a group of identified "corporate raiders" when compared to other filings that are not so readily identified with a potential takeover offer.[19]

Do Target Firms Have Improved Performance After Acquisition?

The evidence presented in the previous section is consistent with the proposition that the stock market perceived increased value flowing from takeovers — particularly hostile ones where the efficiency gains from a reinvigorated management are likely to be the highest. However, the real question is whether the takeover leads to improvements in a firm's economic efficiency — that is, its profitability — as market for corporate control proponents argue.

A number of technical and methodological problems arise in answering this question. First, the acquired firm typically either disappears into a much larger publicly traded entity or, as in the case of LBOs and management buyouts, into a private company. In either case, it is relatively hard to discern what happened to the postacquisition performance of the target firm. The problem is compounded because it is necessary to answer the counterfactual question: How would the company performed had it not been acquired?

Early attempts to answer this question used the event study methodology to examine the stock price history of acquiring firms.[20] These studies generally find either a relatively small return, zero return, or a negative return to bidders on the announcement of a takeover bid. For example, Jensen and Ruback found that for a sample of mergers from the late 1950s to the early 1980s, abnormal returns for successful bidders were in the range of 2.4 to 6.7 percent with a weighted average return of 3.8 percent.[21] However, Jarrell and Poulsen found that bidder returns declined during the 1970s and 1980s to the point where the 159 cases they examined in the 1980s show statistically insignificant losses to bidders.[22] On its face, it appears that the market considers takeovers as value enhancing to the target company, but not particularly to the acquiring company. However, event studies are poorly suited to determining changes taking place over long periods of time. Therefore, a number of studies use other measures, typically various accounting measures of firm performance, to look at the postacquisition performance of the acquirers.

Furtado and Karen looked at management turnover and found that it is greater after a merger — evidence that is consistent with the proposition that takeovers produce governance changes.[23] Ravenscraft and Scherer look at a number of measures of postacquisition performance and find that accounting profitability declines after an acquisition. They find this consistent with the observation that many acquired firms are divested in later years.[24] However, their sample may confound friendly and hostile takeovers and the corporate governance implications are strongest for hostile takeovers. Herman and Lowenstein found a sharp decline in postacquisition return on equity for a sample of takeovers from the 1981–1983 period, and Cosh and coauthors found small, insignificant, postmerger improvements for a sample of acquirers with large institutional holdings.[25]

In an interesting study, Bhagat and coauthors focused on a sample of 62 hostile takeovers from the period 1984–1986 in order to avoid the bias that comes from mixing hostile and friendly takeovers. Furthermore, to solve the information problem discussed above, the authors used an analysis of annual reports, newspaper articles, Moody's and Value Line reports, and so on. "The advantage of this design is that we can attribute the changes we examine, such as layoffs and sell off, to the target firm."[26] One of their conclusions was that bidder returns were negative at more than half of their sample firms. On average, bidders lost $15 million — but the authors note this is a tiny fraction of the average acquisition price of $1.74 billion and is certainly biased upward by the fact that important efficiency improvements may have been impossible to identify using their methodology.

In contrast to the studies discussed in the previous paragraphs, more recent studies such as that by Healy and colleagues and Jarrell have found improvements in postmerger performance.[27] This fact leads Romano to comment that "While earlier studies of post-acquisition performance found no operating improvements in merged firms, more recent studies, which make more careful efforts in benchmark construction and adjust post-merger earnings for changes in accounting methods and acquisition financing, find that performance does improve post merger."[28] However, O'Sullivan reaches a different conclusion. She says that "the empirical analysis of post-acquisition performance fails to produce conclusive evidence that the acquisition process enhances corporate performance."[29] In any case, the evidence does not support the proposition that there were large, unambiguous gains in efficiency flowing from the market for corporate control.

To summarize: In answer to the first three questions posed at the beginning of this section, it appears that (1) it is ambiguous whether target firms in hostile takeovers suffer from corporate governance lapses greater than firms in friendly takeovers; (2) it is clear that stock prices of target firms or potential target firms react positively to takeover interest, consistent with the efficient market hypothesis that provides the rationale for efficiency gains from the market for corporate control; and (3) postacquisition performance appears to be moderately better than preacquisition performance, although the gains are not large, and the methodological difficulties are great. The final question is in many ways the most important and most contentious one: Can the gains to target shareholders be attributed to the prospect of improved corporate governance brought about by the market for corporate control or do they come from other sources?[30]

Are the Gains from Hostile Takeovers Efficiency Gains or Wealth Transfers?

The assumption behind the claim that the market for corporate control is efficiency enhancing for both firms and society is that the gain represents a lower bound on the equity market's evaluation of the improvement in managerial efficiency that will result from the transfer of control. However, other sources of the gains to target shareholders, other than efficiency gains, have been suggested. Most prominent among these are that the gains come from wealth transfers from employees to shareholder or from the government to shareholders. The wealth transfer from employees involves the breaching of various implicit contracts in the form of wage reductions, layoffs, recaptured excess pension funding, more aggressive bargaining with unions, and so on. The wealth transfer from the government arises because of the favorable tax treatment of interest to service debt and the high debt-to-equity ratios resulting from many takeovers. Others have claimed that asset sales or reductions in expenditures, particularly for research and development, have been used to fund the unambiguously observed gain in target firm share prices.

Perhaps most contentious has been the claim that in hostile takeovers labor has provided the gain to shareholders. Some evidence exists to support this claim. For example, as noted in Chapter 4, Shleifer and Summers found that about 150 percent of the premium paid to shareholders in the Carl Icahn's takeover of TWA came from wage concession from the companies unions.[31] In another study, Bhagat and colleagues conclude that "layoffs, which disproportionately affect high-level white-collar employees, explain perhaps 10 to 20 percent of the average premium, although in a few cases they are the whole story."[32] However, other studies fail to find such a dramatic impact. For example, Romano cites studies by Rosette and Kaplan in which Rosette found positive gains in union wealth levels after hostile acquisitions and Kaplan found that in a sample of leveraged buyout firms, employment increased after the transaction — but not as rapidly as that of other firms in their industry.[33] Romano recognizes the difficulties inherent in answering these questions—particularly the construction of a counter-factual benchmark of what would have happened absent the acquisition—but concludes that "what we do know suggests that expropriation from labor does not motivate takeovers."[34]

The tax code allows interest to be paid with before-tax dollars while dividends must be paid with after-tax dollars. Since many takeovers were accomplished with massive amounts of debt, some observers saw the gains to target shareholders coming directly from the U.S. Treasury. Kaplan found that, depending on assumptions about marginal tax rates and debt refinancing, tax savings were important and accounted for 13 to 130 percent of the takeover premium.[35] Bhagat and colleagues also found in their sample that tax savings were "usually somewhat smaller than savings from layoffs (although they are significant in a larger *number* of cases)."[36] However, Jensen and coauthors estimate that the *net* tax effect of LBOs is positive, not negative, when the tax payments of selling target shareholders, the target firm's debt holders, and the firm's future income is considered in the calculation.[37]

In conclusion, the corporate governance properties of the market for corporate control are brought into question by the fact that at least some of the gains to target shareholders might come from wealth transfers rather than from the enhanced profitability of the more efficiently managed post-acquisition company. Furthermore, the fact that it is difficult to identify postacquisition increases in performance also lends support to the proposition that wealth transfer rather than efficiency gains provided the incentive for many of the hostile mergers of the 1980s. This is not to deny that the market for corporate control either through the firms affected or perhaps through its general impact on the business community may have had the beneficial effect of reconcentrating management's attention on shareholder value. At least one observer asserts that the market for corporate control is no longer needed because business has internalized what he sees as the major lessons of the LBO movement: performance-based compensation for management, substantial equity ownership by management, and the use of debt to control the temptation to misuse free cash flow.[38]

In any case, the market for corporate control—at least its hostile takeover aspects—were largely over by the 1980s. In evaluating this period, Romano concludes that "the 1980s was the era of the hostile takeover, which was basically unheard of in prior merger 'wave' episodes, and the burst of intensive acquisition activity dramatically slowed in the 1990s. The collapse of the junk bond market and corresponding credit crunch, caused by weakness in the financial services sector and new governmental policies restricting financial institutions' holding of high-yield debt, surely contributed to the decline in transactions."[39] The enactment of antitakeover statutes by many states and favorable Delaware chancellery court rulings may have also contributed to the end of the hostile aspects of the market for corporate control. The very high level of mergers (as measured by both volume and value) in the 1990s has been overwhelming motivated not by corporate governance concerns, but by strategic impulses in industries such as telecommunications and banking. In addition, the pressure of globalization appears to reward larger scale enterprises. Thus, while the OECD report cited in the beginning of this chapter argued that the U.S. corporate governance model is characterized by the market for corporate control, events during the 1990s suggest otherwise. The market for corporate control remains in place but mostly unused. A variety of governance instruments have either been internalized within the microenvironment of the firm or exist external to it. If it ever was, governance is certainly no longer a matter of a single, dominant mechanism, but rather of a plurality of means.

Corporate Governance and the Board of Directors

In the micro sense, good corporate governance is defined as corporate governance that efficiently solves the principal-agent problem of aligning the interests of managers with those of shareholders. Shareholder activists have developed a series of principles that they support when it comes to corporate governance questions. These include, among others, the independence of directors from excessive management influence, independent directors on the board's compensation and audit committees, some form of equity compensation for directors, the elimination of pension plans for directors, and, for some, the separation of the position of chairman of the board and chief operating officer of the corporation. When it comes to policies, shareholder activists oppose board policies that might reduce the corporation's market value, such as poison pills and other measures to blunt the operation of the market for corporate control, such as incorporation in a state with particularly severe antitakeover laws. As noted above, the model motivating this agenda is that management matters to performance and that good corporate governance does a better job of solving the principal-agent problem than bad corporate governance. It then follows that improving corporate governance at specific companies should improve the economic performance of those companies. At the very least, good governance is a form of rainy-day insurance so that if performance problems do arise, governance structures can ensure that they are dealt with rather than being pushed under the rug.

Director Independence and Corporate Performance

To effectively discharge these duties, many observers believe directors must be independent of any personal, professional, or financial ties to management. If directors are beholden to management, it stands to reason that they may take management's advice and pronouncements with too little scrutiny. They may also be less likely to make tough choices should the need arise. This is particularly true at a poorly performing firm since these choices may very well involve firing top management. Consequently, calls for boards to be made up of a sizeable majority of independent directors are high on the list of many good corporate governance advocates. For example, board independence is the first of three core corporate governance principles enunciated by CalPERS. "Independence," they note, "is the cornerstone of accountability."[40] In fact, on the ideal corporate board as conceived by CalPERS, only one director, the CEO, would be an insider.[41] Others such as the National Association of Corporate Directors (NACD) and the Business Roundtable have called for a substantial majority of nonexecutive directors to be independent of management.[42] For the NACD, the independence of directors is a key element in director professionalism. Similarly, emerging OECD standards call for board members to "exercise object judgement on corporate affairs, independent of management." To be sure, this is different than suggesting that board members be independent of management, but since the OECD is dealing with a variety of national governance systems, it attempts to establish general principles.[43]

These goals are being realized. Director independence is a growing trend at American companies. In a survey of boards of directors at one hundred large corporations, the executive search firm SpencerStuart found that boards were getting smaller, and that "the bulk of this board downsizing is directly attributable to reductions in the number of inside directors."[44] By 1996, fully half of the boards surveyed had only one or two inside directors.[45]

Director independence is often in the eye of the beholder and developing general criteria for independence has become a growth industry in the field of corporate governance. "Management directors" or "inside directors" are easily defined as current employees of the company. Definitions of independent directors, on the other hand, abound.[46] For example, the NACD report states that, "Relationships that may compromise a director's independence may include, but are not limited to; reciprocal directorships (or "director interlocks"); an existing significant consulting or employment relationship; an existing substantial commercial relationship between the director's organization and the board's company; or new business relationships that develop through board membership."[47] An appendix to the NACD report reproduces nine additional definitions of "independence." The CalPERS definition of independence has nine separate items — all but one of which describes the financial or commercial relationship between a director and the company. The one exception is to rule out as independent anyone who is "a member of the immediate family" of someone who fails to meet the other eight criteria. The CalPERS document then goes on to table eight definitions of "independent director."[48]

Mechanical definitions of independence miss what is really desired: directors who can make appropriate decisions in both good times and bad. Being technically independent doesn't guarantee that a particularly director will have the character necessary to stand up to an "imperial" CEO or have the skills necessary to accurately evaluate competing proposals. In fact, a slavish adherence to the concept of independence could produce a board dominated by individuals with little knowledge of the company, its markets, its suppliers, or its special problems. One study has noted that some independent directors might be "more lapdog than watchdog."[49]

The fundamental question governance activists are interested in is: "Does independence matter to corporate performance?" If it does, boards with a significant majority of independent directors (however defined) should be associated with better performing companies while boards dominated by inside, nonindependent directors should perform less well.

Bhagat and Black provide the most recent comprehensive survey of this question. The authors categorized the large number of studies they surveyed into two types. The first type investigates the relationship between board independence and a range of "discrete" board tasks such as replacing the CEO, performance in takeover situations, the granting of golden parachutes, and so on. The second class of studies investigates the direct link between board independence and measures of corporate performance such as stock price.

With respect to the first group, many of these studies show that board independence does matter for the execution of specific tasks in the sense that independent boards are more likely to take certain kinds of actions. For example, boards with at least 60 percent independent directors are more likely to replace poorly performing CEOs than are boards with less than 60 percent independent directors. Also, independence seems to help in takeover situations. Here, the authors report studies showing that firms with a majority of independent directors tend not to overpay for acquisitions. The authors note that "This suggests that independent directors my help to restrain the CEO's tendency to build a large empire even if this means overpaying to buy another company" (p. 285). This is an important finding since the possibility of conflict of interest between management and shareholders is likely to be particularly high in these situations. Finally, golden parachute plans are more likely to be adopted the greater the fraction of the board that is independent. Bhagat and Black interpret this as value enhancing since it reduces the likelihood that management will resist a takeover offer.

While the studies referred to above shed light on the ways the number of independent directors may affect the execution of specify board tasks, the question of the link to enhanced shareholder value generally remains unexplored. As the authors note, "Firms with majority-independent boards could perform better on particular tasks such as replacing the CEO, yet worse on other, unstudied tasks, leading to no net advantage in overall performance" (p. 283). For example, as noted, boards with a majority of independent directors may be more willing to replace an underperforming CEO, but may do a poor job of choosing a successor because of their lack of knowledge about the particular needs of the industry.

The other group of studies that Bhagat and Black investigated attempts to solve this problem by directly investigating the link between board composition and overall firm performance. The argument for a positive relationship between independence and performance has already been made. The argument for a negative relationship focuses on the advantages of insiders and the disadvantages of independent directors. Advantages might come from enhanced information directors get about future (insider) CEO candidates that board members get by working with management directors. They may also flow from knowledge insiders from affiliated firms bring to the board about market conditions and industry trends. Or advantages may be due to the fact that many insiders have generally higher stakes in the financial success or failure of the firm and therefore may discharge their duties more diligently. This is certainly true of executive directors, but it may be true of others who have links to a firm that would disqualify them as independent.

Alternatively, independent directors may have weaknesses that could lower firm performance. One weakness might be a lack of knowledge about the markets in which the firm competes. This is often true of "celebrity" directors — directors chosen because of their high profile in politics, entertainment, or some other area outside of the business world. Another problem centers on the question of how to assure that independent directors will have an adequate financial stake in the firm to motivate them to diligently discharge their duties.[50] Having a significant portion of a director's personal wealth at stake is a marvelous device for concentrating the director's attention on the economic performance of a company, but how to achieve this is a difficult task. Requiring directors to make the investment as a condition for membership would likely rule out many potentially good directors. To compensate directors at a level that would have the same result would, for many directors, require very large director's fees. Very high fees could have the unintended consequence of making directors more timid for fear of losing their fees.

Independent directors may also sit on too many boards and therefore not have adequate time or energy to devote to the needs of any one company. In the early 1990s, Frank Carlucci, an independent director by most definitions, sat on fourteen boards. He became a poster child for director reform after a profile in the *Washington Post* reported that he "attended" a board committee meeting by phone from his doctor's office while attached to an EKG machine.[51] In practice, the majority of independent directors are actually CEOs of other firms. Not only may they have little knowledge of the relevant industries, but they may also have a predisposition to treat management the way they would like their own boards to treat them — that is, with better pay and less oversight. CEO directors, busy people in their regular jobs, may also have little time to devote to the task. An extreme example is John Clendenin, CEO of BellSouth Corporation, who in 1996 sat on the boards of nine Fortune 1000 companies, including his own. The *New York Times* estimated his annual responsibilities for board and board committee meetings *other* than at BellSouth at eight months of forty-hour weeks.[52] Clearly, director independence, however defined, is no guarantee that directors will function effectively.

Bhagat and Black report the results of a number of studies that investigated the link between measures of corporate performance and board independence. Most of the studies report no significant link between the proportion of independent directors on a board and measures of corporate performance used (e.g., stock price performance, Tobin's q, and so on). However, some studies do report a negative correlation between a number of corporate performance measures and the proportion of outside directors. This would lend some credence to the proposition that *non*independent directors can bring value to the firm.

In their own study of the relationship between board composition and firm performance, the authors conclude, "On the whole, our reexamination confirms that the direct relationship between board composition and firm performance, if it exists at all, is weak, and perhaps variable over time." They go on to state that "We find no consistent evidence that the proportion of independent directors affects future firm performance."[53]

There are a number of possible reasons why most researchers fail to find a positive connection between independent directors and firm performance. The link may indeed be there, but the effect of the board of directors may be small or other things effecting performance that go on inside and outside the firm may swamp it. A simple focus on the proportion of independent directors may miss the point that different types of firms might require different board composition. For example, a firm in a slow-growing industry might require more independent directors to prevent management from engaging in low- or negative-return investments. Rapidly growing firms might benefit from the expertise of affiliated or inside directors. Indeed, boards of venture capital-sponsored start-up firms tend to have few if any directors that would be independent by the criteria discussed above. For these firms, where board composition is not subject to shareholder pressure, controlling owners presumably believe it is in their best interests to have inside directors to promote the firm's success. Here, those most effected and most in control opt for skills and knowledge in their directors rather than for the ability to monitor that is presumably provided by independent directors. At the very least, as Bhagat and Black note, "the burden of proof should perhaps shift to those who support the conventional wisdom that ever-greater board independence is an important element of improved corporate governance" (p. 299).

Poison Pills and Proxy Campaigns

Another area of concern to the firm level effectiveness of corporate governance is the influence shareholders have on portfolio companies through the proxy process. The ability to submit a proxy for a shareholder vote at the annual meeting is one of the fundamental rights of ownership. However, the process is proscribed by various SEC regulations. In particular, proxies are generally limited to straightforward governance issues such as separating the CEO and chairman's position. Also, rescinding or requiring a vote to enact poison pills (policies that are designed to make an unwanted takeover bid more difficult or impossible) are frequently the target of investor-sponsored proxy proposals. Occasionally, a hostile takeover will be attempted by proposing an alternative slate of directors followed by a proxy "fight" in which management and the potential acquirer attempt to persuade shareholders to assign proxies for the election of directors to their side.

The "ordinary business rule" prevents proxies that would interfere with the "day-to-day" business decisions of management.[54] Companies can refuse to place a given proposal on its proxy ballot and many that do seek "no action letters" from the SEC validating their decision. Proxies are almost always advisory in nature and even a majority vote does not guarantee adoption by a company. But at many companies even a relatively small minority vote is seen as an important signal of investor sentiment — particularly because of the strong bias in favor of the management's position. Increasingly, however, shareholders are proposing proxies that are binding bylaw amendments as a way to increase their leverage with companies.[55]

In a study of a sample of 866 shareholder-initiated proxy proposals on governance issues at 317 publicly traded companies during the period of March 1986 to October 1990, Karpoff and others used the event study methodology to answer two questions: What types of companies attract these proposals? And, how do the proposals affect firm values?[56]

While all kinds of firms attract all kinds of proxy proposals, the authors found that most proxy proposals tended to be targeted at firms that performed poorly on measures such as market-to-book ratio, operating returns, or recent sales growth. As one might expect, shareholders usually only go to the trouble and expense of a formal proxy campaign when the firm appears to be doing poorly economically. Proxy campaigns at profitable companies are very unlikely to attract much positive support from other shareholders.

Although most proxy proposals submitted by investors fail to receive a majority vote, some have been able to attract substantial support. For example, in 1998 shareholder proposals at Federated Department Stores, Venator

Group (formerly Woolworth), Bristol-Myers Squibb, Fleming Companies, Eastman Kodak, and Jostens all received more than 70 percent of the votes.[57] However, because proposals are generally only advisory the real question is not whether the proposals pass, but whether they have any effect on corporate performance. In contrast to proxy proposal, corporate bylaws amendments, which some activists are now proposing, are mandatory. While binding bylaw amendments have the potential to develop into an extremely important corporate governance tool, they are still subject to legal challenges, so it remains to be seen what will actually happen.

According to Karpoff and others, the answer to whether a proxy fight affects performance is "not much." They "find little evidence . . . of wealth gains that might arise from such improvements. The average wealth effect associated with shareholder-initiated corporate governance proposals was close to, and not significantly different from, zero."[58] Neither do they find much evidence to support the proposition that shareholder proposals actually produce much in the way of observable policy changes such as CEO turnover. The bottom line is that "even the most successful proposals do not significantly alter their target firms' policies or stock values."

The problem with event studies like Karpoff and others' that measure proxy votes is that they may miss the great majority of firms that agree to governance activists' demands prior to proxy voting itself. In other words, measuring only voting disproportionately captures the least effective proxy and other informal pressures on management. In a path-breaking study of CREF's proxy and private negotiation activities Carleton, Nelson, and Weisbach state that "relying [only on] publicly available data on proxy voting is likely to understate substantially the number of times when institutions attempt to influence firms."[59] They go on to conclude that in more than 70 percent of the cases they studied between 1992 and 1996, agreement was reached prior to a shareholder vote. Including those settled privately and those that did come to a vote, nearly 90 percent of the target firms took subsequent actions to comply with the agreements reached with CREF. While the study did not attempt to measure subsequent performance, measuring informally negotiated agreements appears to be a far more accurate way to gauge the actual extent of the pressure institutional investors can bring to bear on portfolio companies, even if it is a methodologically more difficult and complex approach.

Thus, while as yet no clear conclusion emerges concerning the relation between firm performance and the use of proxies as pressure on management, there is good evidence that both the formal and informal negotiations that occur can motivate firms to change their policies and otherwise strongly influences firm behavior. Yet both the formal and informal aspects of proxy campaigns should be seen as part of a larger campaign of "performance targeting" in which investors try to improve the economic performance of poorly performing portfolio companies.

Performance Targeting

As part of the rise of institutional investor activism in the early 1990s, investors began to proactively target companies rather than to react to crises as they occurred. Initially they had chosen targets companies because they had particularly poor corporate governance policies — poison pills or other anti-takeover devices, boards with few independent directors, and so on. While in an abstract sense these companies deserved the reforming ire of institutional investors, the effectiveness of this criteria left much to be desired.

Richard Koppes tells the story of attending, as CalPERS general counsel, a McDonald's Corporation annual meeting to speak on behalf of just such a pure corporate governance proxy proposal. It was a distinctly unpleasant (and ineffective) experience because McDonald's had just completed a record-breaking year and the shareholders at the annual meeting, many of whom were also franchisees, were more interested in holding a "love fest" for management than passing a critical proxy proposal. Shortly after this, CalPERS changed its strategy and began selecting firms for proxy proposals based on economic performance — and not on the abstract shortcomings of a firm's governance structure.[60]

For a number of years CalPERS and other public pension funds, CREF, and two associations, United Shareholders Association (USA) and the Council of Institutional Investors, have run performance-targeting programs. Some of these organizations have been the subject of research that attempts to quantify the effect of this particular type of corporate governance initiative.

CalPERS, the quintessential institutional investor activist, has been targeting firms since 1987, first as part of a general good corporate governance campaign and then, after 1990, as part of a program of performance targeting. Because of its high profile and because of its long record, more studies have been done on its program than on all other targeting programs combined. In the first study to be published, Nesbitt used the event-study methodology to investigate whether the 24 firms CalPERS targeted as "underperformers" in 1990–1992 experienced abnormal stock price returns after targeting. He found that these firms, as a group, underperformed the market by an average of 86 percent over the five years leading up to CalPERS' involvement and in the two years after they outperformed the market by 28 percent.[61] In 1996, Nesbitt extended his analysis to the 62 firms targeted by CalPERS from the inception of the program in 1987 through 1995. For these firms he analyzed the total return for the five years preceding their selection as a target and for the subsequent five years. He found that as a group the stock returns were 34 percentage points above the return on the S&P 500 index for the five-year period. "The performance is found to be statistically significant and marks a dramatic reversal from the very poor returns shown by these same companies for the prior five years which averaged 85 percentage points below the S&P 500 index return (13 percent per year).[62]

Other researchers have also studied the CalPERS targeting program. Crutchley, Hudson, and Jensen looked at two periods in CalPERS history and came to different conclusions about each period.[63] The first period, 1987–1994, was characterized as the "aggressive" period during which CalPERS' CEO Dale Hanson and General Counsel Richard Koppes used high profile methods such as target lists of underperforming firms, press conferences, speeches, detailed letters to CEOs, and proxies and the threat of proxies. In 1994, Hanson resigned and was replaced by James Burton. CalPERS continues to target firms, but now the method of engaging companies has been switched to one of quiet diplomacy. The authors concluded that the method makes a difference: "very visible and aggressive activism does cause substantial increases in shareholder wealth. However, a quieter activism does not yield the same results" (p. 9). Likewise, Smith finds significant, positive, long-term as well as two-day stock returns following the announcement that CalPERS was targeting firms for performance in 1989–1993.[64]

Finally, Wagster and Prevost used the CalPERS target list to investigate the wealth effects of the 1992 SEC rule changes to Rule 14(a)(2).[65] Before 1992, any written or oral communications among more than ten shareholders could be deemed a proxy solicitation. Pension funds, led by CalPERS and the United Shareholders Association (USA), lobbied to have the rule changed, and in 1992 it was liberalized.[66] Now only investors engaged in formal proxy fights have to meet the full SEC requirement. Other investors are free to communicate with each other and with management. Also, subject to a minor filing requirement, they can now send out material or prepared telephone scripts to communicate with shareholders about matters of concern. The authors used the event-study methodology to investigate whether the various announcements associated with the consideration and then the final adoption of revisions to Rule 14(a)(2) had any effect on the firms targeted by CalPERS in 1990, 1991, and 1992. Their conclusion is that the announcements were associated with significant wealth *losses* at "low-compensation" firms targeted by CalPERS (firms that paid their CEOs less that one million dollars) while "high-compensation" firms were not affected. The authors conclude the results suggest "investors perceived the benefits of stricter institutional investor oversight to be less than the associated costs" (p. 23). And that more highly paid CEOs were perceived as being able to resist the meddling of institutional investors better than less well-compensated CEOs. Consequently the wealth effects at these firms was less.

In addition to CalPERS, a number of other institutional investors and two associations have also run targeting programs.[67] One of them, United Shareholders Association (USA), was originally funded by T. Boone Pickens as a way to combine the resources of small shareholders in an attempt to improve their monitoring of management.[68] During USA's existence between 1986 to 1993, part of its program was to develop a Target 50 list of firms characterized by, among other things, poor financial performance, top executive compensation plans that were not sensitive to firm performance, and policies that limited shareholder input on governance issues.

Strickland and coauthors examined the types of firms targeted, the success of proposals, how actions affected firm value, and whether USA was successful at improving the governance structure of targeted firms.[69] In particular, they focused on the proxy proposals that USA promoted. During its existence, members of the association submitted 216 proposals; 53 were negotiated and 163 were submitted to a shareholder vote. In a negotiated agreement, the company agrees to some or all of the proposals in the proxy and the shareholder agrees to withdraw the proxy. A negotiated agreement is a clear-cut instance of investors affecting the corporate governance policies of a company. The proposals at USA most frequently dealt with poison pills, golden parachutes, confidential voting, and the adoption of an independent board of directors with outside directors on the nominating and compensation committees.

In assessing the impact of USA on shareholder value, the authors used the event-study methodology to examine the impact of 53 proposals at the 34 firms at which "negotiated agreements" were reached. They found that "over the two-day event window [the day before through the day of the USA announcement that it had negotiated an agreement with a firm to alter its corporate governance structure] . . . the average USA-sponsored agreement resulted in an abnormal stock price reaction of approximately 0.9 percent. This abnormal return represents a gain to shareholder wealth of approximately $39 million per firm or approximately $1.3 billion in total" (p. 334). Since the authors estimate an upper bound on the cost of the program at $22.75 million, the cost-benefit ratio is quite favorable.[70] Strickland and others also tested for abnormal returns around adoption dates of poison pills and golden parachutes, proxy mailing dates, and the day of the annual shareholder meeting. Abnormal returns around these event dates do not differ from zero. In addition to the wealth gain due to negotiated agreements, the authors state that "Potential benefits from USA-sponsored activism are: (i) competitive pressures on other firms in the target firm industry, (ii) SEC regulation of executive compensation disclosure, (iii) increased activism by public pension funds, and (iv) more outspoken monitoring by some outside directors" (p. 336).

Like USA, the Council of Institutional Investors (CII) is an association, but as its name indicates, its members are institutions and not individuals.[71] It also develops annual lists of underperforming firms that it urges its members to target for improvement. Opler and Sokobin evaluate the effect of this targeting on the 97 firms that appeared on CII's focus lists in 1991, 1992, and 1993. The methodology used by the authors was to calculate mean and median one year holding period returns for the stocks on the CII focus list and then compare these returns to the returns for a number of benchmarks.

One benchmark was the S&P 500. Other benchmark portfolios were created along the following dimensions: size, market risk, short-run performance, long-run performance, book-to-market ratio, and industry performance.[72]

As a result of their analysis, the author's conclude that "Council listed firms significantly outperform all benchmark portfolios." For example, when the CII firms are compared to the S&P 500, the CII firms generated returns that were at least ten percentage points higher in each sample year. "Over the full sample, the CII portfolio exhibits a mean return of 22.99 percent in the year after listing (median 19.4 percent) compared to the market return of 14.01 percent (median 10.46 percent). The results hold up as well when compared to the other benchmark portfolios."

The authors attribute this success to "coordinated monitoring and 'quiet' governance activism by institutional investors" (p. 6). They feel this approach is more successful than programs such as USA's for two reasons. First, the firms on the CII focus list were subject to "coordinated activism rather than individual campaigns run by a single pension fund," and, second, firms are looked at relative to when they first appeared on the focus list (p. 7). The authors felt this was important, because firms subject to public governance events such as proxy proposals are more likely to be the most recalcitrant and least likely to improve. The value of CII's list is that it creates an opportunity for coordinated, quiet governance activism. Poorly performing firms have both the incentive to improve and the nonadversarial support to do so.

While the previous three studies looked at the effects of specific targeting programs of CalPERS, USA, and CII, Wahal performed a pooled analysis of all firms targeted by nine major institutional investors from 1987 to 1993.[73] Over this seven-year period, he identified 365 independent targeting at 146 firms. Wahal then used the event-study methodology to test for the presence of abnormal returns around important dates in the targeting process: the letter date (when the firm was informed it was a target), proxy mailing date, press announcement date, and earliest information date. He also tested for long-term effects on stock price and on accounting measures of performance.

Wahal's results broadly confirm the previous event studies. First, institutions are relatively successful at actually getting corporations to accept their proposals about confidential voting, changing the structure of corporate boards, and redeeming poison pills (p. 2). Second, despite this success, for the sample as a whole there was on average a zero average abnormal return for shareholder proposals. However, Wahal does detect "a positive abnormal return for attempts to influence target firms that did not employ shareholder proposals (i.e. nonproxy targeting)" (p. 16).[74] Finally, on long-term measures of performance — long-term stock price, operating income, and net income — the author found no significant improvement in targeted firm's performance relative to a variety of benchmarks.

In sum, Wahal's "results cast doubt on the efficacy of pension fund activism in improving firm performance." Significantly however, he found that a "subset of firms subject to nonproxy targeting experience[d] significantly positive abnormal returns" (p. 22). The study of CREF by Carleton and coauthors discussed previously suggests scholars need a more subtle and inclusive methodology to accurately gauge influence and behavior. Wahal's study broadly confirms Nesbitt's findings for CalPERS, an institution that moved away from targeting firms for purely governance reasons and to targeting firms for performance reasons — although often using proxies or the threat of proxies on governance issues as part of their overall strategy.

The CalPERS, USA, and CII programs are (or in the case of USA, were) formal, programs designed to identify firms with particularly poor governance structures or particularly poor performance relative to similar firms. Another important feature of corporate governance is the direct pressure institutional investors can bring to bear on boards in order to bring about a change. Firms that attract this kind of attention may be on the aforementioned target lists, but they often stand out as firms with singularly poor economic performance. This tactic is an on-going part of the corporate governance tool kit, but it was particularly pronounced during the period from October 1992 to December 1993, when the CEOs of six major long-term underperforming corporations were forced to resign.[75] It was also used at a number of companies in 1990 and 1991. The power to force changes in top management at poorly performing companies is one of the most powerful tool owners have to align management's interests with their own.

To estimate the importance of CEO turnovers, Grundfest uses a case-study methodology to analyze CEO terminations at four companies: Goodyear Tire & Rubber, Allied Signal, Tenneco, and General Motors.[76] In addition to detailed descriptions of crucial events at these four companies, Grundfest uses the event-study methodology to determine whether excessive stock price changes occurred in the days immediately surrounding the event. He also presents performance data over the year following the event in order to estimate the longer-term impact of CEO turnover on performance. Aggregating the results, Grundfest found the "immediate stock price effects associated with CEO replacements at Goodyear, Allied Signal, and Tenneco totaled more than $1.3 billion . . . adding the gains associated with the April coup at General Motors, but conservatively excluding the gains associated with the October GM termination, brings the aggregate shareholder wealth increase to more than $2.7 billion" (p. 900).[77]

In the longer-term analysis the results are mixed. Goodyear and Allied-Signal substantially outperformed the S&P 500 in the year and a half after the event. At Tenneco, stock performance was not significantly different from the performance of the S&P 500. GM's stock performed slightly worse than the S&P 500 in the months after the events. Grundfest attributes performance to the revelation of continuing problems at both companies and to the fact that the new CEO at Tenneco was diagnosed with brain cancer. In addition, he points out that both companies significantly underperformed the market for a substantial period before the CEO terminations so that merely matching the S&P 500 was an improvement. Grundfest also recognizes that looking for long-term effects of specific events is a difficult conceptual task because of the multitude of other events that may occur subsequent to the event and that can be expected to affect stock price.

Finally, Karpoff surveyed twenty empirical studies that attempted to measure the effects of shareholder activism on target firms' values, operations, and governance structure. He found that the research tends to produce contradictory results. Some studies, such as that by Strickland and coauthors, discussed above show statistically significant increases in shareholder wealth. Others, such as Wahal and Karpoff and others, discussed above disagree. They tend to find little or no support for the proposition that shareholder activism affects performance. After considering the approaches and the methodology of these studies Karpoff concludes that the differences result from the events considered and the ways various authors characterize "success." In the end, "Most evidence indicates that shareholder activism can prompt small changes in target firms' governance structures, but has negligible impacts on share values and earnings."[78] Black reaches similar conclusions: "The best reading of the currently available evidence is that institutional investor activism does not importantly affect firm performance."[79]

Conclusions

The studies presented in this chapter represent well the empirical work that has investigated the linkage between corporate governance on both the macro and the micro level to corporate performance. On the macro level, the market for corporate control appears to have been an effective if sometimes blunt tool for ex post correction of particularly serious lapses in corporate governance. It was especially relevant during the 1980s when numerous companies were taken over and restructured. However, its relevance for the future may be limited to extreme cases.

On the micro level, the results are at best mixed. Studies such as those by Karpoff and coauthors, Karpoff, and Wahal tend to find little or no effect from proxy activity even when the activity is successful at bringing about the desired change. Either the measures aren't directly related to performance or the relationship is swamped by other factors. It may also be that pure governance reform is something like a vaccine — the effect really doesn't show up until the patient is threatened with the disease at a later date.

On the other hand, there does appear to be support for the proposition that active investors or investor associations such as CII or USA can effectively choose target firms and that the act of targeting itself and the actions it brings may enhance shareholder value. Nesbitt, Opler and Sokobin, Strickland, Wiles and Zenner, and Grundfest all provide evidence that targeting or, in the case of Grundfest, direct action at firms that have been identified as underperformers, can generate significant improvements in shareholder wealth. Wahal finds similar results for that subset of proxies that are targeted at underperforming firms, although, like Karpoff and coauthors, he fails to find any wealth-enhancing effects of proxy proposals in general. The implication appears to be that active ownership matters even if specific governance features do not. A related and important implication, but one that has not been tested, is that it may be possible to improve the performance of *all* firms by simply targeting a few firms. The idea here is that expressed by John Biggs, chairman and CEO of TIAA-CREF: "The significance [of shareholder activism] is not the three or four laggards you catch — it's that you get the herd to run. We need to scare all the animals."[80]

This observation leads to the question of the evolving role of institutional owners, not as sponsors of specific proxy proposals to change specific items of corporate governance, but as exercisers of the broad and often informally exercised powers of ownership. Owners may make a difference, not through one mechanism or another, but through the full range of ways that owners interact with companies. This is particularly true since the 1992 reforms to SEC Rule 14(a)(2) allowing informal communication between both groups of owners and between owners and companies. In this environment, proxy proposals or other formal means of communicating with management may be used less frequently.[81] Thus, in the next chapter, attention turns to the evolving relationship between institutional owners and the companies in their portfolios.

Chapter 7
Models of Monitoring and Corporate Governance

Monitoring is the quintessential activity of the professional ownership of corporate equity, and it is coming to characterize fiduciary capitalism. Monitoring can range from the formal (submitting proxies) to the informal (developing positions and communicating them to management). In all cases it is an activity intended to foster organizational accountability on the part of managers to owners or chains of owners. In fiduciary capitalism, agency chains connect a firm's top management to the ultimate owner or beneficiary, such as a pension-fund member or a mutual-fund investor. Yet legally such ultimate "owners" do not have the right to monitor management; only those legally holding shares (and perhaps debt) have such rights. Thus, for all intents and purposes, institutional owners — as professional owners — monitor firms.[1] When exit is blocked as is typically and increasingly the case for most large universal owners, then voice remains the only viable way to attempt to influence a firm's behavior. This is particularly true if the agency problems inherent in the corporate form are to be addressed in ways other than through a market for corporate control — by market monitoring. Thus, there must be some form of monitoring to either supplement or to entirely replace exit as an option.

Commentators have suggested that forms of corporate governance can be identified along several different axes. Perhaps the most commonly suggested spectrum stretches from *liquidity* to *control*.[2] The United States is generally cited as an example of passive corporate governance fostered by liquid capital markets that theoretically facilitate exit. Germany, on the other hand, is often cited as an example of active, or controlling corporate governance typically by a dominant bank in which exit through the market is either blocked or difficult. In this schema, Japan would be mid-spectrum, characterized by a variety of voices that are typically exercised within the structure of the keiretsu.[3]

As noted, the owners of corporations in the United States are generally considered to play a more passive role in corporate governance than banks in Germany. Yet during the 1990s, U.S. institutional investors have proved to be far more active monitors than their German or Japanese counterparts. Indeed, they are often highly effective monitors of the firms they "own." Although U.S. institutional investors in no sense control these firms, either individually or as a group, neither are they as passive as might be suggested by either the market for corporate control model or as they were often seen in the late 1980s and early 1990s.[4]

From Markets to Monitors: Models of Monitoring

Monitoring in all of its forms fundamentally attempts to reduce agency costs that are inherent in the relationship between either owners and managers, or fiduciary agents and other (fiduciary) agents. The form that monitoring can take ranges from the very aggressive or to the very passive. At the aggressive end of the spectrum are controlling block owners who can determine corporate policy. This, of course, is true for partnerships, sole proprietorships, and closely held corporations, but large corporations with controlling block holders are rare in the United States, although they are important in much of the rest of the world.[5] The only exception is the special case of firms with large, founding family interests. At the other extreme is a passive form of monitoring that can hardly be called monitoring at all. This occurs when institutional owners validate management recommendations with little or no attempt to form an independent judgement. Intermediate, but closer to the controlling end is "relationship investing" in which an owner (or groups of owners) hold a significant block of equity in a particular firm, thereby establishing a long-term position and by virtue of their ownership block can exert leverage on management. This is unusual in the U.S. context currently, although some authors believe it will become more important in the future.[6]

In addition to a simple spectrum of passive to aggressive, other observers have developed models of corporate monitoring. An example is Pound's "political model of governance" approach, "in which active investors seek to change corporate policy by developing voting support from dispersed shareholders, rather than by simply purchasing voting power or control," as would be the case in a market- or transaction-based system.[7] While voting remains an important monitoring tool, informal and formal conversation between institutional owners and managers has often proved more effective than formal voting, although the latter buttresses the effectiveness of the former. As noted in Chapter 6, studies suggest that informal and typically off-the-record negotiations are far more widespread than proxy voting, and increasingly common.[8]

While there is a range of monitoring and relationship investing, all have in common the initial (or total) bypassing of the market for corporate control. Most commentators agree with Pound when he writes that a major economic advantage of the "political" model is that it is more flexible than the takeover market since "it can address specific problems at a corporation without imposing changes in control, changes in management, and the enormous transactions costs attendant to them."[9] Similarly, Grundfest argues that "Capital-market behavior is . . . guided by a jointly determined political [regulatory] and economic equilibrium, and an understanding of the political marketplace is essential to appreciate the role that capital-market mechanisms can . . . play in corporate governance."[10] Black argues that shareholder monitoring is part of a series of "imperfect constraints" on corporate managers, which may also include the market for corporate control, the product and capital markets, the market for corporate managers, incentive compensation arrangements, creditor monitoring, and the risk of bankruptcy.[11]

Monitoring by Institutional Investors

Roe suggests there are three general types of board monitoring: hierarchical, collegial, and crisis. Hierarchical monitoring relies on specialization as, for example, when a board financial expert focuses on optimizing financial returns while an operating executive focuses on running the firm. Both voices need to be on the board yet not in the same person. The second form of monitoring is collegial. It depends on directors having proper incentives to be informed and involved. This has been the primary focus of board reform in the recent past. The third type of board monitoring is crisis monitoring. This requires that monitors evaluate the causes of poor results, especially as a means of forestalling crisis and, if a crisis occurs, respond to it appropriately. Well-publicized failures in crisis monitoring have often sparked much institutional investor interest in board restructuring and reform.[12]

Michael Porter, in his 1992 work *Capital Choices: Changing the Way America Invests in Industry,* was unduly pessimistic about the desire and ability of institutional investors (especially those with indexed portfolios) to monitor. He viewed the short-term nature of "monitoring and valuing stocks [through the market] on current earnings" as a destructive and self-fulfilling prophecy. Although the proxy fights could be used and were used as a "direct means of imposing . . . [institutional investors'] views on management," it was an expensive and clumsy means, typically used as a last resort in crisis situations. His conclusion is that "despite their large aggregate holdings, American institutional agents have virtually no real influence on management behavior."[13]

Yet it was exactly beginning in the early 1990s that public pension funds began to actively monitor their "passive" portfolios, primarily because the largest funds had indexed portfolios that reflected the market as a whole.[14] If they could not sell (by definition), they had to care. Porter entirely missed this dynamic of indexed funds due to his singular focus on fragmented aggregated holdings. On the other hand, Pound captured the benefit of monitoring and targeting underperforming firms when he wrote: "The percentage of stock held by a specific investor is largely irrelevant to the decision to monitor. What is relevant is the raw dollar amount at stake, relative to the economic costs and benefits of becoming informed. With a sufficiently high raw dollar level of holdings, the incentive to become active is great, even if the proportion of stock held is very small."[15] Thus, the free-rider problem inherent in collective action situations does not pertain as long as the institution believes that its returns (either firm specific or for all underperformers in its portfolio) will be increased through monitoring.[16] In this sense it appears that Porter mistook an agency problem (which exists in all monitoring situations) for a collective action problem.[17] Richard Koppes, former Chief Counsel of CalPERS, concludes, "the cost-benefit analysis of shareholder activism is an essential step in developing strategy, and that some strategies, such as direct discussions with management at selected corporations [informal monitoring], are an inexpensive means to an effective end."[18]

Institutional Voice

Recently, the largest activist public pension funds, some large private funds, and labor union pension funds (so-called Taft-Hartley funds) have begun monitoring as the sheer size of their holdings permits them to capture gains in spite of having to share the gains from their activism with all other shareholders. Of particular importance was the 1992 reform of the Security and Exchange Commission rules defining permissible communication between owners. This was a watershed reform. Prior to 1992, institutional investors that discussed issues at commonly held companies exposed themselves to the serious litigation risk and onerous reporting requirements that applied to anyone attempting to obtain control of a company. This severely limited institutions' ability to develop a united response to problem companies, although a number of institutions became adept at communicating with their peers through press releases and news conferences. After 1992, restrictions on communication between investors were substantially eased although some impediments still remained. (See the discussion of the 1992 SEC rule changes in Chapter 8.)

Black makes a distinction between what he calls institutional "voice" and institutional "control." The former requires agents to watch agents, often agents such as institutional owners and corporate managers who may not have identical interests, and for that reason this type of monitoring may let greater amounts of daylight into the board room in a sort of checks and balance approach to governance.[19] Institutional control, on the other hand, suggests the domination by one or a small number of institutions over a particular firm, as in the German model. Roe suggests that a structure of multiple intermediaries "can deter opportunism by monitoring one another, impel action in a way that a single blockholder might not, and facilitate power-sharing, not domination."[20] It also avoids or minimizes the political problem in the American tradition of deep distrust of concentrations of wealth and power. Yet what is striking about the current reality is that few large institutions have amassed anything close to the five- percent limit after which severe SEC regulations take effect. As Roe points out, even a number of institutions owning nearly five percent would need to have ongoing coordination in order to "wrest control" from management, were that to be their goal (pp. 244–47).[21]

In order to enhance institutional voice and to overcome the free-rider problem inherent in dispersed ownership, Black advocates that institutions slim portfolios so that they hold between 5 and 10 percent of the stock in a particular firm (but not more than this). Communication among these significant minority holders would then be easier, permitting stronger influence in selecting board members, but at these levels of ownership no single owner is likely to dominate the board or its selection. Thus, a half dozen or so owners could collectively influence major corporate actions, but no one institution could dominate or act effectively alone.[22]

Why have U.S. institutions avoided slimming down portfolios, and not taken larger positions in firms?[23] That is, why have they resisted becoming relational investors with significant stakes rather than coalition, or even individual, monitors? Analysis is divided between the majority who see law and regulation (read: the political tradition) as the primary inhibiting factor and those (most especially Coffee) who see the desire for liquidity (apart from the legal constraints) as the primary factor. On the legal side, concerns abound regarding 13-d restrictions which define (in some highly uncertain situations) two or more persons as a "group" that might be "beneficial owners" of 5 percent or more if their holdings were to be aggregated. The significance of a group designation is that, regardless of their intentions, it subjects group members to the rules and regulations that govern a takeover attempt. These include, among others, stringent reporting requirements and limits on the institutions' ability to sell positions.

The chilling effect on voice results from the fact that such an aggregation, in Briggs' words, can be determined by the courts "if they have agreed to act together 'for the purpose of acquiring, holding, voting or disposing' of the issuer's equity securities." Such agreement need not be in writing and can be inferred ex post from circumstantial evidence.[24] The danger of triggering a "group" is clearly an inhibiting factor for accumulation of even relatively small percentages, and an incentive for caution around voting and other strategies.

Multiple Monitors

A special problem for monitoring corporations is realizing the potential of multiple monitors and overcoming the natural barriers to collective action. In this context, Grundfest advocates that multiple monitors use "just vote no" campaigns directed against management director slates as a whole, or individually targeted directors, as CalPERS did in 1995 and 1996, and the Teamsters' Union has done since 1996. "Just vote no" campaigns are effective monitoring tools because they are easy to coordinate and require a minimum of resources. While these campaigns typically achieve only minority support — often upwards of 35 percent — they are highly symbolic and usually attract considerable attention from management. Grundfest argues that symbols are often effective as public flags that something is wrong, and can be important first steps toward correcting perceived problems by putting pressure on the board. One example of a "just vote no" campaign was the 1994 campaign directed against the Westinghouse corporation initiated by the New York City Teachers Union pension fund, which gathered more than 35 percent of the proxies in a "just vote no" campaign.[25] The Westinghouse campaign was relatively successful in that it allowed shareholders to effectively cast a no-confidence vote at a firm where, in Grundfest's words, "there [was] general consensus that management or strategy [was] deficient."[26]

Roe also argues in favor of multiple monitors in a somewhat different vein. "Multiple blocks may induce intermediaries to act in a way that a single isolated blockholder [as in Germany] might not. The multiple blocks may solve the weakness problem without creating a dominating block that recentralizes authority in a dominating intermediary."[27]

The idea of multiple monitors is central to Pound's idea of the political model of corporate governance. He suggests seven types of evidence that monitoring is increasing and "strengthening" the political model. First, proxy contests are moving away from control as the goal to sending a message, increasingly settled by negotiations between dissidents and management. Second, the use of formal voting challenges are being used to provoke debate over specific policies (as in "just vote no" campaigns), rather than as an attempt to get control. Third, some monitors are using public lobbying campaigns without a vote, such as forming a "shadow board." Fourth, private, informal negotiations, as CalPERS, CREF, and other large institutional investors have been conducting since 1995 are becoming more common. Fifth, the development of "smart voting systems" that target firms on the basis of economic performance, are being used by monitors such as New York's, Wisconsin's, and California's pension funds. Sixth, management is now actually responding to these initiatives in a variety of ways, such as by establishing an "investor ombudsman." Finally, Pound suggests that there is a "new dynamic" between large investors and large corporations that is reflected in the meetings that began in 1993 between various investors and CEOs at various firms such as GM, Westinghouse, IBM, American Express, and others.[28] As the *Institutional Investor* noted at the time, "The biggest single spur to the growth of the shareholder movement . . . occurred when pension fund activist began linking governance issues . . . to concerns about cooperate performance."[29]

The Monitoring Firm in a Market for Monitoring

Most monitoring models take the structure of the typical firm's board of directors for granted. However, many reformers propose a variety of changes making more independent various committees of the board, including the nominations committee and the compensation committee. Some of these reform proposals are discussed below. A more fundamental reform and one that is consistent with the professionalization of ownership is the call for a "monitoring firm" proposed by Latham.[30] He argues that to be effective governance activists need to separate the actual nomination of board members from the board itself. Currently, the typical board nominates a slate of directors for shareholders to vote on. The process is heavily influenced by the chairman of the board, who is often the CEO of the company. Under this system all an institution can do is to vote for or against individuals or for or against the slate as a whole. There are no other ways, save informal pressure, to affect the nomination process as such. In short, the board is seen as self-perpetuating, and in its strongest case, a self-perpetuating oligarchy.[31]

Latham's proposal is to create an agency or agencies outside of the firm to nominate company directors. By moving the nominating process out of the boardroom, directors would become more responsible to owners. By creating specialized firms to identify and nominate directors, the free-rider problem that would exist if institutions did this individually would be mitigated. The role of monitoring director performance would then fall to these independent monitoring firms. There is a certain parallel to the idea of a "professional director" in the proposed British system, the so-called PRO-NED proposal — PRO-NED standing for professional non-executive director. While the PRO-NED system would make available certified and qualified directors from a central clearinghouse, Latham suggests creating a competitive industry of director-selection firms: "Think of accounting firms as having similar investments in reputation. The typical shareholder would be hard pressed to name a good director candidate, but most can name a good accounting firm."[32]

The usual means investors have to influence boards and to align director's interests with the shareholders' tends not to solve the problem of board responsiveness. Instruments such as takeovers, lawsuits, compensation schemes, informal shareholder pressure, and director independence, even taken together, do not and cannot make directors truly independent of the CEO. With the partial exception of compensation schemes, all are ex post forms of monitoring that tend to work only after a major problem has surfaced. By making directors accountable to owners, what Latham desires is ex ante monitoring, thereby avoiding or minimizing problems before they arise and before the market value of stock has suffered.[33]

Not only would proactive monitoring be more efficient, but it would also have the effect of promoting social welfare since large, indexed institutional investors — as universal owners — could more efficiently pursue the generalized monitoring of their portfolios. "The reason is that a well diversified investor shares the profits of a company in about the same proportion as the investor shares in the company's social and environmental effects, such as pollution, community service. . . . A CMF [corporate monitoring firm] that pursues a policy of balancing all these effects would thus be in the selfish interests of [indexed] investors."[34]

The Partial Institutionalization of Insurgency: Who Monitors Most and Most Effectively

Although proxy voting and quiet activism have increased substantially over the past decade among mutual funds and some other institutional investors, the most consistent and effective monitors have been those institutional investors that are not dependent on commercial networks and ties: public and not-for-profit funds (e.g., CREF) and labor union funds. These core institutions in the emerging fiduciary capitalism are those that Monks characterizes as the "new owner."[35]

Activist institutions have continued filing proxies, conducting "just vote no" campaigns against incumbent directors, and engaging in increased reliance on informal lobbying and monitoring. In the United States, monitoring practices have developed into a partial institutionalization of insurgency based on the highly fragmented ownership patterns of institutional shareholders. Under these circumstances monitoring must take the form of widespread coalitions rather than either a controlling interest or even an institutional voice form. Since it is unlikely that the underlying ownership structure will change rapidly, a number of proposals for better coordination among monitors have been offered. For example, some authors have suggested that various "trade groups," such as the Council of Institutional Investors (CII), should play a more important, albeit informal role in coordination, as they did in the Westinghouse case. A number of proposals for increasing monitoring while reducing the fragmentation of ownership have suggested that there should be "lead monitors" whose holdings are greater than those typically held by the large indexed funds. Such institutions would reduce their portfolios from approximately 1,000 or more to a few hundred positions, without increasing risk, assuming the capital asset pricing model is correct. This would enable institutional holders to divide up monitoring responsibility to a greater extent than currently, thereby minimizing the free-rider problem attendant with ongoing, and especially ex ante monitoring.[36]

While coordinated monitoring offers promise, a variety of factors have impeded its implementation. Among public funds each fund is jealous of its autonomy, and while a great deal of informal conversation occurs, coordinated standards and action are the exception rather than the rule. Second, funds exist in a political world, so the priorities naturally differ from fund to fund. Third, nonpublic funds vary widely in their makeup and "personality" (e.g., CREF and Fidelity), and in turn differ fundamentally from public funds. Thus, while coordination is possible, it usually only occurs on issues that fundamentally unify funds, such as when the SEC attempted to change proxy-voting rules in 1997 and 1998. Public, Taft-Hartley, and other funds, among other groups, were able to get the SEC to reconsider its proposals. (See Chapter 8 for a discussion of these proposals.)

Even with these difficulties, the institutionalization of insurgency has continued apace through the late 1990s. For example, in late 1997 CalPERS announced the use of an Economic Valued Added (EVA) approach to searching out underperforming managers. EVA calculates a company's after-tax net operating profit, minus the cost of capital for one year. Negative EVA destroys wealth, regardless of a firm's stock price (which can be pumped up by various forms of creative accounting). A negative EVA three years in a row makes a firm a candidate for CalPERS' "target 10" list, provided it is also underperforming in the market and has poor governance features.[37]

In late 1998, CalPERS proposed that all firms undergo corporate governance performance audits as an additional indicator of good governance. Such an audit would require a firm to hire independent consultants to evaluate the firm, and to report back to all shareholders. Included in the audit would be a detailed analysis of audit committees to provide shareholders with information on the financial auditors (e.g., nature of independence from the firm). The principle behind the firm itself hiring a governance auditor is to avoid the free-rider problem inherent in making available to all shareholders the results of an audit paid for by a single investor or group of investors. Additionally, CalPERS expanded its international corporate governance program, forming alliances with a number of governance activist funds in the United Kingdom, including the largest quasi-public fund, Hermes. For the first time, CalPERS is funding a number of leading edge areas of research on topics such as, can voting rights be legally unbundled and traded separately from share ownership? Other research topics included the voting practices of mutual funds and the dilution effect of widespread share option grants and pricing.[38]

One of the most significant developments in the late 1990s was the role of labor unions (so-called Taft-Hartley funds) as governance activists. This significantly expanded the base of institutionalized insurgency, and added a number of important dimensions. The AFL-CIO's Capital Stewardship program, a coordinating center for activism, has also articulated performance criteria for activism, including voting proxies that promote long-term value, public policy advocacy before public agencies such as the SEC and the Department of Labor, and "high-performance" workplace competitiveness strategies that emphasize the potential partnership between employees, shareholders, and communities.[39] In addition to traditional governance issues, executive compensation, director independence and political soft-money reporting have been on labor's governance agenda.

In the late 1990s, labor union funds have been among the most active and most effective of all funds in obtaining passage of their proposals. Neverthe-less, it is likely that CREF, CalPERS, and other nonunion funds are more effective in obtaining informal changes.[40] Most importantly, the Teamsters Union pioneered the binding bylaw amendment. This technique is poten-tially the most important new tool developed for institutional investors in a long time. Traditionally, proxy proposals are advisory and management is under no obligation to implement them. In fact, even proxies that received majority votes are often ignored either in whole or in part. But, in 1997, after seeing their proxy proposal at the Fleming Company, which called for a shareholder vote on the company's adoption of a poison pill, receive 64 percent of the vote only to be ignored by management, the Teamsters Union submitted a proxy as a binding amendment to the company's bylaws. The measure passed and was upheld by the Oklahoma Supreme Court, but as of 1999 is on appeal.[41] In the mean time, the number of binding bylaw proxy proposals has risen sharply. By the 1999 proxy season, at least thirty such proposals had been submitted.

Relationship Investing as an Alternative to Monitoring a Fragmented Portfolio

A number of authors have suggested that "relationship investing" would be a beneficial alternative to the informal monitoring of fragmented port-folios.[42] In relationship investing, an institution takes a significant, although not controlling, stake in a firm and, in Koppes' and Reilly's words, has a "long-term commitment, and reciprocity between owner and management over business policy decisions." While ex post monitoring is widespread, influential, and growing, relationship investing is, to date, the rare excep-tion, at least partly because of formidable legal and historic-cultural bar-riers.[43] Monks and Minow summarize some of the most important legal barriers for all types of financial institutions.

With commercial banks, there is the prohibition of Glass-Steagall; mutual fund hold-ings are limited by the Investment Company Act of 1940; insurance companies are limited by state law; private pension plans are required by ERISA to diversify as widely as possible; the federal system under FERSA [Federal Employment Retirement Sys-tem Act of 1986] is limited to equity investment through index funds. These provi-sions, enacted independently, have a cumulative impact of preventing the financial sector executives from being able to exercise control over commercial sector execu-tives — to keep Main Street independent of Wall Street.[44]

Kleiman and coauthors review the performance of a number of "patient" capital investors (loosely, "relationship investors"). These investors range from "white-squire" funds that assist firms targeted for hostile takeovers to straightforward purchases of major equity positions. The review concludes that early evidence suggests a generally positive benefits to all shareholders, but warns against a possible future backlash if the issue is not handle carefully. It also points out that there may be possible "corporate inefficiencies" if relational investors attempt to micromanage firms.

A distinction is often made between *negotiated* and *non-negotiated* forms of relational investment. The former describes a long-term investment in return for a board seat, for example, while the latter typically offers unsolicited suggestions about what should be done. Negotiated positions typically have been taken by investment banks or investment companies (e.g., Corporate Partners, GE Capital, 1818 Fund, Warren Buffett/Berkshire Hathaway, Inc.). The State of Wisconsin Investment Board singularly among public pension funds holds 5 to 10 percent of outstanding shares in a cross section of medium-size high technology firms.

Non-negotiated forms have often been pursued by corporate governance funds (e.g., Lens Fund), which focus on underperforming firms. These funds often use issues such as shareholder rights, executive compensation, equal voting rights, and board of director independence as a means of leverage. Kleiman and coauthors conclude that the negotiated positions have been moderately successful, while governance funds (fewer and smaller capitalized firms) less so. They conclude skeptically that "Relationship investing that focuses on a shareholder value perspective undoubtedly will play a major role for a few more years . . . [yet] investors may discover that relationship investment, not unlike the diversification movement of the 1960s and the LBO activity of the 1980s, is nothing more than a fad of the 1990s."[45]

Increasing the Focus on Boards of Directors

Governance activities and much analytical commentary have been directed at examining the role of the board of directors in either implementing or impeding the various demands of institutional investors. A large and rapidly growing literature exists on these aspects of governance, especially in the United States and the United Kingdom.[46] A passive, CEO-dominated board has traditionally been seen as the logical, albeit not the legal, result of managerial control.[47] In spite of the political language and legal procedures of democratic process (votes, elections, ballots), the reality in managerial theory and corporate procedure was shareholder disenfranchisement and a CEO-dominated, self-perpetuating, and passive board.

Accountability in the Board Room

As boards have increasingly come to be seen as the key link between institutional monitors or would-be monitors (whether of a "relationship investment" or "monitor as catalyst" nature) and operational management, the aim of reformers has been to create a situation of accountability in the boardroom. Dale Hanson, former CalPERS' CEO, characterized this as simply "letting the sun shine in."[48] Along these lines a 1999 blue-ribbon panel of stock market regulators, accounting officials, and some corporate officials proposed rules making the audit committee of the board significantly more independent.[49]

There has also been some interest in the German dual boards that codify a clear division between managers who manage and nonexecutives who monitor them. While dual boards are unlikely to be imitated in the United States, institutionalization of truly independent directors as effective monitors has become a primary focus of reform. Measures to increase board independence include the creation of independent board committees on key issues such as CEO compensation and board nomination.[50] Despite attempts at reform, the core problem remains: boards are self-perpetuating and self-selecting, even in those cases where the once near absolute power of the CEO has been dramatically reduced. As Monks writes, "Directors are not 'nominated,' they are selected by the incumbent directors (however independent) and the chief executive officer.[Therefore] independence is a matter of personal character. This is not acceptable. We cannot have a system that depends on the luck of stumbling across an occasional honest man."[51]

While directors have the legal authority to execute almost all the reforms that various corporate critics, monitors, and would-be monitors desire, they have failed to do so. The problem, in the words of one chairman of a large firm, is that boards have the power "to govern, but not the process."[52] The issues are what should boards do, how they should do it, and in whose interests (and how conceived) should they act? An important, if difficult to overcome, part of board reform is sociopsychological and cultural. As *The Economist* notes:

Whatever people's stated roles, small group dynamics tend to make them agree with each other and to forget their role representing outside interests. Nonexecutives come to respect the judgment of a successful boss too much, or suppress misgivings so as not to upset him. A better way for shareholders to make a board work for them is to make it their direct responsibility to see that it does.[53]

The Critics' Agenda

The critics of CEO-dominated boards have focused their attention on a number of problematic areas and practices. For some time now, one of the highest priorities for boardroom reform has been the role of independent or outside directors. Independence is often in the eye of the beholder, but typically has come to mean having no direct or indirect connection with the firm. Independent directors are thought to enhance the objectivity of the board, to provide a defense against co-optation by the CEO, and to be better able to act in times of crisis.[54] Here, there has been real success over the last twenty years, at least as measured by the ratio of independent/outside directors to insiders. However, as discussed in Chapter 6, there is much debate as to whether this has had any significant impact on board performance.

In order to carry out their fiduciary duty, directors need better information if they are to do their jobs effectively. Inevitably, directors can not know as much about the firm as management because they do not devote their entire professional efforts to a single company and therefore are not enmeshed in the day-to-day information flow of the company. This shortcoming is compounded by management's control of the information that is allowed to reach the board. Too often the result can be a board knowing too little, too late and, even if it is willing and able to act to confront a growing problem or crisis, it is often unable to do so.[55]

Board independence is seriously compromised by the common practice at the great majority of U.S. corporations where the CEO is also the chairman of the board. This provides the CEO the opportunity to manipulate the board both through agenda setting and through control of information flow to directors. The United States has a history of strong CEOs acting as individuals. Thus, a board can, although it need not be, manipulated by a powerful and skillful CEO as chairman of the board. Similarly, a former CEO who sits on a board (of his or her own company or of another firm) may become part of a network of managerial insiders who go along with the dominant managerial culture.[56] The penchant for appointing ex-CEOs as directors tends to make for acquiescence, since such individuals may be reluctant to assert leadership in opposition to the reigning CEO (whom they may even have appointed). Appointment of the former CEO of a company clearly retards a fresh break with the past.

The nominating process for directors has attracted the critics' attention. In the vast majority of U.S. firms, candidates for the board originate in a board-nominating committee, and are subsequently ratified by shareholders in uncontested proxy elections. Even though the selection of directors is nominally in the hands of the board, a 1991 study found that more than 80 percent of board vacancies were filled by CEO recommendations.[57] Concerns with the nominating process were at the heart of the problem that led Latham to the proposals discussed in an earlier section.

Another area of concern is executive compensation in general and CEO compensation in particular. Pay-for-performance is increasingly the common standard. In some corporations compensation is set by an independent board committee with sufficient expertise to make recommendations, but in others compensation is set by management-friendly directors. In that case, abuses such as repricing stock options to maintain their value in the face of a decline in stock price or selecting performance measures that are easy to achieve or do not accurately reflect corporate performance are a danger. Performance criteria are often too narrow and limited, typically based on stock performance only. Many critics argue for multiple measures of long-term performance.[58] The issue of proper and effective compensation is a large and difficult one, but any solution is compounded by CEO-dominated boards with limited information flows.

Another area of concern is director compensation. Here, the problem is walking the fine line in compensating directors so as to focus their attention on performance while not compensating them in a way or to an extent that discourages director independence. The problem is compounded by multiple board membership and the resulting relatively large incomes and variety of perquisites for individual board members. If multiple board membership is reduced (which is a slowly emerging trend), reexamination of pay may also have to occur. Compensation for outside directors in the form of stock grants and/or options is becoming increasingly popular, but may generate some of the same kinds of problems that stock options for management have created.[59]

The practice at some boards of holding staggered board elections—often called "classified boards"—in which only a fraction of the board stands for election each year has attracted the vigorous criticism of institutional investors. Prior to the 1980s takeover era, the near universal practice was to elect boards at annual shareholder meetings. However, in the early 1990s this practice was changed to staggered elections as part of the antitakeover defenses at many corporations. This procedure meant a disgruntled shareholder or would-be acquirer could not unseat the entire board at a single election, thus insulating directors from shareholders.

Since management control of the proxy processes is nearly total, agenda setting and all phases of the proxy process have attracted the attention of numerous critics. Confidential voting, greater access to the proxy statement, and reforms challenging the way management can alter the rules and even sometimes the content of proxies as they are being voted on are just a few of the concerns often voiced.

Critics have also raised questions about the personal accountability of directors. Traditionally, directors have been prominent individuals from business and academia and were presumed to be well qualified by virtue of experience and training. Furthermore, shareholders usually voted for the entire board or, in the case of a proxy fight, against the entire board. Recently, questions have been raised about the maximum number of boards on which a director should server, the director's individual contribution to a board, and other issues of professionalism. As a complement to this increased interest in the quality of individual board members, some institutions such as CalPERS have begun to monitor individual director performance as a means to encourage them to act as catalysts, as well as to "urge directors to devote more time to fewer boards."[60]

Case Study: A Response to Institutional Investor Pressures

It is only natural that as institutional investors began to act as professional owners other power centers in corporate governance triad—directors and managers—began to react. The reaction from different elements in the triad has often been to try to come to agreement on codes of good practice. This in itself is an example of professional behavior. For example, in 1996 the National Association of Corporate Directors (NACD)—an influential professional organization closely aligned with corporate interests—issued a report on director compensation and professionalism.[61] The report incorporated some important demands that institutional investors had long wanted. This section critiques the report and its recommendations in some detail because of the report's influence as a benchmark and standard setter, and as an example of the fact that a single reform cannot adequately align directors' interests with those of shareholders nor can the monitoring problem be solved through simple incentive alignment.[62]

The overriding concern of the NACD report is how best to align the agency chains in fiduciary capitalism as fully as possible to maximize shareholder returns. Conventional wisdom in the institutional investor community suggests that if such alignment succeeds, the long-term return to shareholders is maximized and agency and governance problems are thereby ameliorated. As investors, particularly institutional investors, looked more closely at boards of underperforming companies—and at some individual directors on those boards—they found a number of disturbing practices that might broadly be characterized as unprofessional. To begin with, many boards contained directors whose independence from management, and thus their ability to effectively represent the interests of shareholders, was severely compromised.[63] Not only were current members of top management board members, but frequently CEOs were also chairmen of the board responsible for leading the very body charged with monitoring and evaluating their own performance.

While a lack of director independence has been an important issue in corporate governance for some time, two other attributes of individual directors also raised concerns. First, some directors lacked the necessary expertise in the company's businesses and the industries it competed in to provide proper managerial oversight. Second, and contributing to the first problem, a number of directors held an excessive number of seats on different boards. This limited their ability to perform their duties with regard to any one company and limited their ability to gain the knowledge necessary to be an effective director. Owners now want directors who are not only independent of management, but who also know the business and the industries in which the company operates—or who are willing to put in the time necessary to learn them. They also want directors who have special expertise to contribute to the monitoring and oversight function of the board. Areas such as finance, marketing, or international competition, depending on the firm's business, are often mentioned.

How Does the NACD Propose to Solve These Problems?

The NACD report argues that the key corporate governance problem has been to align the interests of directors with those of shareholders. At the same time it articulates a general set of professional standards to which the corporation institutionally and each director individually should be committed. When these standards are operationalized, the proper alignment of directors' financial (and other) interests will more likely result in the proper execution of their duties to evaluate and monitor management.

The report makes a number of recommendations to promote a "culture of professionalism." First, all directors should have specific competencies (e.g., finance, accounting, strategy, industry knowledge). Second, the board should maintain its independence from management (e.g., set its own agenda, hire outside experts, and so on). Third, the great majority of nonexecutive directors should be independent of management. Fourth, each director should have a significant personal, long-term equity stake in the firm. Fifth, there should be a strict, explicit limitation on the number of other boards on which a member may serve. In sum, a director should be independent, have specific and useful competencies, devote significant time and energy to the board(s) he or she serves on, and over time come to possess a significant ownership stake in the firm.

Before turning to a critique of these recommendations, it will be useful to make explicit a number of assumptions implicit in the report. First, higher levels of director independence reinforced by greater professionalism are assumed to increase firm economic performance and to maximize the wealth of all shareholders. Second, shareholders are assumed to be the only important stakeholders who should be on the board. Excluded are debt and other nonequity financial stakeholders, suppliers, employees, and others who may have a significant stake in the well-being of the firm, or who may be in a position to uniquely contribute to maximizing firm-level productivity. This exclusion is, of course, consistent with the finance model. Third, shareholders are assumed to be a homogeneous group. There is no discussion of, for example, traders versus investors (short- and long-term holders), small holders versus institutional investors, or beneficial holders versus individual investors. All shareholders are assumed to have identical interests.

The Question of Independence

Independence, which plays such a central role in the NACD's recommendations, raises a number of important questions. They include what is independence? Independence from whom? And, independence to what end?

The definition of independence has become a mini-industry in the corporate governance community and an appendix to the NACD report provides nine definitional examples.[64]

The goal is to make directors independent from management in order to prevent managerial opportunism from lining up with director self-interest. However, one can easily imagine other types of relationships not specified by the NACD's definition as discussed in Chapter 6 that could severely compromise a director's independence. Perhaps the most obvious is a personal friendship or family relationship between a director and a CEO. This is closely followed by a glorified employee relationship where a director owes his or her seat to the CEO/chairman and where the director is richly compensated with fees and other perquisites of board membership.

In the mid-1990s, investors' desire for a majority of independent directors on boards was well illustrated by the boards of two companies: Archer Daniels Midland (ADM) and the Disney Corporation. At ADM, a board heavy with inside directors and led by "the iron hand of 78-year-old Chairman Dwayne O. Andres" failed to provide the oversight necessary to prevent the company from first engaging in and then effectively responding to a major price fixing scandal that ended up in a $100 million fine.[65] This is a simple example of lack of independence by any definition. At Disney, CEO Michael Eisner placed on the board the principal of his children's elementary school, the president of a college attended by one of his children, and his *personal* attorney. Furthermore, the attorney was the chairman of the compensation committee that negotiated Eisner's pay package.[66] While independent of business relationships with Disney, clearly their board status was due entirely to personal relationships with the CEO. In these two cases shareholders were right to wonder whether the directors they elected to represent their interests would be able to exercise the oversight necessary to keep their companies out of difficult situations or to make the tough choices that may be necessary should they fall on hard times. Thus, a second and most necessary element of independence is that directors have a positive incentive to *act* independently from the CEO. The NACD report addresses this issue through a number of recommendations. First, that most or all of a director's compensation be in the form of equity. The intent is to tie a director's remuneration to overall firm performance. Second, that each director be required to own a substantial amount of stock in the company. This is to concentrate the director's attention on creating shareholder value (p. 13). And finally, the report recommends limiting the number of boards on which directors serve in order to provide adequate time to be devoted to each company and to more closely identify a board member's personal reputation with the success of a particular company. This reputational "equity" is intended to reinforce the other elements of director independence recommended by the NACD. These recommendations have received significant support from many governance activists and represent what in the late

1990s is broad agreement on the issue. However, their implications are more complex than immediately meet the eye.

While the report's recommendations go a long way to assuring director independence from management, they may also have the unintended and potentially perverse effect of exaggerating director independence from shareholders. In one of the few references to shareholders, the report notes that "the board does more than mechanically link those who manage the corporation to those who own it, rather as a *surrogate for dispersed ownership*, the board is at the very center of corporate governance itself."[67] This is the traditional statement of the divorce of ownership and control. The report explicitly adopts the dispersed ownership view. Professional directors should therefore rely on independent expertise and advice and have a "significant equity position" in the company so that directors come to closely resemble Plato's "philosopher-kings," motivated by nothing more than their own self-interest and a professional commitment to discharge their duty as honorably as possible. Such directors may also become independent of ties to any of the other elements of the corporate governance triad. Such a structure with its heavy emphasis on director professionalism may serve the interests of shareholders well—or it may not. However, it does potentially reduce monitoring to a board function only. Might the proposed reforms and new standards simply result in a class of professional directors who effectively insulate the true owners from the companies they own?

The question of empirical support for a clear, direct link between director independence and corporate performance was presented in Chapter 6. As noted, the link remains unverified. However, independence may matter to corporate performance in ways that are too subtle to be easily detected. For example, independent directors are often cited as important actors in crisis situations, such as the removal of the CEO of an underperforming company. There is some support for this in the literature, but these are relatively rare events and the effect of director independence might not show up clearly in large, cross-sectional studies. The problem is more difficult since each crisis tends to have a large number of unique factors.[68] Also, the very categorization of directors as independent or not independent may be too imprecise to capture the real differences between directors that might contribute to performance. Finally, independence as commonly defined may not reflect the most salient characteristic of an effective director—independence of mind.

Where Are the Fiduciary Institutions Represented?

While concentrating on director independence, the NACD report ignores the rise of fiduciary institutions. As fiduciaries their sole responsibility is to act as agents for their beneficiaries. However, beneficial ownership is divorced from fiduciary ownership, creating a chain of "agency owners."[69]

The fiduciary duty of prudence requires that institutions exercise all of the legal rights of ownership (buying and selling, voting proxies, filing proxies, and so on) with the result that the power and responsibility of ownership, while diffuse in terms of the beneficiaries, has, in fact, become reconcentrated into the hands of relatively few decision makers. Indeed, it was the activity and publicity around corporate governance generated by some of the largest "fiduciary activists" that put the nature of boards and director independence on the reform agenda.[70] The NACD report's silence on these historic developments is a striking omission.

The NACD recommendations could well be seen as a counterrevolution against the intrusion of active institutions. After all, little if any of the information on individual director performance is to be shared with large institutional owners, even though they must decide how to cast their votes in director elections if they are to properly discharge their monitoring duty. (In this regard CalPERS, the Teamsters Union pension fund, and others focus on post-1996 individual directors is a noteworthy counterpoint.) The report also makes no mention of the need and currently frequent practice to represent institutional interests or even to seek their input on important corporate issues. Institutions, of course, will continue to have the power they have always had to vote "no" on the election of a particular director or slate of directors, and they can still wage proxy campaigns to get the attention of underperforming boards. But, to the extent the board is viewed as the fair and independent representative of some Platonic investor, institutions who feel their interests are not being correctly served may find it harder to influence corporate decisions.

Furthermore, the report implicitly assumes that all investors are identical—small, diffuse, disinterested, and disenfranchised—but this simply is not true. Shareholders are a diverse—if not diffuse—group with many different interests: a young, single individual building a retirement nest egg is a very different investor from a retired couple trying to live on their life's savings. This divergence of interests is particularly significant for institutional investors, which, as has been noted, typically hold well-diversified portfolios of common stocks and, in the case of pension funds, have very long time horizons. The report implicitly rejects the proposition that these diverse interests should receive any particular weight in board decisions or should share in any of the information generated by the evaluation process proposed by NACD. Yet, as these institutions come to represent a larger and larger fraction of all equity, their interests as owners become more and more important. Thus, a central concern of reform should not be just the alignment of directors' interests with the firm's long-term performance, but the development of multidimensional linkages between the board and shareholders.[71]

Moreover, the assumption that directors represent diffuse shareholders whose only goal is to maximize the long-term stock market return on their holdings in a particular company ignores the fact that most investors (certainly all institutional investors) hold portfolios of stock. The holder of a portfolio is interested in total portfolio returns, not solely in individual returns. The proposals for independence and their accompanying recommendations about compensation might adversely impact portfolio returns in at least two ways.

First, by tying a director's compensation more closely to firm performance, it may have the undesirable (and likely unintended) effect, from a diversified owner's point of view, of making the board more risk averse. Second, many institutional investors are universal owners who effectively own the *entire* economy. For them, long-run investment returns depend as well on macroeconomic performance as on firm-level performance. As has been discussed previously, these institutions internalize social costs and benefits in ways that individual firms cannot. Thus, the fact that the broader interests of universal owners might not be represented on the board may lead to suboptimal decisions both from society's point of view and from the point of view of the fiduciary owners as universal owners of corporations.

In an attempt to align the interests of shareholders and directors, the NACD report places great emphasis on requiring stock ownership by all directors. The reason for this suggestion is that "A significant ownership stake leads to a stronger alignment of interests between directors and shareholders, and between executives and shareholders. . . . [such arrangements] should emphasize stock over benefits."[72] However, implementing these reforms raises a number of thorny issues with possible unintended consequences. For example, if these stakes are to be significant, how are directors to acquire them? Are directors to buy their stake with personal funds? If so, does that limit directorships to the very wealthy? If they are to acquire their stake through stock as compensation, the compensation is likely to have to be quite large to achieve the desired alignment of interest. At the same time, the report argues for increased equity ownership by directors, it calls for a reduction in the number of boards individuals serve on. This, of course, would concentrate individual director's personal portfolios in fewer baskets and raise the very real possibility of capture through equity buy-in. But will a large paycheck compromise director independence? The result may be that previously independent directors, unlike the typical diversified shareholder, may become *too* coupled to the economic fortunes of a single firm. This has the potential to make the principal-agent problem worse by further weakening the director's accountability to shareholders. The overall danger is that instead of becoming effective, independent monitors, directors could become glorified employees—deferring to the chairman/CEO and protective of their rich compensation packages.

Clearly, even the most sensible-sounding "professional reforms" require careful scrutiny since aligning the directors' interests with shareholder interests and providing them with sufficient incentives to act independently is a difficult task to accomplish. The proposals require careful consideration, for in the absence of pressure from extra-board monitoring from professional owners well-intended reforms may result in a variety of abuses that benefit *both* directors and top managers at the expense of shareholders in general and institutional shareholders in particular.

Alternatives to the Board Professionalization Model

Even with perfect alignment of individual director's interests with the firms' long-term performance, institutional investors who on the whole cannot use the market to sell must exercise voice options.[73] Voice necessitates more than the directors' aligned interests, which is problematic in any case, since directors' interests are not necessarily identical to those of all classes of shareholders. Thus, voice proposals and frequent informal practices have in common the assumption that both the market for corporate control and/ or individual director alignment with long-term firm performance are inadequate to completely resolve agency and agency-chain problems. What is required is some form of direct monitoring or relationship investing whereby an owner (typically a large institution) holding a significant block of equity for the long-term has the ability to exert leverage on management and/or the board of directors.

This nonmarket or political form of governance has many possible modalities. For example, Pound proposes an approach "in which active investors seek to change corporate policy by developing voting support from dispersed shareholders, rather than by simply purchasing controlling power or control," examples of which can be found in the "just vote no" campaigns launched by various institutional owners against boards of directors as a whole, or targeted at individual directors. Along these lines, *The Economist* has argued editorially that "A better way [than relying only on alignment of interests] for shareholders to make a board work for them is to make it their direct responsibility to see that it does."[74] This is similar to a proposal Jensen makes calling for the resurrection of "active investors" who hold large debt and/or equity "positions in a company and actively participate in its strategic direction. . . . They have incentives to buck the system to correct problems early rather than late . . . but they have been shut out of board rooms by the legal structure, by custom, and by their own practices."[75]

In short, many of the recommendations of the NACD Blue Ribbon Report on Director Professionalism are logical and well founded and reflect some of the best of current thinking in a new wave of ownership expectations sweeping through the boardrooms of America. They also clearly address some of the more egregious situations in which directors are beholden to management, have little personal financial stake, and received little compensation based on company performance, and where directors are either simply unqualified or are stretched too thin to devote the necessary time to their responsibilities. Common sense demands that these situations be rectified.

However, as empirical conformation that good governance leads to superior performance has yet to be demonstrated, it is important to note that some of the reforms proposed by the NACD report may, in fact, have unintended consequences. Compensation systems designed to align directors with shareholders may result in directors becoming too financially dependent on one particular company and therefore inclined to be more risk adverse than would be in the best interests of diversified shareholders. It may also give directors an unintended incentive to protect their personal economic interests at the expense of the economic interests of all shareholders. By treating ownership as diffuse and disinterested, some of the proposed reforms have the potential to insulate the board from important shareholders and stakeholders. Institutional investors have worked hard over the past decade to make their voices heard in the boardroom and can, with little exaggeration, claim credit for most of the governance changes that have been adopted. Since these institutions have substantial fiduciary responsibilities, a professional orientation, large equity positions, and, at least in some cases, a demonstrated desire to exercise their ownership responsibility, it would be unfortunate — in the name of reform — to develop governance structures that might potentially freeze them out of the process.

Conclusion

This chapter has reviewed monitoring, relationship investing, and board of director "best practices." It concludes that while the terms of ownership and control are strongly contested primarily between institutional owner/agents and manager/agents, there is often little agreement on the forms of monitoring, on the nature of monitoring, and on how to evaluate the relative success or failure of monitoring. Additionally, a number of topics have yet to be addressed — in particular, monitoring when an institution owns a broadly diversified portfolio that, effectively, makes it an owner of the entire economy. This issue is examined at the conclusion of this work.

Many observers and institutional activists (e.g., Black, Pound, Koppes, and CalPERS) have pointed out that there are economies of scale to monitoring that tend to overcome the inherent free-rider problem and therefore make the costs and benefits of monitoring underperforming firms weigh in on the benefits side. Also, the raw dollar amounts involved are often sufficient to justify action, even in the presence of free riders. At the same time, Koppes and Black, for example, among many others, have simultaneously argued that active monitoring "keeps the herd moving" at a rate that (ceteris paribus) it would not otherwise have. In short, it is claimed that the market and the economy as a whole are positively affected by monitoring the underperformers. It is not clear how one would substantiate such a broad claim, although it is a plausible hypothesis. Nor is it clear that the most effective way to affect the market as a whole is to target the underperformers, or only target them, especially since there are many possible forms of monitoring and relationship investing. Reactive (ex post) monitoring is clearly important and relatively well established at the turn of the millennium, but is not necessarily the only strategy. Proactive (ex ante) monitoring in the form of a more effective board of directors is also advocated by, among others, Latham with his proposal for establishment of independent corporate monitoring firms that would monitor individual directors and make voting recommendations to institutional owners. In a different vein, Kester, Porter, Roe, and others argue that economic performance and competitiveness would be improved if (in addition to what we can call financial monitoring) various forms of contractual-relationship investing were developed and formalized. This would expand the "nexus of contracts" to include vendors and suppliers, employees, and other key stakeholders.

The dramatic growth of various forms of institutional voice in the last five years, and of the scholarly analytical and advocacy literature concerned with it, will continue to have major public policy implications. In certain areas it will call for federal and state deregulation while in other areas there may be a need for increased regulation. In addition, the private decisions and changes made by corporations and institutional investors may have significant social and economic consequences that raise new public policy issues, or change the consequences of existing public policy made under often dramatically different conditions. The next chapter considers some of the most important aspects of these developments.

Chapter 8
Policy Currents:
Regulatory and Proposed Regulatory
Reforms, and Voluntary Standards

The catastrophic event of the 1929 stock market crash increased Americans' long held suspicion of concentrated wealth and their general mistrust of the treatment afforded small investors by the various financial institutions of the time: banks, securities brokers, and insurance companies. A direct result of the stock market crash was a flood of legislation that included the Securities Exchange Act of 1934, which established the Securities and Exchange Commission (SEC), an independent, nonpartisan, quasi-judicial regulatory agency given the responsibility for administering federal securities laws. Robert Denham and Michael Porter, the authors of a major study on U.S. competitiveness in the global economy, noted that those effects are still with us when they wrote, "The major features of the [U.S.] legal and regulatory framework governing relationships among owners, institutional investors, and managers have their roots in the political backlash to the stock market crash of 1929."[1] The purpose of the various securities acts passed during the 1930s was to restore the confidence of the individual investor who, as Berle and Means observed at the time, had become the backbone of the market. The massive growth of institutional ownership since the late 1970s challenges many of these Depression era standards and procedures. This emerging new ownership pattern has had and will continue to have a major impact on policy currents. As Bernard Black has written, "A major paradigm shift in corporate law seems to be underway."[2] He argues that "we need partly to reduce the legal obstacles that now exist. But we also need to affirmatively encourage voice. We need not just to *regulate* but to *differently regulate*—to *redefine* the role of institutional shareholders so that the institutions *will* monitor if monitoring is valuable" (emphasis in original).[3]

Writing in the early 1990s, Porter and Denham argued that the main legal and regulatory goal was to strike the proper balance between liquidity and control in order to "reproduce the perceived attributes of the continental

European and East Asian systems without compromising the unparalleled liquidity and 'efficiency' of our financial markets."[4] In light of the Asia crisis of the late 1990s, they might also have added that a critical prerequisite for liquidity is transparency of information, and indeed the downside of both Asian and (some) European institutional involvement has been both lack of liquidity *and* a lack of transparency. As Lowenstein suggests, "disclosure compensates remarkably well [in the U.S.] for the absence of a body of large-stake, long-term, knowledgeable shareholders able to sit on boards of directors or otherwise to act as proxies for shareholders generally."[5]

Generic Impediments to Monitoring: Exit and Voice

The previous chapter discussed how activist institutional investors have become monitors of U.S. firms. Much of this monitoring has focused on issues internal to the firm and in particular on the role and structure of the board of directors. However, monitoring is also affected by the external legal and political environment. Consequently, it is important to analyze the role public policy plays in monitoring. In the United States, federal regulations that provide impediments to monitoring fall into two broad categories: those that regulate voice and those that regulate exit.[6] As the authors of "Lifting All Boats" observe,

a fundamental tradeoff exists between "exit" and "voice" . . . if voice is more feasible and attractive, institutions will rely less on exit and have an incentive to hold larger equity stakes in individual companies and monitor them more closely. The challenge for public policy is to strike a balance of incentives within the market for exit and voice. Too little liquidity can prevent the deployment of resources . . . but where liquidity is the only choice . . . this can impose costs in the form of excessive transactions costs and shortened investment time horizons.[7]

The following section examines some other current aspects of the regulation of voice and exit, while later sections discuss proposals to deregulate voice and exit, and to establish new regulations in other areas of exit and voice. The area of legal and regulatory impediments to effective monitoring contains a vast and complex legal and political literature. What follows is not an attempt to comprehensively review all topics, but rather an attempt to highlight some of the most important issues and trends.

Regulation of Voice: Four Examples

Section 13(d) of the 1934 Securities and Exchange Act

Section 13(d) of the 1934 Securities and Exchange Act requires "any person or group" that beneficially owns 5 percent or more of a public company's stock to file a disclosure statement with the SEC. Black writes that "while the filing isn't complex it involves substantial litigation risk which means heavy legal bills win or lose."[8] These requirements are in place to protect investors in contests for corporate control. Specifically they are designed to signal the market that a contest for control may be occurring, and to provide transparency with respect to ownership and control. In 1992, this section was changed in what was the single most significant proxy rule reform of the last two decades. (Apart from proxy reform, antitakeover statutes and rulings have been extremely important.)

Before these reforms were enacted, institutions that communicated with one another about substantive issues at commonly held companies ran the serious risk of inadvertently tripping the regulations that covered acquisitions. While it never happened, it was conceivable that the heads of the right pension funds chatting together at a cocktail party could bring down upon all of the members of the "group" the expensive and onerous provisions of the securities laws. The very possibility had a chilling effect on voice. The institutions most concerned with their ability to communicate, the public pension funds, had no intention of acquiring companies. However, if they tried to coordinate their activities they might be subject to being forced to communicate with all shareholders though tightly structured, legalistic proxy materials that had to be approved by the SEC and that would be cumbersome and expensive to prepare. Furthermore, under the provisions of Section 16(b) discussed below, being cast in the position of an acquirer could trigger restrictions on the institution's ability to trade in the stock of the "target" company. Institutions led by CalPERS enthusiastically sought these reforms because they felt that freer communication would greatly facilitate monitoring and lead to better coordination on a variety of corporate governance efforts. The reforms were equally vigorously opposed by business groups, particularly the Business Round Table, but in the end they were adopted.

However, some important questions concerning 13(d) still remained. As Briggs notes in his discussion of the 1992 communication liberalization, the problem regarding communication still arises under 13(d) since there is a new "risk calculus" between the post-1992 communication standards and the potential liability under 13(d). He goes on to say that "The SEC's reforms [on communication] probably do not go far enough. Shareholder free speech of all sorts, especially speech advocating action, continues to be chilled by the proxy rule and by section 13(d)."[9] The authors of "Lifting All Boats" agree: "the real threat . . . is that the information disclosed [between shareholders] can easily become the subject of securities litigation brought by the target company. . . . [The rules under 13(d)] have a substantial regulatory barrier to collective action by shareholders (if the group agreeing to vote together collectively owns 5 percent or more)."[10] The concern is that while the rule change allows for significantly greater speech, it might have a chilling affect on action that results from freer communication, thereby triggering the classification of a "group" acting as an acquirer.

Section 16(b) of the 1934 Securities Exchange Act

This section of the act limits the ability to sell after a 10 percent threshold has been passed, whether for an individual or a "group." Coffee argues that the law is very imprecise about the specific circumstances under which a group of holders become subject to the law. Similarly, the definition of a group itself is vague. For instance, such a group could be a voting group that had coordinated its positions through private (or possibly public) discussion that would be allowed under the 13(d) reforms. While the intent of this provision of the law is clearly to regulate exit to prevent price manipulation by short-term movements in and out of the market, it does affect voice because group status may be inadvertently triggered by communication. If this happens, the law requires a reporting company (a company in the legal sense of an investment company) to turn over profits made on a purchase and sale within a six-month period. In yet another section of 16(b), as the authors of *Lifting All Boats* state, "even if they [institutions] stay below the 10 percent threshold, they may still be subject to its recapture provision if they have participated in nominating and electing a member of the corporation's board. . . . Thus, an institutions owning only 1 percent may be subject . . . if it belongs to a shareholder group that has elected a director."[11]

ERISA and Fiduciary Liability

The fiduciary standard under which pension plans operate requires that all actions be taken in the sole interest of the beneficiaries and that actions should be those of a "prudent person." Failure to properly discharge a fiduciary duty exposes pension fund administrators to *personal* liability. Thus, Black points out that under the 1974 Employee Retirement Income Security Act (ERISA), which explicitly adopted the "prudent person" rule as well as under the common law of trusts, the "prevailing watchword . . . is caution," thereby favoring broad diversification and passivity, while concentrated ownership and activism with its accompanying voice are "dangerous." These rules reinforced similar provisions in the 1940 Investment Act, which had codified such conservatism and its chilling effect on shareholder voice.[12] Whether the prudent person rule actually prohibits governance activism and higher levels of concentrated holdings is the subject of debate and doubt, especially considering the impact of modern portfolio theory. Nevertheless, the chilling effect remains the dominant impression.

Section F of the 1934 Securities and Exchange Act:
Proxy-Voting Procedures, Access, and Agenda Setting

The traditional avenue for shareholders to express their voice has been the proxy system under which proposals are submitted to a vote of the shareholders. Consequently, any proxy-voting rules that significantly limit the scope of proxies or limit shareholder ability to communicate with each other over proxy matters are a severe limitation on shareholder voice. A number of rules do. In particular, proxy rules define solicitation such that a shareholder is exposed to onerous reporting requirements and potential liability so broadly that even a communication that seems on its face not to solicit can still be ruled a "solicitation." This is still a problem even though the SEC's 1992 revisions in communication rules loosen this restriction to some degree. SEC Rule 14(a)(8) protects the limited rights of shareholders to use a company's proxy statement to offer proposals while severely limiting such statements in a variety of other ways by predetermined standards on what is "appropriate" substance for such resolutions. Rule 14(a)(7) limits the ability to gain access to shareholder lists. The cumulative impact of these and other restrictions makes the costs of, for example, electing a single nonmanagement slate director or making a counterproposal to management extremely expensive. It also opens up various types of institutions to legal liability. Roe concludes: "Managers control the proxy machinery [thereby effectively controlling agenda setting, and] . . . managers can find out how shareholders vote."[13]

Taken as a whole these four instances of the regulation of voice create significant formal barriers. It is interesting to note, however, that with the exception of the 1992 communication ruling by the SEC even the most activist institutional investors have neither lobbied for reform nor seemed particularly interested in such reform. Many institutional investors are either happy with the regulatory environment as it relates to their ability to exercise their voice as owners or they have made their peace with the existing system, perhaps because of a lack of a desire for a stronger voice. This is particularly true of institutions such as bank trust departments, corporate pension programs, and insurance companies that have traditionally tended to be passive owners. Other institutions, particularly some of the more active ones, appear to be able to do much of what they want within the existing regulatory framework. Furthermore, these institutions may prefer the status quo to uncertain change, particularly if, as might happen, that change provoked hostility from the business community or a backlash by the public at large. Even prior to the 1992 communication reforms, institutions that wanted to communicate with their peers could do so through press conferences, speeches, and articles in the trade press. In fact, even under the old rules there was probably a considerable amount of direct communication among activist institutions.

Regulation of Exit: Four Examples

If selective deregulation and further regulation of voice is seen as improving monitoring, similarly deregulating certain types of exit (with the aim of improving the liquidity of the market) is taken by reformers as improving the ability to effectively monitor. Improved liquidity should, all else being equal, also lower the cost of capital. Exit regulation especially affects an individual investor or a "group" deemed to control a firm. Since there is some legal ambiguity about exactly what constitutes a group, institutions could arguably be discouraged from taking larger positions that might be construed as "controlling." The reluctance to take large positions could reinforce the tendency of institutional investors to hold widely diversified portfolios. As long as these barriers to exit remain in place, it may well be difficult to know whether there is either an interest in or the potential for a relatively small group of large institutions to take substantial positions in a smaller number of firms with the intention of monitoring more effectively.

Insider Information Restriction on Long-Term Indexed Investors

Coffee argues that since indexed investors are of necessity long-term investors (and thus potentially effective monitors), regulation that prohibits access to insider information is an effective restraint on good monitoring since such monitoring logically requires, or at least would be greatly facilitated by, insider information. The purpose of the restriction on trading on insider information is to prevent short-term investors from profiting at the expense of less well-informed shareholders. But, by definition, long-term investors don't trade short term and, therefore, they cannot profit from short-term uses of insider information. Thus a distinction between traders and long-term investors would better govern insider information rather than the current blanket prohibition.[14] Access to insider information for long-term holders could well improve their ability to monitor. The difficulty, of course, is sorting out the long-term holders from the short-term holders. If long-term holders do not trade short term, there is no need for them to be concerned about receipt of insider information. The real issue is how long-term holders might use inside information to better effectively monitor. Institutions that follow a strict index strategy might logically fall into the latter category, but what about the vast majority of institutional investors that adopt a mix of index and discretionary strategies? A possible solution might be Latham's proposal, discussed in the last chapter, to create director selection firms. Directors, of course, have access to inside information, and if Latham's proposal would prove effective, it might substitute for the need of long-term investors to have access to insider information.

A primary focus of exit proposals has been on insider trading rules. One likely consequence of deregulating voice and the consequent increased monitoring would be the possibility of regular access to insider information by the direct and indirect representatives of institutions. Trading on inside information is for short-term gain; long-term holders should have little interest in it. Currently there are complex regulations, backed up by severe penalties, that prohibit various forms of trading on inside information.

Coffee notes there is concern that deregulating exit might lead not only to greater insider trading but also to stock market manipulation. Thus, he proposed a reform of Section 16(b) that would create a safe harbor by exempting institutional investors who are not short-term traders. This would involve reinterpreting and loosening "deputation theory" so that individual representatives of institutions could function on boards of directors or in other interactions with firms more effectively. Deputation occurs when an individual is taken to be a representative of an investor, although there may be no formal relation and the institution may only be soliciting proxies for such an individual who is, for example, a nominee for the board. Coffee argues that the easiest solution would be to exempt from 16(b) rules trades made simply to maintain an indexed portfolio, which must be adjusted "automatically" as the market changes to keep the index balanced. Such trades are not motivated by insider information. The authors of "Lifting All Boats" also call for revision in Section 16(b)'s deputation theory.[15]

The Securities Act of 1933

The 1933 act addresses the issuance and initial marketing of securities, while the 1934 act regulates subsequent trading. Under the 1933 act, an individual or group in "control" of a firm is taken to be an "affiliate," and is restricted in its ability to resell *any* of its shares except after a registration statement is filed or an exception permitted. The effect, according to Coffee, is to place a degree of restriction "on liquidity before resale is likely to be economically feasible" for the individual or group, potentially forcing the individual or group to hold equity longer than they otherwise might.[16]

Section 16(b) of the Securities and Exchange Act of 1934

While a disincentive to voice as discussed above, Section 16(b) operates by effectively creating a six-month period of illiquidity in order to prevent insider trading against "short-swing" trading profits, that is, profits potentially earned by speculating on short-term movements. This, of course, is a restriction on exit that, in itself, potentially discourages institutions from taking larger stakes that might lead to more effective monitoring. Again the effect for long-term holders is compounded because of uncertainty. In Coffee's words, "because current law is conspicuously imprecise as about when members of a loose association of institutional investors become subject to it" (p. 1344).

Insider Trading Liability

An institution that has an employee or agent serving on a corporate board is potentially liable if it trades with insider information, *even* if "those making the trades did not use or have access to it." The effect of this is that in order to maintain liquidity, "the institution must delegate its monitoring role to an outside agent, with whom it must have only limited contacts" (p. 1345).

Thus, both exit and voice are impeded by long-standing restrictions, which date back to the reaction to the 1929 stock market crash, and were perceived as needed to protect small individual investors from the machinations of stock market manipulators. Times have changed, and significant regulatory reform in an era characterized by the mutual existence of both small individual investors and large institutional owners may well be worthwhile. A number of regulatory and legal reforms have occurred during the 1990s. However, they do not fundamentally transform a regulatory system built on the Berle and Means' assumption of the small shareholder as typical and widely diversified holdings as the norm.

Regulatory and Legal Reforms of the 1990s

Reforms typically require action by either Congress, the SEC or the Department of Labor. In particular, the SEC plays a determining role concerning the principal-agent alignment issue and voice issues. Black notes that "the Securities and Exchange Commission — sometimes intentionally, sometimes not — has been a principal purveyor of shareholder pacification."[17]

The SEC 1992 Communication Rule

As noted above, the single most important reform of the 1990s affecting the deregulation of voice was the 1992 communication ruling by the SEC. Significantly, the reform was initiated by a CalPERS letter to the SEC in 1989, itself indicative of the increased influence of public pension funds. The CalPERS' initiative was vehemently opposed by corporations. The liberalization had significant impact on the ability of institutional investors to better coordinate both formal and informal activities, and to more quietly influence boards of directors and top management. In Pound's words: "The new rules exempt communications by 'disinterested' parties — parties who are not actually soliciting votes — from the proxy statement filing and delivery requirements."[18]

However, few observers have been completely satisfied with the outcome. As Sharara and Hoke-Witherspoon note, "The SEC struck a balance between institutional investors' desire for unrestrained communication and management's desire to monitor backroom decision by large shareholders."[19] Similarly, Black suggests the reforms were a "middle range" between the original CalPERS proposals and the massive corporate lobbying against them. He calls for completing the "much work undone . . . with a view to further deregulating communications among shareholders."[20] He also notes that the "political counterattack" by corporate lobbying groups such as the Business Roundtable may have stalled a reexamination of other reform proposals.[21]

SEC "Cracker Barrel" Ruling and Other Actions

The so-called "Cracker Barrel" ruling by the SEC refers to the 1992 decision in which the SEC ruled that the Cracker Barrel Old Country Stores could exclude from a shareholder proposal under the "ordinary business rule" issues of discriminatory hiring practices, in this particular case employment discrimination against homosexuals. The ordinary business rule refers to Rule 14(a)(8)(c)(7). Prior to 1992, however, the SEC had permitted various groups to raise issues related to employment practices such as equal employment and affirmative action. These were allowed on the grounds that they were policy issues that might be considered a proper subject for a proxy filing. But the issue also shaded over into micromanaging the business decisions made by management that would be shielded from shareholder actions by the ordinary business rule.

The Cracker Barrel decision was based on the perception by the SEC that "the line between includeable and excludable employment-related proposals based on social policy considerations has become increasingly difficult to draw."[22] And drawing the lines is important because the method that a company typically uses to keep an item off of its proxy statement is to submit a "no action" letter to the SEC, which must then decide whether to accept it. Most institutional investors accepted the proposition that the SEC was increasingly being drawn into drawing fine distinctions between ordinary business and social policy. But some strenuously objected that this was no excuse for, in O'Connor's words, "why the staff should consequently exclude all employment-related proposals, even those that involve significantly policy considerations" (p. 1354).

Nevertheless, after the 1992 Cracker Barrel ruling the SEC did not see a diminution in employment-related proxy filings. Some were withdrawn after agreement; others were placed on the proxy without objection. In any case, they increased because few firms were willing to face the negative publicity that would likely come in reaction to a heavy-handed rejection. Furthermore, the SEC did find that institutions were complaining that Cracker Barrel case had a chilling effect on institutions' willingness to use the proxy process to raise legitimate concerns with some employment policies (p. 1354).[23]

In 1997, after five years of pressure, the SEC was prepared to reverse

Cracker Barrel decision, but it initially tried to tie the reversal to greater restrictions on minority shareholder proposals by raising the threshold necessary to both put a proposal on the ballot and then to resubmit it in following years. A broad coalition of institutional investors successfully lobbied the SEC to reverse the Cracker Barrel decision while withdrawing its more stringent standards for shareholder resolutions.[24] The logic behind many institutional investor's opposition to the Cracker Barrel decision was based on the very large monetary settlement resulting from lawsuits against Texaco and Shoney's, indicating that such suits, a forms of contingent liabilities, have the potential, in McCann's words, to "seriously harm the financial condition of a company and diminish shareholder value. . . . The shareholder proposal process achieves accountability by forcing management to address the employment issues." Thus, ordinary business cannot veil potential shareholder harm.[25] Institutional activist pressure on the SEC continued with a first of its kind meeting between fifty members of the Council of Institutional Investors and the SEC's top staff and commissioners in 1998.[26]

While the Cracker Barrel and other shareholder resolutions — like most proxy resolutions — have been nonbinding, a potentially significant 1999 ruling from the Oklahoma Supreme Court held that shareholders may introduce *binding* resolutions concerning corporate governance issues. Consequently, binding resolutions have been introduced with increasing frequency, rising from only seven in 1997 to thirty by early 1999.[27]

Another major area that was initially considered by some observers to have potential significance in the relation between large investors and the firms in which they have stakes is a provision in the Private Securities Litigation Reform Act of 1995, specifically its lead plaintiff provision. The intent of the lead plaintiff provision was to provide an incentive for large institutional investors to increase their monitoring of firms. Prior to 1996, the principle of "first to file" (and the resulting dynamic of a "race to the courthouse") meant that the attorney who filed first had the greatest chance of becoming the lead plaintiff in a securities class action suit. This principle provided a perverse incentive for attorneys to find small investors (often called professional plaintiffs) to become lead plaintiffs and thereby reward themselves with lucrative legal fees.[28] The act replaced the first-to-file principle with the "most adequate plaintiff" principle. Under this rule, after all interested parties had filed within the given deadline, the court would determine who was to become lead plaintiff and the lead plaintiff would select the attorney for the class as a whole. The logic was that since large institutional investors theoretically have the most to gain from meritorious litigation, they should represent the class.[29] No large institutional investors testified during the hearings that this would be the likely outcome or that such an outcome was especially desired by them, nor by the late 1990s has it resulted in large institutions taking on this role. Indeed, what seems to have occurred, according to Grundfest and Pirino, is that "competing groups of individual plaintiffs have tended to vie for the lead plaintiff position . . . [so that] traditional plaintiffs' law firms . . . cobble together large numbers of smaller claimants who, in aggregate, have the largest financial interest."[30]

It is interesting to note that as another reflection of the sea change that has taken place in equity ownership many congressional members and attorneys considered institutional investors especially fit to play this role. The statement of the managers of the bill explained that:

The Conference Committee seeks to increase the likelihood that institutional investors will serve as lead plaintiffs by requiring courts to presume that the member of the purported class with the largest financial stake in the relief sought is the "most adequate plaintiff." The Conference Committee believes that increasing the role of institutional investors in class actions will ultimately benefit shareholders and assist courts by improving the quality of representations in securities class actions.[31]

The principle underlying this thinking is suggested by the title of Weiss and Berkerman's article, "Let the Money Do the Monitoring." They argue that the act creates a fiduciary obligation for institutional investors. When informed about a pending class-action suit or the possible initiation of a suit, they have a duty to determine whether it has merit and is likely to result in a substantial recovery for the institution. If it does, they have a fiduciary duty to become a lead plaintiff.[32] Whatever the merits of institutional investors becoming lead plaintiffs under the principle of letting the money do the monitoring, the total sums involved in securities fraud and insider trading cases is a quite small proportion of the potential gains available through performance monitoring.[33] This probably explains the relative disinterest of large institutional investors since monitoring for fraud and monitoring for economic performance are quite distinct. The significance of the passage of the act is that it was the first securities reform since the original New Deal legislation in the 1930s, and while so far its impact has been either small or nonexistent, it could set a precedent in devising ways to create incentives for other types of lead monitoring by large institutional investors.[34] In any case, it is clear evidence that Congress is likely to turn to institutional investors, perhaps in their role as universal owners or in other roles, to participate more actively in the monitoring of corporate behavior.

Proposals for Improving Monitoring by Institutional Investors

As was discussed above, the most significant recent change in regulatory policy was the SEC's 1992 communication rule. For some legal observers this policy opens a potential legal liability for institutional investors. Some have therefore called for an explicit redefinition of "control" by the SEC. Coffee, for example, suggests that the current definition is overly broad and inherently vague.[35] Securities Act Rule 405 defines control as the "possession, direct or indirect, of the power to direct or cause the direction of the management and policies of a person, whether through the ownership of voting securities . . . or otherwise." This means the *potential* to influence control is sufficient to be considered control itself. The authors of "Lifting All Boats," following Coffee, Black, and others, propose a "safe harbor" provision that would explicitly exempt institutional investors (or, alternately, certain institutional investors) from being "controlling" by simple virtue of their attempts, for example, to monitor, and hence "influence." Similarly, the power to elect even a single board member may be considered control. Thus, various reformers propose an increase in the shares a financial institution can hold from the present 5 percent to 10 percent or 15 percent without being considered a controlling person or group if they hold long term and monitor.[36]

Kester arrives at a similar conclusion by focusing on governance from the perspective of transaction-cost economics. He argues that the logic of increased vertical contractual governance (e.g., linking to suppliers), which he favors, leads to the commingling of debt and equity held by financial institutions, which can and should consequently act as effective monitors. Thus, he calls for the "removal of existing impediments to the establishment of closer ties between the industrial and financial sectors." Antitrust law that limits vertical relations should be loosened while antitrust legislation that limits horizontal competition is essential and should be maintained.[37]

These are two examples of the way some current regulation potentially inhibits the full development of both monitoring and relationship investing, whether by financial institutions or by nonfinancial firms. Thus, deregulation in these areas is a way to increase the strength and effectiveness of the monitoring of large institutional investors.

While significant deregulatory proposals of voice are seen by many scholars as facilitating monitoring and relationship investing, so some observers see regulatory proposals (as both incentives and disincentives) as necessary complements. For example, Coffee suggests there are insufficient positive incentives for money managers to exercise voice. This suggestion has two aspects: an information overload problem for large indexed funds; and, a problem of thin margins for money managers who sell indexing services to those funds. This gives them a strong incentive to cut costs and engage in price competition, thereby avoiding monitoring since they would not be able to carry the inevitable free riders. Coffee proposes to remedy this by reducing the size of a typical indexed portfolio. Additionally he proposes to make monitoring *mandatory*, including a market for proxy advisers and creating a market for monitoring services. However, a structural and legal obstacle to this idea exists. Structurally large funds could then have huge blocks, and appear like German banks, which he believes politically undesirable. He therefore suggests an ownership cap of 3 to 5 percent in order to encourage institutional voice without control. Legally ERISA requires an unsophisticated form of diversification that focuses not on net loss, but only on a potential loss of a sizeable magnitude. Thus, concentrated ownership is dangerous in terms of potential trustee liability, which, he argues, should be reformed.[38]

The authors of "Lifting All Boats" also argue that prudence needs to be explicitly redefined in terms of the "facts and circumstances of the process by which the portfolio is constructed." They note that the State of New York has already moved in this direction, and urge a similar reform of ERISA.[39] Some observers urged passage of a law that would either require or encourage institutions to retain voting power rather than creating trustee accounts. These proposed proactive regulatory and legal reforms have as their goal making monitoring both more direct, more powerful, and in some cases, mandatory. Under the 1994 Department of Labor's Interpretive Bulletin 94-2, the duty to monitor, in Koppes and Reilly's words, "is subject to greater scrutiny" than previously. The mandate by the 1994 Department of Labor Bulletin extended the logic of the 1988 Avon letter, which required the voting of proxies. The 1994 rule required informed voting, that is, some ability to monitor the firms that institutions owned. They argued that the monitoring of delegates is inherent in the standards of prudence and that therefore the logic of the 1994 bulletin is that a "new standard would impose a continuing duty to monitor *prior* investment decisions," not just current and future ones. He supports such interpretations by the courts.[40] Similarly, the authors of "Lifting All Boats" propose that the SEC and relevant banking and state insurance regulators issue a "statement of obligations" with respect to proxy voting similar to the Department of Labor ones.[41]

Disclosure and Democratization of Voting and Proxy Procedures

The most direct avenue that institutional investors have for expressing their views to portfolio companies is through their proxy votes. Consequently, a number of changes in current rules, regulations, practices, and procedures with regard to the proxy process have been urged. Some of these suggested reforms require Congressional or SEC actions, while others do not. Related are proposed reforms to the operation of key board of director committees. The goal is to improve institutional voice, often by permitting a freer flow of information to those wishing to exercise voice and by assuring at least a minimum degree of independence of the board and its key committees from the potentially heavy hand of the CEO. Blair summarizes these proposals as being concerned with equal voting regardless of class of shares, limitation of powers of the board to impose changing terms of directors' appointments in order to protect shareholder rights, and deciding elections on the basis of votes actually cast rather than counting unvoted proxies as proxies cast in favor of management's position. Many of these proposals could be instituted by corporations themselves without changes in law, but some could not, and many advocates argue for national standards for best practices, thus requiring SEC and or Congressional action. More broadly, Blair cites a proposal for tying corporate democracy to relationship investing in order to reduce the adversarial quality often associated with interest group politics.[42]

Coffee suggests that the power of incumbent management to manipulate the proxy agenda may need to be regulated, especially regarding corporate management's ability to bundle issues. That is, for example, to offer shareholders a generous one-time dividend tied to a promanagement board revision or bylaw restructuring.[43] In a similar vein, the authors of "Lifting All Boats" call for improving access to the proxy statement by institutional investors by changing Section 14(a)(8) of the Securities Act of 1934 to make utilization of the proxy process less expensive. This section of the act permits shareholders to use the corporation's proxy statement for some purposes, but not for others. Especially prohibited is using the proxy statement in relation to election of directors. They propose that in order to make use of the proposed provision a floor of, for example, 10 percent of all shareholders be required to sign on to a proposal prior to submitting it to the general shareholder population. This would prevent tiny, minority shareholders from offering frivolous or nuisance proposals. Such reform would enable institutional holders to comment on individual board members up for election, and thereby raise substantive issues in a public manner. The "Lifting All Boats" authors also propose greater disclosure of information regarding the independence (or lack thereof) of nominating and auditing committees of boards of directors, under Section 14(a)(7) of the 1934 Securities Act.[44]

Further Regulation of Exit

While selective deregulation of exit is regarded as important some (and typically different) governance reformers would restrict exit through either incentives for holding long term or by disincentives for selling short term. Thurow, for example, would link equity voting rights to the length of time a security is held, for example, one-third voting rights if held more than two years; two-thirds voting rights if held for four, and so on. While contradicting some other reform proposals promoting liquidity (see above) Thurow's suggestion would orient voting toward long-term interests while creating a barrier to exit.[45] The result would be that short term, liquid investors would have little or no influence on a company while long-term investors would be empowered.

Reforms on the Corporate and Institutional Investor Level

A wide variety of reforms have been proposed by scholars and activists that do not require either changes in regulatory administrative rulings or in law.

To varying degrees some of these have been implemented by corporations and institutional investors while others have not. Below are summarized some of the most important of these proposals.

Corporate Reforms

Here, the focus of concern is to align the interests of management, key professionals, employees generally, and other resource suppliers with those of the firm's owners in order to maximize the potentials of teamwork. The Organization for Economic Co-operation and Development argues that "Corporate performance is a function of teamwork." Thus, the alignment of key resource groups is an important governance factor.[46] Porter extends this argument by forcefully arguing for expanding boards to reflect contractual representation of suppliers, customers, and employees. Kester makes similar arguments for encouraging contractual governance systems as "close, vertical commercial relationships [which] can be sources of efficiency in contractual exchange."[47] Porter suggests that the stated mission of the firm should be the "long-term shareholder value as [the] goal of the firm rather than current stock price." This would discourage short-term trading and promote long-term holding. He proposes a series of recommendations that would primarily encourage firms to seek out long-term owners, and to accept their role in governance. He also advocates changes in accounting practices to facilitate this, such as an Economic Value Added (EVA) analysis.[48] It is worth noting that in 1997 CalPERS began to use EVA analysis to screen its holdings in addition to five-year equity returns (capital appreciation plus dividends).

There are numerous proposals for linking management remuneration to long-term performance, in particular by requiring managers (and sometimes others) to have direct, long-term, and significant stakes in their firms. Since the mid-1990s stock options have proliferated widely for top management, and especially in high technology and start-up firms for many other employees as well. While offering strong incentives to employees and managers, stock-option proliferation often dilutes nonemployees' holdings, and it is open to the abuse of management repricing the options should the stock price decline below the exercise price. Other means of encouraging stake-in-the-firm proposals for lower-level management and employees are ESOPs and other employee stockholder devices discussed below.[49]

In Chapter 7, board of director compensation and structure were discussed. More broadly, board of director reform proposals tend to focus on greater accessibility to institutional owners, greater and more direct representation for institutional holders, and responsiveness to their policy concerns. The growth of governance "best practices" statements, guidelines, codes, and white papers in numerous countries illustrate these developments.[50]

The "best practice" reforms fall into two groupings: those directed at the internal workings of the board of directors, and those directed at proxy reform and the relation between the firm and large institutional investors. Reforms focused on the internal working of the board have stressed the elimination of staggered board elections, thereby permitting owners to replace an entire board at one time should that be necessary. As discussed in Chapter 7, reforms have also stressed linking long-term pay with long-term performance in one manner or another. Similarly, many proposals have argued for a reduction in the size of the board so that meetings are manageable, while at the same time limiting the number of boards a director should serve on. Some reformers have stressed the importance that directors should meet on a regular basis with large owners apart from the CEO and other inside directors, while mandating that only outside and truly independent directors should serve on the compensation and nominating committees of the board. By the late 1990s many if not most of these reforms have come to be accepted by large numbers of corporate boards. The singular one that has not been widely accepted is the reform proposal that the CEO and the chairman of the board should be different individuals.

The second groups of "best practices" reforms concern the relation of the firm to its large shareholders and the proxy-voting methods. Reform proposals have argued for confidential voting, typically monitored by an independent voting firm. It is not unusual for management to be able to monitor voting, and in some instances stop the vote if it is not going in management's direction and then send out another ballot with different wording or entirely different proposals. Some have proposed cumulative voting to ensure minority representation on the board while others have proposed making shareholder lists available to all shareholders upon request. Some proposals suggest that the board designate one independent director or a special subcommittee of the board to communicate with shareholders at company expense, in exchange for limitation of individual liability in order to institutionalize direct communication between independent board members and large institutional investors. More radical proposals (often not desired by many institutional investors) would place representatives of large institutional investors on the board, a form of what is often called "constituency" representation.

Institutional Investors Reforms

As discussed in previous sections, some analysts and governance activists have called for a significant reduction in the average number of positions in institutional portfolios in order to facilitate better monitoring. Porter recommends creating special funds such as relational investing funds to test new investment approaches. In 1995, CalPERS established such a relational fund. Koppes and Reilly conclude that the problem for all public funds is over-, not underdiversification, and advocate a significant reduction in portfolios.[51]

There has been widespread discussion as to the merits and demerits of professional board of directors' members. Some reformers do not like the idea while others are in favor of it. The basic idea is to confront the problem of "who hold[s] real power in corporate governance." in order to break the "club ethos" of today's outside, yet too often only nominally independent directors who may function more independently in name than reality.[52] Coffee argues that creating a market in professional directors is an adequate but limited response to the problem, since without making the director financially dependent on the institutional owner rather than on the firm on whose board they sit, an agent-principal problem is re-created. He argues that this avoids aligning incentives at the institutional level, since all institutions have principal-agent problems themselves. Institutional managers may well be "rationally apathetic" given the free-rider problems inhibiting institutional activism.[53] Black proposed that institutions select an institutional representative(s) to the board. This could be done formally through a registry of directors, or the process could be more informal. Such a system would help permit minority board representation and also institutionalize voice. Black makes clear that his idea is not for public-interest shareholders, but rather for institutional representatives only. He suggests a careful study of the United Kingdom's Promotion of Non-Executive Directors (PRO-NED) system.[54] Monks argues for "shareholder directors," a similar notion to Coffee's, and for the creation of professional directors' organizations, and for the development of a market for directors.[55] In Chapter 7, Latham's proposals to create a market for monitoring addresses some of these same problems.

The logic of these proposals is to create greater levels of coordinated monitoring. One way is to encourage the growth of formal and informal blockholders. Black, for example, suggests establishing so-called "white squire type" funds that would take substantial "relational" stakes in firms, perhaps coordinated by trade groups such as the Council of Institutional Investors, the Institutional Shareholders Service, or activist consulting groups like Madison and Gordon Groups.[56] To date there are few actual example of such funds, although there are a number of governance funds, such as the Lens Fund, that take positions in underperforming firms that the fund believes could be turned around through governance reforms. The principle of the Lens Fund, Robert Monks, suggests that one or more institutional monitors undertake primary responsibility for monitoring a particular firm as a lead monitor, and coordinate with other lead monitors joint activity and information sharing across broad portfolios. Various trade groups could serve as clearinghouses for such joint monitoring. Porter makes similar proposals as well.[57]

While most attention has been focused on the relation between institutional investors and firms, Romano proposes that public funds, which have been viewed by most observers as leading the "corporate governance revolution," be as insulated from political pressures as possible. This issue regained salience when in 1999, President Clinton proposed that a small proportion of Social Security funds be made available for investment in equities by an independent government agency, in ways similar to the large state public pension funds. Romano is concerned about politicization of public funds and their capture by either legislative or gubernatorial interests. As antidotes she proposes that membership on fund boards include elected representatives of fund beneficiaries (which might be an interesting principle to apply to corporate funds as well) and that ERISA standards be extended to explicitly include public funds, that are now exempt. She also suggests constitutionalizing public funds' independence from political authorities (as happened in 1992 in California at CalPERS' initiative). She advocates shifting funds from defined benefit to defined contribution forms while mandating passive strategies for portfolios.[58] This increase in the size of the defined contribution plans might shift the monitoring responsibility more squarely to institutional investors who are better equipped to discharge it as professional owners. Monks argues the Department of Labor should be explicit in requiring ERISA trustees to act in the "exclusive benefit of" and "solely in the interest of" plan participants in monitoring, he suggests may "spur the creation of special purpose fiduciary institutions in the future."[59]

As a final point it is worth noting that a number of scholars and policy analysts have argued that the growth of Employee Stock Ownership Plans (ESOPs) should be seen as a potentially important factor in corporate governance debates.[60] They propose that both governmental and private sector policy actively encourage ESOP growth as well as make ESOPs directly representative of and responsive to employees, rather than management dominated and controlled as is often the case currently. Blair, Monks, and Minow, and the authors of "Lifting All Boats" in particular link governance reform proposals to giving employees a stake in the firm. They argue that this will increase firm-level productivity and provide a different yet important voice in governance, much like the dual tier boards of German firms that institutionalize employee voice and interests. As discussed in Chapter 5, Blair and the authors of "Lifting All Boats" argue that as firm-specific human capital increases in importance (for both the economy as a whole and for a firm's competitiveness), providing adequate incentive alignment for human capital is a critical part of governance reform.

The authors of "Lifting All Boats," for example, strongly support various forms of "enabling working people to share in the long-term growth of U.S. equity markets [which] may help to mitigate the impact of declining real wages" and in the aligning the interests of employees and shareholders as well as increasing firm productivity. Specifically, they suggest amending the tax code for ESOPs to take advantage of capital gains to a greater degree, and to guarantee full proxy-voting rights to employees in ESOPs by amending ERISA.[61] Under current law, a variety of voting schemes are possible: from a one share, one vote by all employee-owners, to a completely management-controlled ESOP, including exclusive management voting.

Conclusion

This review of recent policy proposals and currents suggests a shift may be emerging in corporate law toward a more active and effective monitoring by professional owners. Such a shift would reflect and respond to the sea change that has occurred in the ownership of U.S. publicly held corporations. Already universal owners realize that their ability to trade in and out of the market is both limited by their size and by the indexing strategies many have adopted. Thus, voice — that is, monitoring — is not only often the most effective way to improve returns, but it may also be the only effective avenue available in many situations.

This chapter has reviewed a number of areas in which reforms are being considered. However, it is impossible to say what shape the future might take since many of these issues strike at the heart of the duties, responsibilities, rights, privileges, and powers of what it means to be a shareholder. Furthermore, many of these proposals bring powerful institutional investors into conflict with powerful managerial interests, and the legal and regulatory environment in which this conflict will be played out is necessarily a political one. Nonetheless, fiduciary institutions will continue to grow in size, complexity, and power. And in the exercise of their obligations to their beneficiaries, they are likely to be driven toward seeking more effective ways to monitor.

The shift has not and is not likely to take place in a short period, but rather it is part of a large agenda that will move in fits and starts in a number of venues over a long period of time. Indeed, most of the reform proposals have not been adopted. Those few that have, most notably the 1992 communications liberalization, significantly improved the ability of professional owners to coordinate their monitoring efforts, have themselves raised additional concerns and problems. Outside of the legal and regulatory framework, the paradigm shift in corporate law and government policy underway is also reflected in policy changes and debates among institutional investors and corporate management. In practice, the various forms of new relations among these institutions are being developed informally and behind the scenes. While change in nongovernmental, private sector policy has been more rapid than changes in law and regulatory rules and rulings, it too remains limited in scope.

Chapter 9
Summary and Conclusion

The history of equity ownership in the United States in the twentieth century as detailed in Chapter 3 is one of dispersal followed by concentration. Equity ownership in the first half of the century, while concentrated by economic class, was on a firm-by-firm basis highly dispersed. This led Berle and Means to observe early in the 1930s that this pattern had resulted in the "dissolution of the old atom of ownership into its component parts, control and beneficial ownership."[1] The result was the transfer of effective control from individual owners to professional managers: their famous observation of the separation of ownership from control. By the end of World War II at the latest, managerial capitalism had come to replaced entrepreneurial capitalism. Then starting a bit after midcentury, corporate ownership began to reconcentrate — this time, not into the hands of individuals, but into the hands of financial institutions, notably public and private pension funds and mutual funds.

Driving this reconcentration were a number of powerful political, economic, and demographic forces. First, the expansion of private company pension plans was stimulated by public policy. Specifically, war-time wage and price controls during both World War II and the Korean War and the favorable tax treatment of corporate contributions to pension programs during a time of high excess profits taxes contributed to this effect. The former prevented higher wages, but allowed firms to compete for workers with more generous fringe benefits. The latter meant deferred compensation in the form of pension benefits that could be offered at pennies on the dollar. Second, mutual funds became a more acceptable investment vehicle to a growing fraction of the population. Third, civilian public employment, particularly at the state and local level, grew rapidly over this period. This factor was accompanied by a shift in investment strategies on the part of the public employee retirement systems from "safe" investments in bonds and real estate to an increasing reliance on investments in the equity markets. Finally, in 1974, ERISA was passed. This legislation brought substantial federal regulation to private pension systems. And among other features it required full funding of pension liabilities and diversification as one of the central features of plan portfolios.

Financial assets held by financial institutions exploded after 1980 and especially after 1990. The result is that for the first time in the history of the country, institutions own more corporate equity than individuals. In fact, by 1998 they owned more than half a trillion dollars more than individuals.[2] By 1997, the latest year for which data is available, total assets held by institutional investors had reached $14.3 trillion or 21.2 percent of all financial assets in the United States. This was an eight-fold increase from 1980 as compared to only a five-fold increase in total financial assets.[3] At the same time institutions were shifting their asset allocations toward equities. In 1988, 26.5 percent of total assets were in equities. Ten years later this number had risen to 43.6 percent or about $6.2 trillion (p. 20). By 1997, reconcentration of equity holding had proceeded to the point where institutional investors collectively owned almost 60 percent of the outstanding equity of the one thousand largest U.S. corporations and almost 50 percent of the equity of all of the corporations in the country (p. 20).[4] In fact, institutions held more than 50 percent of the equity in 71.3 percent of the largest one thousand corporations (p. 28). While any one institution typically owned a relatively small portion of a corporation's equity, some institutions — particularly the public employee retirement systems in the largest states, TIAA-CREF, mutual funds, and FERSA — have come to hold substantial blocks of stock both individually and, certainly, taken as a group. Furthermore, institutional ownership is concentrated in the largest companies. By 1997, their ownership share had grown to the point where they owned on average almost half (48.7 percent) of the twenty-five largest U.S. corporations. The holdings of the largest institutions are concentrated in the largest companies. By the late 1990s, the largest twenty-five institutions owned about 28 percent of the largest twenty-five companies.[5] By virtue of the sheer size of their portfolios and the importance of diversification the largest of these institutions have become owners of the economy as a whole. In short, they have become universal owners whose fortunes are closely tied to the overall macroeconomic performance.

A central fact about these institutional investors is that they are professional owners. That is, they actually own the equity — the companies — and they exercise almost all of the rights and privileges of equity ownership. They buy and sell. They vote proxies, make proxy proposals, and monitor portfolio firms, and communicate their concerns to management. However, there is a crucial difference between professional owners and individual owners. Individual owners receive the profit or loss from an equity investment whereas professional owners do not. Instead, as the managers of other people's money, professional owners make investments on behalf of ultimate beneficiaries — retirees, future retirees, or individuals who have purchased shares in mutual funds. These professional owners have a positive incentive to carry out their ownership responsibilities in a manner that assures the institution will be able to meet its obligations to beneficiaries. These obligations are defined by the common law of fiduciary duties and are heavily influenced by the embodiment of these duties in ERISA.

These institutions are, therefore, called fiduciary institutions. Because of their important position in the economy, this stage of American capitalism might well be characterized as fiduciary capitalism. In fulfilling their duty on behalf of their beneficiaries, fiduciary institutions are governed by the twin duties of care and loyalty. Furthermore, they are legally required to take only those actions a "prudent person" would take to further the best interests of the beneficiary. This, coupled with the fact that many of these institutions have very long-term liabilities and therefore long-term horizons and that about one-third of the assets of the 200 largest defined benefit funds are invested in indexed portfolios, has important implications.[6]

Fiduciary duty empowers and legally requires institutions to act vigorously to promote the beneficiary's interests. The prudent person rule also encourages institutions to act conservatively since actions deemed imprudent can result in personal liability to the fiduciary. The safest course of action for a professional owner is to take *only* those actions generally accepted as prudent — which historically has led institutions to adopt a conservative view of their responsibilities as owners. This conservatism is well illustrated by the indexing of portfolios, a practice of a great many institutions under which investments are chosen to mirror a market index such as the SP 500 index. With an indexing strategy, trading is passively driven by the need to conform ownership to the index, not by a desire to hold any particular stock.

One might expect that the reconcentration of ownership in the hands of institutional owners coupled with fiduciary rules and an indexed portfolio would complete the divorce of ownership from control. But that hasn't turned out to be the case. The requirement to act in the beneficiary's best interest has increasingly led fiduciary institutions to act as active owners. At a minimum, financial institutions have been required to vote the proxies on the equities they own. Some institutional investors have been much more active. They have opposed management polices that reduce shareholder wealth (poison pills, for example), filed proxies to change company bylaws, and lobbied for changes in management at severely underperforming companies. In other words, they have acted as serious professional owners. Some institutions feel that the only way they can discharge their fiduciary duty when maintaining an indexed portfolio is to actively attempt to improve the performance of individual companies.[7] This has led professional owners to promote corporate governance reforms that strengthen their ability to act as owners, to vigorously monitor underperforming portfolio companies, and to oppose management when they determine that it is not acting in the best interest of the shareholders.

The Finance Approach to Corporate Governance

The appropriate role of the corporation in American society is the subject of a large and active debate. However, as far as fiduciary institutions are concerned, the "finance" view of the corporation, grounded as it is in a traditional view of private property, accords closely with their views. From its perspective, the *only* goal of the corporation is to maximize long-term shareholder wealth. The agency problem that the separation of ownership from control presents is that individuals charged with making the operating decisions that affect shareholder wealth — the managers — may systematically behave in ways contrary to the interests of the owners. The solution to this problem is to strengthen the institutions that seek to align the desires of owners with the actions of agents. Thus, the finance model provides the fundamental justification for many legal, regulatory, and procedural proposals.

Many who support the finance model regret the passing of the "market for corporate control" that characterized the 1980s. In that era, hostile takeovers were seen as the ultimate mechanism for aligning manager's actions with owner's wishes. Managements that didn't take every action to maximize shareholder wealth faced the real possibility that a more aggressive manager would come along, buy the company, fire current management, and proceed to reap the economic gains from correcting managerial inefficiency. However, the market for corporate control was roundly criticized for disrupting companies and communities, and the efficiency gains that were claimed to flow from the takeovers were challenged by researchers who found wealth transfers instead. Furthermore, hostile takeovers occurred in only the more egregious cases because the difference between private and public values, the takeover premium, had to be large enough to cover both the substantial costs involved and the real possibility of failure.

The market for corporate control was severely weakened at the end of the 1980s by the adoption of a range of antitakeover measures by corporations, the enactment of rules by key state legislatures that made takeovers more difficult, the collapse of the junk bond market, and governmental restrictions on the ability of financial institutions to hold high-yielding debt.[8] Owners — institutions — were then forced to turn their attention to the removal of these impediments to the market for corporate control, to the enactment of governance reforms to give owners more influence on boards, and to initiatives to influence the Securities and Exchange Commission, the Department of Labor, and other agencies to adopt rules that either forced institutions to act aggressively as owners or rules that allowed institutions to better coordinate and pursue collective action against individual companies. These were all taken in the name of the ultimate beneficiaries by professional owners driven by their fiduciary duties.

The Implications of Universal Ownership

As the exclusive benefit rule dictates, fiduciary institutions have a duty of loyalty to take only those actions that are in the sole benefit of their beneficiaries — mutual fund shareholders, pension plan participants, or insurance policyholders. Today most institutions view their focused adherence to the goals of the finance model as satisfying the exclusive benefit rule. However, many of these institutions are emerging as universal owners, owners of a broad cross section of the economy. In addition, many have a particularly long investment horizon because of their size, purpose, or choice of investment strategy. Consequently, they need to reconsider the finance model's injunction to maximize shareholder value on a firm-by-firm basis.

To begin with, because they own the economy as a whole, universal owners should care about the overall health of the economy, not just the economic health of individual firms. In the long run, the performance of their large, diversified portfolios will depend more on the overall performance of the economy than it will on the performance of any individual company in those portfolios. The spectacular performance of the stock market in the middle and later years of the 1990s has been driven by monetary policy that has led to lower inflation and lower interest rates and has been complemented by fiscal policy that has reined in central government deficits.[9] In addition to appropriate fiscal and monetary policy, sustained economic growth depends on factors such as a well-trained labor force, an effective infrastructure, and a legal and regulatory environment that encourages efficiency in the business sector.

Consequently, a universal owner that really wants to maximize the shareholder value of its portfolio would need to develop public policy–like positions and monitor regulatory developments and legislation on a number of key issues to the economy as a whole. This is not to argue that fiduciary institutions should lobby in Congress, although they might, but rather that individually and through associations of institutions such as the Council of Institutional Investors universal owners should monitor a broad range of issues that affect the economy as a whole, and they should lend their weight to those initiatives that they come to understand as promoting sustained, long-run economic growth.

In addition to a concern about economy-wide issues, universal owners will, of course, need to monitor individual companies. This focus will continue to include the traditional monitoring for managerial slack and managerial malfeasance that can arise because of the agency problems created by the separation of ownership from control. However, what a universal owner must also appreciate is that by owning the economy as a whole, it in effect internalizes both the positive and negative externalities generated at individual portfolio companies. This broadens the monitoring task from individual companies to the entire portfolio as an integrated whole. Consequently, while employee training programs or research and development activities, to name two obvious examples, might not be undertaken to a socially optimal degree by an individual company, a universal owner might find it worthwhile to encourage these types of activities in companies across its portfolio because of the positive external benefits they generate — benefits that a universal owner would capture because it holds a portfolio that reflects the economy as a whole. Failing widespread positive responses from large firms, institutional universal owners might also turn their attention directly to public policy in these areas.

The largest pension funds have taken some tentative steps in this direction — steps that can be considered indications of an awakening of universal owner consciousness, which is an awareness that the actions of individual companies can have spillover effects that impact the owner's entire portfolio. Perhaps the best current example is that institutions have for a number of years justified much of their corporate governance activism not only on the basis of what it does at a particular target company, but by the positive externalities it generates at other companies. In the words of the John Biggs, Chairman and CEO of TIAA-CREF, one of the largest fiduciary institutions and an emerging universal owner, "The significance [of shareholder activism] is not the three or four laggards you catch — it's that you get the herd to run. We need to scare all the animals."[10] Thus, "CalPERS seeks to 'move the herd' rather than to follow it, while still retaining the risk-reward reliability of an indexed portfolio."[11]

In addition, fiduciary institutions acting as professional owners have for a number of years developed proxy-voting guidelines that embody universal owner elements. For example, the proxy guidelines for the combined New York City Funds require a vote against shareholder proposals that "prohibit corporate funds to be given to any charitable, educational or other similar organization, except for the purposes in direct furtherance of the business of the corporation." The reason given is that "charitable contributions by corporations are consistent with the Funds' philosophy which holds that companies should be good corporate citizens and must recognize their responsibilities to adhere to accepted moral standards."[12] Thus, the fund recognizes that actions that might be narrowly profit maximizing at individual firms, such as refraining from charitable contributions unless they can be tightly linked to the bottom line, may, in fact, contribute to a higher return for their portfolio as a whole.

Furthermore, as universal owners come to the understand that maximizing shareholder value requires a more holistic approach to managing their portfolio, they increasingly need to appreciate that fulfilling their fiduciary duty to their beneficiaries also requires that they come to understand that the sharp line the finance model draws between stockholders and stake-holders may be breaking down. In fact, beneficiaries and mutual fund inves-tors are both stakeholders and shareholders at the same time. Thus, the stand on charitable contributions referred to above can also be interpreted as a recognition that shareholders have stockholder-like claims on the cor-porate sector.[13] However, the interests of various stockholder as stakeholder groups are neither clear cut, simple, or unambiguous. Indeed, these "inter-ests" have barely begun to be articulated or conceptually formulated either by ultimate recipients and "owners" or by most senior institutional man-agers themselves. Most importantly, there are demographic, regional, class, employment, and other factors that cause, or in the future may cause, signif-icant divisions among different classes of shareholders and beneficial claim-ants. What is interesting is that these divisions cut across both groups rather than divide them neatly into stockholders and stakeholders.

As has been indicated previously, although this book argues that there is great potential for universal owners if they recognize and act on their unique status, there is also concomitant danger that currently exists, given their vast and perhaps growing power as a result of this unprecedented financial concentration. Two key questions arise: Who will watch the watch-ers, and to whom are these fiduciaries not only accountable but responsible?

In summary, universal owners must first be aware that they own the econ-omy as a whole and then realize that this has implications for the way they monitor their investments. Firm-by-firm monitoring continues to be very important, but a universal owner also needs to augment firm-by-firm moni-toring with a concern for the broader economic environment. These con-cerns include but are not limited to general monetary and fiscal policy, regulatory policy, and the provision of important public and quasi-public goods such as education, tort law, and the transportation and communica-tion infrastructure. It also needs to pay particular attention to the activities of individual firms in its portfolio that may generate either positive or nega-tive externalities. It needs to support companies that are engaged in ac-tivities that generate positive externalities, because it will capture the benefit across its portfolio. At the same time it needs to oppose companies that generate negative externalities because it will bear the cost across its port-folio. Furthermore, in managing their portfolios universal owners need to appreciate the ambiguous role of their beneficiaries as both stockholders, although once removed by the mediation of the institutions and as stake-holders, with a concern for the quality of social, political, and economic life in which they receive their benefits.

A Modest Plan of Action for Universal Owners

Once universal owners recognize that they must consider both economy-wide and portfolio-wide issues in order to successfully maximize wealth in the long run, they will need to find ways in which to act on this realization. Constraining this action is the often repeated refrain of institutional investors: "We are small and we must carefully consider whether we can add value at a reasonable cost." But as Kim Johnson, general counsel for the Colorado Public Employee Retirement Association, puts it, this calculation can be made more sophisticated.

That is, you do not look only at events in isolation, but look at them in the context of your portfolio as a whole. That's explicit fiduciary law. If you use that same philosophy in making decisions about governance, which is an economic activity as far as I'm concerned, then we are prepared to take individual actions that in the narrow sense may not be cost effective if we believe that our action coupled with other actions by other funds over a period of time will indeed lead to a long term benefit.[14]

While Johnson's statement is specifically about traditional corporate governance issues, it can be directly generalized to other issues that have similar spillover effects. However, the problem of considering company-specific costs in light of portfolio-wide benefits is compounded by the well-known collective action or free-rider problem that arises because all owners of the equity of affected companies benefit, while only those owners who take an action bear the cost. This problem is mitigated to some extent for large institutional owners because the absolute size of their holdings may be sufficient to justify action even if most of the benefit accrues to other institutions.[15]

The problems posed by the cost/benefit calculation for large and small institutions alike can be reduced in several ways. First, institutions can choose from a range of responses, some of which are relatively inexpensive to initiate; some examples are given below. Second, institutions can work through coalitions such as the Council of Institutional Investors. This would reduce the duplicate cost and effort that would result from several institutions analyzing the same issue and would promote communication and coordination among the institutions. Third, institutional investors can "coat tail" on other institutional investors that have developed skills and a reputation for expertise in a particular area. For example, the State of Wisconsin Investment Board has developed a reputation for effectively monitoring companies on compensation issues, particularly with regard to option programs. Other institutions have joined in when called upon to support proxies and other actions the board has taken at companies it has targeted for abusive compensation policies. In a similar vein, at the Colorado Public Employee Retirement Association, Kim Johnson reports, "We are trying to pick areas where we can be cooperative with others because we really believe that the road to success is through cooperative action."[16] This semiformal division of labor could be an efficient response to the collective-action problem.

Some professional owners already have policies and programs and are taking actions that reflect a consciousness of their role as universal investors. What follows is a list of examples of some of these programs and the ways in which they might be used to monitor portfolio companies.

Develop policy guidelines on a particular issue. These guidelines could be to be used in proxy voting or other policy issues. Currently, the trustees of CREF have adopted a statement on environmental issues that they sent to the companies in their portfolio.[17] Policy guidelines can lead to "quiet diplomacy" and to other informal, off-the-record discussions with individual corporations, or they can be used for a variety of more public actions.

Survey portfolio firms on particular policies. This kind of action allows for results to be published with or without comment. This is similar to the report CalPERS commissioned on high-performance workplace issues.[18] The results can then be circulated to the portfolio companies, the press, and other institutional investors.

Monitor the lobbying efforts of portfolio companies. Lobbying efforts on behalf of individual companies can be narrowly self-serving or they can support much needed reforms. A universal owner should be alert to the possibility that one company may be gaining an advantage at the expense of other portfolio companies. Universal owners could publish reviews of their monitoring efforts and, possibly, express their approval or disapproval of particular lobbying campaigns.

Grade portfolio firms on a particular issue. This action would require that an institution develop a position on a issue and develop a criteria with which to rate performance, which is more proactive than simply monitoring portfolio firms. An example of this type of action is a program in which CalPERS surveyed and graded portfolio companies from "A" to "F" on how well they adhered to the GM board's list of corporate governance guidelines. It then published the results.[19]

Target specific portfolio companies on specific issues. This action requires an institution to take a stand vis-à-vis practices at a particular company or group of companies. Once targeted, the institution would take the appropriate action, which could include communicating with management, meeting with boards, filing proxy resolutions, or appealing to the public at large through press conferences. For example, when CalPERS had questions about management's actions in the controversy surrounding the logging of ancient redwood trees in the headwaters forest in Northern California, it sent a letter expressing its concern to the Maxxam corporation.[20] In a very early example CREF communicated with General Motors concerning the company's response to safety issues around its Corvair automobile.[21]

Do nothing. This kind of action (or nonaction) is a constructive policy when it is taken in full consideration of the facts. It is not a constructive policy when an institution fails to take a position because it has failed to inform itself on the issues involved.

Different institutions will, of course, adopt different approaches with regard to their overall response to the responsibilities of universal ownership. They will almost certainly apply different strategies in different situations with respect to different firms. For example, deciding consciously to do nothing may be the appropriate response to many issues and many firms, while only a few firms might warrant specific targeting. In any case, the herd effect that has been so successful on issues of traditional corporate governance can be expected to apply to universal owner issues as well.

A Final Question: Who Will Watch the Watchers and for What Will They Watch?

The reconcentration of ownership into the hands of institutional investors may, superficially, appear to solve the Berle-Means problem, but in fact it adds one more layer of agents between the "real" owners and the firms they own. Beneficial owners, the ones owed the duty of care and the duty of loyalty by the fiduciary institutions, are now separated from the corporations they own by another set of agents—the fiduciary institutions themselves. Instead of a principal-agent problem between owners and managers, they must now solve a principal-agent-agent problem between owners, professional owners, and managers. On its face an agency chain of this type would seem to make everything much more difficult.

Institutions are, of course, charged to act in the best interest of their beneficiaries, but how is this determined and who determines it? As has been noted, beneficiaries are a very diverse group with interests that cut across traditional stakeholder and stockholder categories in ways that have yet to really emerge. To determine what is in the "best interest" of any group of beneficiaries may be a difficult or even impossible problem to solve with certainty. However, one thing is certain. Its solution will, in the broadest sense, be a political one in the sense that the ultimate beneficiaries and owners will have to assert that universal owners begin to act as such. This could take the form of direct pressures on fiduciary agents as well as pressure on legislative bodies (at the state and federal levels) to mandate such actions.

The problem of the potential co-optation of fiduciary institutions by the corporations they are supposed to monitor does present serious problems. Indeed, large classes of institutions, corporate pension funds, and bank trust departments are written off as strong advocates of shareholder interests because they are thought to have been captured by management or to exist in a tight commercial network of firms in which they own stock and debt and with which they conduct other business. The remaining active institutional investors—primarily public pension funds—are relatively free from corporate pressure, but may be subject to political pressure.[22] In any case, co-optation can be a subtle process. For example, one of the unintended results of the 1992 communication reforms designed to facilitate coordination between institutions and thereby improve their ability to monitor portfolio firms may have been a subtle co-optation of institutions. Institutions can communicate directly with one another and with management behind closed doors, but as activism has moved out of the public spotlight it has become more difficult to monitor the initiatives of institutional investors. In turn, this may have reduce their effectiveness.[23] Because of this perception, some observes believe that in an attempt to reestablish distance from the firm they are trying to influence, institutional investors may try to revitalize the publicity tool that they so effectively wielded in the early 1990s.[24]

The crux of the issue is: Who will monitor the monitors and what will they monitor them for? The ultimate beneficiaries of most institutional investors are an even more diffuse, disinterested, and disenfranchised group than the traditional Berle-Means shareholder. Thus, it is unlikely that beneficiaries as a group will ever to be able to effectively "watch" the fiduciary institutions. So it remains to be seen whether the oversight available from various governmental agencies will be sufficient. ERISA funds, for example, are subject of federal regulation that may provide some oversight for these institutions. Public employee retirement funds are normally under the supervision of their respective legislative bodies, but this can be a mixed blessing. To date, most funds have been able to remain relatively independent of political influence, but the danger still exists. Some, such as CalPERS with its referendum mandated independent funding, have more autonomy than many. As discussed in Chapters 7 and 8, Congress controls the financial institutions through the various securities acts, particularly through the definition of a group in acquisition situations. Changes in this legislation would probably have profound effects on the behavior of universal owners, although Congress' most recent attempt — the legislation governing lead plaintiffs — has yet to produce the results desired by its proponents. The Securities and Exchange Commission doesn't control the fiduciary institutions per se, but it has substantial influence over their ability to act as owners through its regulatory control of the proxy process.

Perhaps the best hope for effective monitoring is transparency coupled with competition between the institutions. As public entities, the state and local retirement funds are admirably transparent. They are accountable to the citizens of the state as well as to the legislature and to their beneficiaries. Other institutional investors, particularly the mutual funds and the private pension funds, are much less transparent. Consequently, monitoring them effectively is a much more difficult problem. Growing professionalism may also contribute to a kind of internal monitoring that, while not a substitute for effective external monitoring, may still prevent egregious abuses. Yet this cannot deal with the growing power of influence that comes to the managers of fiduciary institutions, a direct consequence of the growing concentration of financial assets. Such influence has always accompanied wealth, whether privately or institutionally held. Unless great care is taken by both the ultimate beneficiaries as well as their political representatives, such political, social, and economic power (over media, the political process, business, and the like) is likely to engender a backlash against these institutions.

Thus, in the end, the rise of universal owners with their accompanying concentrations of great wealth and power into the hands of relatively few professional owners raises serious concerns about monitoring the monitors.

Should this be a governmental function? Should it be left to the "market"? What role would the market play in monitoring monitors and how might it play this role? If the role of institutions is strengthened to make institutions more effective monitors, what kind of safeguards should be enacted to protect beneficiaries from institutional abuse? Is "fiduciary duty" enough to assure appropriate behavior? In the end, these may be the most important questions to ask about the rise of fiduciary capitalism at the end of the twentieth century.

Notes

Introduction

1. Alfred D. Chandler, *The Visible Hand: The Managerial Revolution in American Business* (Cambridge, Mass.: Belknap Press of Harvard University Press, 1977).

2. This shift is discussed in detail in Chapter 3.

3. See Table 3.3.

4. "Institutional Investment Report" (New York: The Conference Board, 1998), p. 37.

5. Monks and Minow coined the term *universal owner,* but have not developed it beyond their initial insight (Robert A. G. Monks and Nell Minow, *Corporate Governance* [Cambridge, Mass.: Basil Blackwell, 1995]).

6. Mark J. Roe, *Strong Managers, Weak Owners: The Political Roots of American Corporate Finance* (Princeton, N.J.: Princeton University Press, 1994).

7. Louis D. Brandeis, *Other People's Money and How the Bankers Use It* (New York: Harper & Row, 1967).

8. See, for example, Max B. E. Clarkson, *The Corporation and Its Stakeholders* (Toronto, Canada: University of Toronto Press, 1999), for a good collection of both "classic" and contemporary stakeholder essays.

9. James M. Poterba and Andrew A. Samwick, "Stock Ownership Patterns, Stock Market Fluctuations And Consumption," *Brookings Papers on Economic Activity,* no. 2 (1995): 295–372.

10. It should be noted that some non-U.S. institutional owners possess large proportions of shares in a few firms, while others have a more universal type of portfolio. An example of the former would be German banks, while an example of the latter would be large Dutch pension funds. See Rafael La Porta, Florencio Lopez-de-Silanes, Andrei Shleifer, and Robert W. Vishny, "Corporate Ownership Around the World," NBER working paper 6625 (Cambridge, Mass., National Bureau of Economic Research, 1998).

Chapter 1. The Universal Owner

1. James M. Poterba and Andrew A. Samwick, "Stock Ownership Patterns, Stock Market Fluctuations and Consumption," *Brookings Papers on Economic Activity,* no. 2 (1995): 295–372.

2. James P. Hawley, "Political Voice, Fiduciary Activism and the Institutional Own-

ership of U.S. Corporations: The Role of Public and Non-Corporate Pension Funds," *Sociological Perspectives* 38, no. 3 (1995): 415–35.

3. The finance model is discussed in more detail in Chapter 4.

4. Adolph A. Berle and Gardiner C. Means, *The Modern Corporation and Private Property*, Revised ed. (New York: Macmillan, 1967).

5. Jon Lukomnik, former deputy comptroller for Pensions of New York City, "denied the theory of mutual exclusivity" between the primacy of either stockholder or stakeholder, especially in the case of long-term pension (and similar fund) holdings (Personal communication, January 26, 1998).

6. Robert A. G. Monks and Nell Minow, *Corporate Governance* (Cambridge, Mass.: Basil Blackwell, 1995), pp. 268–70.

7. A truly universal portfolio would own a properly weighted selection of all of the financial assets in the world — stocks, bonds, real estate, etc. The focus here is on equity, but the largest public pension funds such as CalPERS hold a portfolio approximating true universality with about 20% of its assets invested in the equity of non-U.S. companies. Another 4.5% is invested in real estate and about 28% in fixed income assets (http://www.calpers.ca.gov/invest/asset/asset.htm, accessed May 5, 1999). Delineating exactly which institutions are universal owners is a future task of some significance. Jon Lukomnik suggests that there are perhaps 25 such public funds, plus CREF. Whether large mutual funds are also universal owners needs to be studied. One might also add Taft-Hartley funds, at least in some regards (Personal communication, January 26, 1998).

8. "The California Public Employees' Retirement System (CalPERS) grows about $1 billion every two months — more than four times the median market value of a *Fortune* 500 industrial company; in a year, enough to buy all the common stock of General Motors with enough left to buy five tankfuls of gasoline for each vehicle it makes" (Monks and Minow, *Corporate Governance*, p. 124).

9. An index strategy (or "passive" strategy) seeks to mimic the performance of a broad index of stocks and can be based on any broad index of market performance such as the S&P 500 or the Russell 2000. Once an index strategy is put in place, the only trading that occurs is that necessary to adjust the weighting of the various components of the index to keep them in line with their participation in the target index.

10. See James P. Hawley, Andrew T. Williams, and with John U. Miller, "Getting the Herd to Run: Shareholder Activism at the California Public Employees' Retirement System (CalPERS)," *Business and the Contemporary World* 6, no. 4 (1994): 26–48.

11. Interview with Jon Lukomnik, deputy comptroller for pensions, New York City, December 15, 1997.

12. Robert A. G. Monks and Nell Minow, *Watching the Watchers: Corporate Governance in the 21st Century* (Cambridge, Mass.: Blackwell Publishers, 1996), p. 121.

13. They add that in addition to corporate governance focusing on competitiveness and minimizing agency costs, "the most important task for the corporate governance system is ensuring a balance between the freedom to maximize wealth (power) and the limits of doing so without imposing disproportionate costs on others (accountability). In this sense, corporate governance must both protect corporations from society and society from corporations" (p. 265).

14. State government (indeed all government) pension funds are a peculiar type of "third party" since, both directly and indirectly, governments at various levels bear part of the costs of negative externalities via the tax system. In a formal sense, government is an indirect party to the contract rather than an "innocent" third party. The complexity is furthered since many, but not all, state and local government pension funds are not constitutionally direct "arms" of government, but have a quasi-autonomous relation to government.

15. In a similar vein, a 1997 OECD conference on "institutional modernization for effective and adaptive corporate governance" concluded that "developments in corporate governance and capital markets are sometimes coupled with transition problems, for example in terms of employment adjustments, as an outcome of improvements may also create resource allocation suboptimalities when social vs. private returns of investments happen to differ significantly (for example in certain areas of R&D, employee training, investments in declining regions, etc.)." This relates more generally to the "social capital" issue, which raises collective action problems. This formulation was in response to the staff-developed question: "Do you see growing difficulties for financial institution and business corporations to fund possibly high social — but practically low private — return investments in areas such as precompetitive R&D, employee training, etc., where return divergences are not bridged by tax incentives, reputations effects, or remedied by public relations applicable to all enterprises? Might such 'market failures' become important in modern economies" (OECD, "Report from the OECD Business Sector Colloquium on Corporate Governance," September 1997, Paris, pp. 8, 12, memo).

16. *Institutional Investment Report* (New York: The Conference Board, 1998), tables 8 and 14, pp. 25, 29.

17. See also *Business Week*'s annual survey of institutional ownership for the largest 1000 firms ("Investment Outlook Scoreboard," *Business Week*, December 29, 1997, pp. 161–88).

18. Many pension funds that primarily follow an index strategy often keep a small proportion of their funds, typically less than 25%, to manage actively. In contrast to a "passive" indexing strategy, an "active" strategy involves selecting investments based on the investment managers' judgement about what will be good investments.

19. When the 1990s bull market runs its course and declines markedly we expect the institutional share of the market to increase, since large investors have nowhere else to go, while individuals and small institutions have greater flexibility in their asset allocation. For similar reasons, we expect the indexed percentage of large institutional portfolios to increase.

20. A defined benefit retirement program is a "traditional" pension in which the program has an obligation to pay a benefit defined by a retirement contract. A defined contribution plan is one in which the contributions to the program are defined, but in which the actual retirement benefit depends on the investment performance of each individual plan participant's portfolio. IRA, KEOGH, and 401(k) plans are examples of defined contribution programs. Most importantly, in a defined benefit plan the plan administrator has sole discretion over investment decisions — the administrator is a professional owner. In a defined contribution plan, the owner of the plan (the "participant") frequently makes the investment decisions, though they are often limited to choosing from a menu of mutual funds offered by the plan. If the investments are mutual funds, then the mutual fund company is the professional owner.

21. The Conference Board, *Institutional Investment Report*, p. 22.

22. http://www441.fidelity.com:80/about/world/manage.html, accessed May 5, 1999, and http://www.pionline.com/moneymanager/, accessed May 5, 1999.

23. *Institutional Investment Report* (New York: The Conference Board, 1998). As a retirement program, TIAA-CREF is a hybrid of both the defined benefit and the defined contribution approaches. During one's working years a participant contributes to a CREF account. The amount available at retirement depends on individual contributions and the allocation choices a participant has made between the various CREF accounts. At retirement, the balance in a participant's CREF account is converted to an annuity that is the financial responsibility of TIAA.

24. CREF is invested in a smaller number of companies since some individual positions represent different equity issues of the same company.

25. "Semi-Annual Report: College Retirement Equities Fund" (New York: College Retirement Equities Fund, 1998). On June 30, 1998, the total assets in the CREF stock account were divided as follows: common stock, 94.88%; short-term investments, 4.92%; preferred stock, 0.16%; and bonds, 0.04%.

26. Paul A. Gompers and Andrew Metrick, "How Are Large Institutions Different from Other Investors? Why do these Differences Matter?" (Cambridge, Mass.: Harvard Business School Working Paper, August 1998), p. 30.

27. "Uniform Management of Public Employee Retirement Systems Act (1997)" (National Conference of Commissioners of Uniform State Laws, 1997).

28. One major public pension fund defines the duty of loyalty and the duty of care as follows: "The duty of loyalty is sometimes referred to as the 'sole purpose' doctrine. This means the Board and other CalPERS fiduciaries must act solely in the interests of members and beneficiaries. For this reason, CalPERS cannot base its corporate governance actives on social or political causes. Instead, it must focus on the 'bottom line' of enhanced shareholder returns. . . . Under the duty of care, the Board and other CalPERS fiduciaries must manage fund assets as a 'prudent investor.' Essentially, this means with the care, skill and diligence that a prudent person, familiar with the matters, would exercise under similar circumstances in managing a pension fund of like size" ("Why Corporate Governance Today? A Policy Statement," [Sacramento, Calif.: California Public Employees' Retirement System, 1995], pp. 3–4).

29. "Interpretive Bulletin 94-2 (Title 29)" (Washington, D.C.: U.S. Government Printing Office, 1994), 38860–38864.

30. Of course, fiduciaries receive compensation for the services they provide. These are the costs of running public pension funds or the management fees that are charged the holders of mutual funds.

31. Joann S. Lublin, "CalPERS Considers Seeking Board Seats," *Wall Street Journal*, December 26, 1997, p. A3.

32. Interview with Michael A. McGrath, Minnesota State Treasurer, December 8, 1997.

33. Lilli A. Gordon, "Active Investing in the U.S. Equity Market: Past Performance and Future Prospects: A Report Prepared for the California Public Employees' Retirement System" (Cambridge, Mass.: Gordon Group, 1993).

34. This position should not be confused with what has been termed "the stakeholder fiduciary principle" or the "multiple fiduciary stakeholder synthesis" that argues, according to Goodpaster, that "management bears a fiduciary relationship to the stakeholders and to the corporation as an abstract entity. It must act in the interests of the stakeholders as their agent, and it must act in the interests of the corporation to ensure the survival of the firm, safeguarding the long-term stakes of each group" (Kenneth E. Goodpaster, "Business Ethics and Stakeholder Analysis," *Business Ethics Quarterly* 1, no. 1 [1991]: 53–73, as quoted in John Hasnas, "The Normative Theories of Business Ethics: A Guide for the Perplexed," *Business Ethics Quarterly* 8, no. 1 [1998]: 19–42).

35. According to *Pension and Investments*, the largest U.S. retirement funds (excluding TIAA-CREF) had combined assets of almost $800 billion in late 1998. Accessed at http://www.pionline.research/r100.shtml on November 19, 1998.

36. Bernard S. Black, "Shareholder Activism and Corporate Governance in the United States," in *The New Palgrave Dictionary of Economics and the Law*, ed. Peter Newman (New York: Macmillan Stockton Press, 1998), 459–65.

37. Joseph A. Grundfest, "Just Vote No: A Minimalist Strategy for Dealing with Barbarians Inside the Gates," *Stanford Law Review* 45, no. 4 (1993): 857–973.

38. "Why Corporate Governance Today? A Policy Statement" (Sacramento, Calif.: California Public Employees' Retirement System, 1995), p. 14.

39. Interview with Kim Johnson, General Counsel, Colorado Public Employee Retirement Association, December 4, 1997.

40. Interview with Kurt Schaht, General Counsel, Wisconsin State Investment Board, December 2, 1997.

41. The controversy arose out of Maxxam's desire to log old growth redwood trees, which provoked strong opposition from environmental groups and other concerned citizens. The issue was presented to the board of the California Public Employee Retirement System as Agenda Item 16 on April 14, 1997. See also Mitchel Benson, "Fund Warns Maxxam Not to Log," *Wall Street Journal*, February 19, 1997, p. CA1.

42. The term was used by Jon Lukomnik.

43. Interview with Kim Johnson, General Counsel, Colorado Public Employee Retirement Association, December 4, 1997.

44. In economic terms, the optimal investment for a firm occurs when the marginal private cost to the firm just equals the marginal private benefit the firm receives. When the benefit to the economy at large — the social benefit — exceeds the private benefit, as it does with education, firms will underinvest from the point of view of society at large.

45. See Robert E. Lucas, "On the Mechanics of Economic Development," *Journal of Monetary Economics* 22, no. 1 (1998): 3–42, and James E. Rauch, "Productivity Gains from Geographic Concentration of Human Capital: Evidence from Cities," *Journal of Urban Economics* 34, no. 3 (1993): 380–400.

46. CalPERS news release, June 15, 1994, "CalPERS Adopts Study on Workplace Practices," Sacramento, Calif.; The Gordon Group, "Report to the California Public Employees' Retirement System, High Performance Workplaces: Implications for Investment Research and Active Investing Strategies" (May 30, 1994, Cambridge, Mass.) (Xerox); and, City of New York, Office of the Comptroller, "High Performance Workplace Practices: A Recommendation for Institutional Investor Action," January 1995.

47. "The Changing Nature of Entrepreneurship," a conference sponsored by the Center for Economic Policy Research in association with the Chemical Heritage Foundation, May 30, 1997, at the Donald L. Lucas Conference Center, Ralph Landau Center for Economics and Policy Research, Stanford University. The title of the talk was "Regional Linkages, Silicon Valley and the Networked Firm." The most famous case of a company failing to capture the benefits of its research and development expenditures may be Xerox Parc, a basic research facility for the Xerox Corporation in Palo Alto, Calif., which invented, among other things, computer networking and the graphical user interface with a mouse as an input device.

48. *Pensions and Investments*, "Funds Say Clinton's Actions Snuffing Out Tobacco Stock Allure," September 29, 1997, pp. 3, 49.

49. William Crist, personal communication, January 1998.

50. Interview with Kayla Gillan, CalPERS General Counsel, September 8, 1997.

51. In this case, Crist said, "You are almost micro-managing. This is a management decision, but why are they doing a very expensive advertising campaign . . . the fact of the matter is they make mistakes . . . when it gets to the level that it's more of a media issue, a total macro issue, it becomes an externality. Then you have a responsibility to look at it. [It can be said] . . . 'that's just BS,' since you're still reacting to complaints on the social side. OK, [but] that calls it to your attention" (Interview with William Crist, President, Board of Administration, California Public Employees' Retirement System, October 24, 1997).

52. Interview with Michael A. McGrath, Minnesota State Treasurer, December 8,

1997. McGrath and others felt the case against tobacco was not a fiduciary one, but rather a "social" one.

53. Personal communication with Michael A. McGrath, January 1998.

54. Interview with Linda Scott, Director of Investment Affairs, New York State Retirement Fund, December 19, 1997.

55. Interview with Jon Lukomnik.

56. Similar interests in transparency practices and social accounting standards and monitoring were the motivation for an OECD conference in February 1998 titled, "The Role of Disclosure in Strengthening Corporate Governance and Accountability."

57. These issues were mentioned by representatives of CREF, the New York City Fund, New York State Teachers' Fund, New York State Common Retirement Funds, and others.

58. CalPERS and The New York City Fund have active and relatively large ETI programs, usually in real estate development for moderate- and low-income housing development.

59. Interview with William Crist.

60. Interview with Jon Lukomnik.

61. Interview with William Crist.

Chapter 2. Proxy Voting

1. Joann S. Lublin, "Oklahoma Court Affirms Holders' Right to Pursue a Binding Bylaw Proposal," *Wall Street Journal*, January 28, 1999, p. B2.

2. Individual owners who hold substantial positions are more likely to vote those shares if for no other reason than the fact that management can solicit individual stockholders directly and are most likely to solicit votes from larger shareholders. For a discussion of the antidemocratic nature of proxy voting, see Bernard S. Black, "Shareholder Passivity Reexamined," *Michigan Law Review* 89, no. 3 (1990): 520–608.

3. U.S. Department of Labor has stated that "the fiduciary act of managing plan assets that are shares of corporate stock includes the voting of proxies appurtenant to those shares of stock" ("Interpretive Bulletin 94–2 [Title 29]," [Washington, D.C.: U.S. Government Publishing Office, 1994], 38860–38864, p. 38860).

4. Bernard S. Black, "Shareholder Activism and Corporate Governance in the United States," in *The New Palgrave Dictionary of Economics and the Law*, ed. Peter Newman (New York: Macmillan Stockton Press, 1998), 459–65.

5. State of Wisconsin Investment Board "Proxy Voting Guidelines," n.d.

6. Cover memorandum for Agenda Item 15 submitted to the CalPERS Investment Committee on September 14, 1998, p. 15-2.

7. California Public Employees' Retirement System. "Domestic Proxy Voting Guidelines," March 16, 1998. CalPERS and most other funds have separate, though similar policies for voting domestic and international proxies.

8. "Statement of Procedures and Policies for Voting Proxies," November 1987 (last amended June 1998), New York City Combined Funds. The New York City Combined Funds are the New York City Board of Education Retirement System, the New York City Employees' Retirement System, the New York City Fire Department Pension Fund, and the New York City Police Department Pension Fund. The combined funds have separate procedures and policies for voting domestic and international policies.

9. Father Sean McManus, president of President of the Irish National Caucus, a Washington, D.C., lobbying group, developed the MacBride Principles. The principles seek to end religious discrimination in employment in Northern Ireland. The

Community for Environmentally Responsible Economies is an environmental group based in Boston that seeks to encourage sound environmental policies at corporations throughout the world.

10. There are a great many more corporate governance issues that institutional investors vote on than those listed in Table 2.1. For example, CalPERS' proxy-voting guidelines list more than 60 different corporate governance issues.

11. A "no action letter" is in response to a request by a company to take "no action" on a proxy proposal because it regards an inappropriate matter or otherwise doesn't meet SEC standards.

12. At a classified board (or staggered board) only a fraction of the directors are elected each year. A typical classified board has board members who hold three-year terms so only one-third of the board is elected in any one year. This poses an all but insurmountable obstacle to a takeover candidate using the tactic of replacing the existing directors with a board of directors favorable to the takeover.

13. Institutional investors typically look beyond raw performance numbers. A company could be in a slump and thus do poorly relative to a benchmark index such as the S&P 500, yet still out perform the other firms in its industry group. Institutions would consider such a firm to be well managed.

14. Lublin, "Oklahoma Court Affirms Holders' Right."

15. "Poison Pill Bylaw Proposals Pending at 14 Companies," *Corporate Governance Highlights* 10, no. 2 (1999) p. 5.

16. As quoted in Lublin, "Oklahoma Court Affirms Holders' Right."

17. California Public Employees' Retirement System, "Domestic Proxy Guidelines," p. 9.

18. Florida State Board of Administration, "Proxy Voting Guidelines," December 1995, mimeo, p. 89.

19. California Public Employees' Retirement System, "Domestic Proxy Guidelines," pp. 25, 32.

Chapter 3. The Rise of Institutional Ownership in the United States

1. Robert A. G. Monks and Nell Minow, *Corporate Governance* (Cambridge, Mass.: Basil Blackwell, 1995). See chapter 6, "Case Studies: Corporations in Crisis," for a detailed discussion of the role du Pont played at General Motors during this period. See also Mark J. Roe, *Strong Managers, Weak Owners: The Political Roots of American Corporate Finance* (Princeton, N.J.: Princeton University Press, 1994), pp. 124–32. For an interesting description of the role J. P. Morgan personally played in resolving the financial crisis of 1907, see Jean Strouse, "The Unknown J. P. Morgan," *New Yorker*, November 23, 1998, p. 13.

2. Adolph A. Berle and Gardiner C. Means, *The Modern Corporation and Private Property*, revised ed. (New York: Macmillan, 1967), p. 8. A "beneficial owner" is the ultimately or "real" owner of an equity. Trust departments, brokers and dealers, or nominees may be the "owner of record," but the beneficial owner is the owner of fact.

3. Alfred D. Chandler, *The Visible Hand: The Managerial Revolution in American Business* (Cambridge, Mass.: Belknap Press of Harvard University Press, 1977), pp. 484–98. While Chandler's thesis is generally accepted, some authors have challenged the extent of the "managerial revolution." For example, Burch concludes that as late as the mid-1960s, about 40 percent of the largest 450 firms were probably under family control and an equal number probably under management control (Philip Burch, Jr., *The Managerial Revolution Reassessed: Family Control in America's Large Corporations* [Lexington, Mass.: Lexington Books, 1972], p. 103). He believes

that family control through direct ownership, directors controlled by families, and family members in management positions has been and continues to be relatively stable. However, the substantial rise in equity ownership by institutional investors in the latter half of the century, particularly pension funds and mutual funds, suggests that the trend has been away from the family control of American corporate enterprises.

4. Stefan Reichelstein, "Agency," in *The New Palgrave Dictionary of Money and Finance,* ed. Peter Newman, Murray Milgate, and John Eatwell (London: Macmillan Press, 1992), p. 23.

5. Ronald Gilson, "Cooperate Governance and Economic Efficiency: When Do Institutions Matter?" (Columbia and Stanford Universities, Schools of Law and Business, 1995), p. 5.

6. Peter Drucker, *The Unseen Revolution: How Pension Fund Socialism Came to America* (New York: Harper and Row, 1979), p. 1. While Drucker saw the coming of workers' socialism, the result might better be characterized as workers' "capitalism."

7. In 1995, business receipts of corporations totaled almost $14 trillion while those of all other non-farm businesses totaled only $1.75 trillion (U.S. Census Bureau, *Statistical Abstract of the United States: 1998* [Washington, D.C.: U.S. Government Printing Office, 1998], table 855, p. 540).

8. Monks and Minow, *Corporate Governance,* p. 11.

9. Morton Keller, "The Making of the Modern Corporation," *Wilson Quarterly* 21, no. 4 (1997): 58–69, p. 58.

10. See "The South Sea Bubble: A Short Sketch of Events" at http://is.dal.ca/~dmcneil/sketch.html, accessed April 11, 1999.

11. Keller, "The Making of the Modern Corporation," p. 60.

12. Berle and Means, *The Modern Corporation,* p. 126.

13. Incorporation in the United States is a state activity. However, the rules of the major stock exchanges and the Securities and Exchange Commission do exert some unifying influences on corporate charters.

14. Berle and Means, *The Modern Corporation,* p. 12.

15. These financial institutions hold shares for many clients or beneficiaries. However, only the institution appears on a corporation's shareholder list as a single owner of record. The statistical problem is to attribute this equity to the beneficial owners — individuals or institutions who actually own the stock. A common technique was to use data on dividend income received as reported in the *Statistics of Income* to link equity ownership to individuals and to ignore that portion of equity that was owned by other than individuals.

16. Edwin Burk Cox, *Trends in the Distribution of Stock Ownership* (Philadelphia: University of Pennsylvania Press, 1963), p. 197.

17. Lewis H. Kimmel, in *Share Ownership in the United States* (Washington, D.C.: Brookings Institution, 1952), attributes this to the speculative boom of the late 1920s. "The principal reason for the marked increase from 1929 to 1932 [in the number of shareholdings] was a change in the manner in which shares were held. In the period of the speculative boom, many people in the market had their securities listed in broker's names for convenience in switching their investments and in getting in or out of the market. By 1932, when speculation was at a low ebb, many buyers had shifted their holdings from brokers' accounts to outright ownership in their own names. In this manner the number of shareholdings could expand enormously, even though there was no change whatever in the total number of investors adjusted for brokers' holdings" (p. 129).

18. Kimmel, in *Share Ownership,* attributes at least some of this decline to the success of the wartime effort to divert individual savings to the government through the use of war bonds as a patriotic alternative for individual wealth holding (p. 131).

19. Quoted in Cox, *Trends in the Distribution of Stock Ownership*, p. 207.

20. The figures in Table 3.1 are for "record shareholdings." A record shareholding represents one owner in the records of one company. Thus, if an individual owned shares in five different companies, he or she would have five "shareholdings."

21. United States Federal Trade Commission, *National Wealth and Income*, 69th Cong., 1st sess. Senate. Doc. 126 (Washington, D.C.: Government Printing Office, 1926).

22. "A typical nominee company is a partnerships consisting of three individuals who were employees of a bank or trust company" (Kimmel, *Share Ownership*, p. 48).

23. Kimmel, in *Share Ownership*, states that "The troublesome problem of nominee holdings has not, to the best of our knowledge, been analyzed in any study of share ownership" (p. 47).

24. Cox, *Changes in the Share*, p. 53.

25. E-mail from H. Garth Dickey, former director of the Indiana Public Employees' Retirement Fund, February 11, 1999. Dickey notes that when he took over as director in November 1995, before the constitution had been changed, "we were 100% domestic fixed income with diversification consisting of ⅓ Government, ⅓ mortgage backed and ⅓ investment grade corporate bonds." Indiana, South Carolina, and West Virginia were the last three states to be prohibited from investing in equities—all have since changed their policies.

26. See Geof P. Stapledon, *Institutional Shareholders and Corporate Governance* (Oxford: Oxford University Press, 1996), for a discussion of the rise of institutional ownership in the U.K. and Australia.

27. Trustees normally fulfill these functions, but depending on the terms of a particular trust, the rights of ownership may be influenced to a greater or lesser degree by the beneficiaries of the trust.

28. In Table 3.3, bank personal trusts and estates are included in the household sector until 1969.

29. See, for instance, John C. Coffee, Jr., "Liquidity versus Control: The Institutional Investor as Corporate Monitor," *Columbia Law Review* 91, no. 6 (1991): 1277–1368, pp. 1329–1336, and Monks and Minow, *Corporate Governance*, p. 121.

30. Equity mutual funds come in basically two types: open end and closed end. An open-end mutual fund sells and redeems shares on demand. When investors buy shares of the fund, the fund has more money to invest in the market. When shares are redeemed, the fund must, in principle, sell equity to honor the redemption. Thus, the number of shares outstanding at any one time is determined by the demand for shares by would-be investors. A closed-end mutual fund issues a fixed number of shares that are tradable like shares of stock, but are not redeemable. Closed-end funds were more important in the past, accounting for about a third of equity owned by mutual funds during the 1950s. By the end of the period covered by Table 3.3, closed-end funds accounted for only 2 percent of the equity owned by mutual funds.

31. However, some mutual funds, notably those created by Michael Price, have adopted a more long-term, activist approach similar to that played by public pension funds. See Andrew E. Serwer, "Mr. Price Is on the Line," *Fortune*, December 9, 1996, p. 70.

32. Benjamin M. Friedman, "Economic Implications of Changing Share Ownership" (National Bureau of Economic Research, Inc., 1995). esp. section III: Institutionalization and Volatility.

33. Named for the section of the Internal Revenue Code authorizing the plans. Mutual-fund assets in IRAs grew by about 15 times between 1985 and 1996 (U.S. Census Bureau, *Statistical Abstract of the United States: 1998* [Washington, D.C.: U.S. Government Printing Office, 1998], table 845, p. 533).

34. According to Carole Gould, "Fund Watch: At the 401(k) Forefront," *New York Times*, December 31, 1995, Section 3, p. 4, "Mutual fund companies have become the dominant force in the 401(k) retirement plan market, accounting for about 37 percent of plan assets."

35. However, the liquidity needs are not eliminated entirely. First, many mutual funds can be held in either taxable or nontaxable accounts so the liquidity needs of a fund may be driven by the motives of taxable investors. Second, many tax-deferred retirement accounts allow investors to switch between a limited number of funds. For some retirement accounts, such as individual IRA accounts, the range of choice is almost unlimited. In these cases, liquidity to redeem shares from investors who wish to change positions is still an important consideration.

36. Interview with Richard Koppes, Chief Counsel, CalPERS, Sacramento, Calif., November 1995, and R. C. Pozen, "Institutional Investors: The Reluctant Activists," *Harvard Business Review* 72, no. 1, January—February (1994): 140–149.

37. The first of the modern pension funds and in many ways the model for subsequent private pension funds was created at General Motors by Charles Wilson in 1950. Its guiding principle was to invest in a diversified portfolio of common stock — and not to be overinvested in the equity of the company creating the pension system (Drucker, pp. 5–11).

38. Mark J. Roe, "The Modern Corporation and Private Pensions," *UCLA Law Review* 41, no. 1 (1993): 75–116, p. 114.

39. "Company Relations with Institutional Investors," (Conference Board, 1994), p. 38.

40. Taft-Hartley pension funds, named for the act authorizing them, are an exception. These multiemployer pension plans are designed to provide "portable" pensions to union members such as carpenters and plumbers whose work takes them from one employer to another in the same industry.

41. However, in 1998 the experts were surprised when assets of defined-benefit plans grew almost 50 percent faster than defined-contribution plans. According to an article in *Pensions & Investments*, defined-benefit plans were more heavily invested in equity and thus benefited from the strong equity markets. They also benefited from superior returns on nonstock holdings, which are not found in traditional 401(k) plans (Vineeta Anand, "Defined Benefit Assets Surge 20.3%," *Pension and Investments*, March 22, 1999, pp. 1, 45).

42. Margaret M. Blair, *Ownership and Control: Rethinking Corporate Governance for the Twenty-First Century* (Washington, D.C.: Brookings Institution, 1995), pp. 161–162.

43. Bernard S. Black, "Agents Watching Agents: The Promise of Institutional Investor Voice," *UCLA Law Review* 39, no. 4 (1992): 811–893, p. 827

44. Among the most important are "Interpretive Bulletin 94-1 (Title 29)" (Washington, D.C.: U.S. Government Printing Office, 1994), 32606–32608, and "Interpretive Bulletin 94-2 (Title 29)," (Washington, D.C.: U.S. Government Publishing Office, 1994), 38860–38864.

45. Teresa Ghilarducci, James Hawley, and Andrew T. Williams, "Labor's Interests and The Evolution of Corporate Governance," *Journal of Law and Society* 24, no. 1 (1997): 56–43.

46. See Stewart J. Schwab and Randal S. Thomas, "Realigning Corporate Governance: Shareholder Activism by Labor Unions," *Michigan Law Review* 96, no. 4 (1998): 1018–1094.

47. Edward Regan, former New York State Comptroller, quoted in Monks and Minow, *Corporate Governance,* p. 134.

48. See also Roberta Romano, "Public Pension Fund Activism in Corporate Governance Reconsidered," *Columbia Law Review* 93, no. 4 (1993): 795–853. Figure 10 in

Romano's article shows the percentage of ETI investment of total assets for the largest 20 public funds as of 1994; the average was 4.6 percent.

49. CalPERS: California Public Employee Retirement System; CalSTRS: California State Teachers Retirement System, New York City Combined Funds: New York City Board of Education Retirement System, New York City Employees' Retirement System, New York City Fire Department Pension Fund, and the New York City Police Department Pension Fund; SWIB: State of Wisconsin Investment Board.

50. However, some recent proposals to invest portions of the Social Security Trust fund may yield an even larger pension fund.

51. Monks and Minow, *Corporate Governance,* pp. 139–142. The current administrator is Barclays PLC, in turn the largest trust fund in the U.S., and one recently involved in informal monitoring of selected underperforming firms.

52. Bernard S. Black, "Shareholder Passivity Reexamined," *Michigan Law Review* 89, no. 3 (1990): 520–608, p. 606.

53. Roberta Romano, "Public Pension Fund Activism."

54. "Share and Share Unalike," *Economist,* August 7, 1999, 18–20.

55. Foreigners own most of the remaining equity; see Table 3.2.

Chapter 4. The Finance Model and Its Implications for Corporate Governance

1. "The principal-agent, or finance, model is the dominant academic view of the corporation" (Kevin Keasey, Steve Thompson, and Mike Wright, *Corporate Governance: Economic, Management, and Financial Issues* [New York: Oxford University Press, 1997], p. 3). The finance model is sometimes referred to as the shareholder primacy model to indicate the central role of shareholders in the corporate governance process.

2. Here the concern is with investor-owned corporations—the IBMs, GEs, and Microsofts of the world. However, the answers to the questions of who owns whom and to what purpose can lead to a number of different organizational forms such as cooperatives, nonprofit corporations, partnerships, etc. These forms of business organization aren't the focus of this study. For an interesting analysis of why particular organizational forms are adopted in particular settings, see H. B. Hansmann, *The Ownership of Enterprise* (Cambridge, Mass.: Harvard University Press, 1996). For a discussion of some of the more important alternative views of the firm, see Chapter 5.

3. For a statement of the finance model, see Oliver Hart, "Corporate Governance: Some Theory and Implications," *Economic Journal* 105 (1995): 678–89, and Oliver Hart, *Firms, Contracts and Financial Structure* (Oxford: Clarendon Press, 1995). See C. K. Prahalad, "Corporate Governance or Corporate Value Added? Rethinking the Primacy of Shareholder Value," in *Studies in International Corporate Finance and Governance Systems,* ed. Donald H. Chew (Oxford: Oxford University Press, 1997), 46–57, for another perspective on what is inside the black box.

4. Michael C. Jensen and William H. Meckling, "Theory of the Firm: Managerial Behavior, Agency Costs and Ownership Structure," *Journal of Financial Economics* 3, no. 4 (1976): 305–60.

5. See Eugene F. Fama, "Agency Problems and the Theory of the Firm," *Journal of Political Economy* 88, no. 21 (1980): 288–307, and Adolph A. Berle and Gardiner C. Means, *The Modern Corporation and Private Property,* revised ed. (New York: Macmillan, 1967). Many others have questioned whether shareholders of large corporations are "owners" in the sense referred to in the text. In particular, see Oliver E. Williamson, *The Economic Institutions of Capitalism* (New York: Free Press, 1985). The famous

Berle and Means quotation about splitting the atom of ownership into its constituent parts questions whether ownership in the traditional sense survives this "nuclear" reaction. Chapter 5 explores this issue in detail as part of a general critique of the finance model.

6. Hansmann, *The Ownership of Enterprise,* p. 11.

7. Adam Smith, *Wealth of Nations,* Cannan ed. (New York: Modern Library, 1937), p. 700. Indeed, the temptation to abscond with other people's money is so great that it is in some sense remarkable that managers return anything at all to their investors. To a large extent, corporate governance is the body of law that seeks to ensure that investors won't be excessively exploited by the natural avarice of managers. Other writers have voiced similar opinions including Alfred Marshall in *Industry and Trade* (London: Macmillan, 1920).

8. For an early discussion of the problem of shirking and managerial perquisites, see Oliver E. Williamson, "Managerial Discretion and Business Behavior," *American Economic Review* 62, no. 5 (1963): 1033–57. For a recent review of the controversy, see *Wall Street Journal,* April 7, 1999, special insert on "Executive Pay."

9. Robert A. G. Monks and Nell Minow, *Corporate Governance* (Cambridge, Mass.: Basil Blackwell, 1995), pp. 412–416. Unfortunately, "A shareholders suit challenging the museum was settled — over the objections of the large institutional investors — because the court found it likely that the contribution would be protected by the business judgment rule" (p. 416). For a popular treatment of Armand Hammer and his museum see Edward Jay Epstein, "The Last Days of Armand Hammer," *New Yorker,* September 23, 1996, p. 36.

10. Stock options are not a panacea for solving the principal-agent problem. In fact, some observers view the abuse of stock options as a severe form of managerial malfeasance: "Never before in history has there been a greater transfer of wealth from one class in a society to another [shareholders to managers] without a revolution" (Robert Monks' remarks to the International Corporate Governance Network annual conference, San Francisco, July 1998).

11. Fundamental to modern financial analysis is the proposition that in an efficient financial market greater risk is rewarded with greater return. By coupling this observation with diversification, it is possible to construct a portfolio of risky assets having less risk overall than any of its components taken individually and, therefore, delivering a higher risk-adjusted return. Managers, because they have both their human capital and often much of their financial capital invested in only one asset — the firm they work for — are denied many of the risk-reducing possibilities of a diversified portfolio.

12. Y. Amihud and B. Lev, "Risk Reduction as a Managerial Motive for Conglomerate Mergers," *Bell Journal of Economics* 12, no. 2 (1981): 605–17.

13. James P. Hawley and Andrew T. Williams, "The Westinghouse Corporation and Institutional Investor Activism" (paper presented at the International Association for Business and Society, Vienna, June 26–29, 1995), p. 10. In early 1993, the board of directors backed by major institutional shareholders forced the then CEO of Westinghouse from office; one of the primary issues was excessive diversification. By 1997, Westinghouse had almost completely refocused its business on broadcasting, the most successful of its 135 divisions. By then it had sold most of its nonbroadcasting divisions, purchased CBS, and changed its name to the CBS Corporation. The remaining engineering business, the traditional core of the company along with the Westinghouse name, was sold to a joint venture headed by the Morrison Knudsen Corporation.

14. A. Shleifer and R. Vishny, "Management Entrenchment: The Case of Manager-Specific Investments," *Journal of Financial Economics* 25, no. 1 (1989): 123–39.

15. Margaret M. Blair, *Ownership and Control: Rethinking Corporate Governance for the*

Twenty-First Century (Washington, D.C.: Brookings Institution, 1995), p. 95. Lazonick also argues that the separation of ownership from control is desirable since it allows managers to achieve "organizational integration" and to use retained earnings to build dynamic, innovative enterprises free from the meddling demands of owners (William Lazonick, "The Anglo-Saxon Corporate System," in *The Corporate Triangle: The Structure and Performance of Corporate Systems in a Global Economy*, ed. P. H. Admiraal [Malden, Mass.: Blackwell, 1997], 1–35).

16. Before the modern corporate form with its limited liability became prevalent, the growth of many enterprises was constrained by the ability to find family members with the necessary skills and inclination to staff any increase in plants, offices, or shops. In a world of unlimited personal liability, it was one thing to have your son place your entire wealth at risk; it was an entirely different matter to entrust your entire wealth to a stranger — particularly if the stranger were located in another city or on another continent. Today similar restraints hamper some Asian business enterprises where opportunities must be forgone because there isn't another son to manage an expansion. Nevertheless, fictive business-capable "sons" are often de facto adopted into families to compensate. See Richard Whitley, *Business Systems in East Asia* (Thousands Oaks, Calif.: Sage, 1995), p. 197.

17. See Peter Temin, "The Stability of the American Business Elite," *Industrial and Corporate Change* 8, no. 2 (1999): 189–209. Hewlett-Packard set a precedent when it was the first Fortune 500 company to appoint a woman as its CEO (John Markoff, "Hewlett-Packard Picks Rising Star at Lucent as Its Chief Executive," *New York Times*, July 20, 1999, p. C1).

18. For a seminal critique of managing by the numbers, see Robert H. Hayes and William J. Abernathy, "Managing Our Way to Economic Decline," *Harvard Business Review* 58, July–August (1980): 67–77.

19. Since managerial compensation is highly correlated with revenue, one of the easiest ways for a CEO to grow revenue — and to give himself a raise — is to acquire other companies. See Murray Weidenbaum and Steven Vogt, "Takeovers and Stockholders," *California Management Review* 29, no. 4 (1987): 157–168, and S. R. Reid, *Mergers, Managers, and the Economy* (New York: McGraw-Hill, 1968).

20. Michael C. Jensen, "Takeovers: Their Causes and Consequences," *Journal of Economic Perspectives* 2, no. 1 (1998): 43–64.

21. The concept of the market for corporate control was first used by H. G. Manne, "Mergers and the Market for Corporate Control," *Journal of Political Economy* 73 (1965): 110–120.

22. Alfred Rappaport, "The Staying Power of the Public Corporation," *Harvard Business Review* 68, no. 1 (1990): 96–104, and Michael C. Jensen, "Eclipse of the Public Corporation," *Harvard Business Review* 67, no. 5 (1989): 61–74. See also the Organization for Economic Cooperation and Development, *OECD Economic Surveys: United States* (Paris: OECD, 1996), chapter iv, "U.S. Corporate Governance: The Market as Monitor."

23. The efficient market hypothesis comes in several forms. The semistrong form of the efficient market hypothesis says that equity prices accurately reflect the economic value of all public knowledge about a company. The strong form says that the prices reflect all information, private as well as public, and the weak form says that an equity's current price reflects all of the information contained in past price movements of that equity (Stephen A. Ross, Randolph W. Westerfield, and Jeffrey F. Jaffe, "From Corporate Finance," in *Foundations of Corporate Law*, ed. Roberta Romano, Interdisciplinary Readers in Law [New York: Oxford University Press, 1993], 45–62).

24. In theory, only a small premium of private over public value is needed to call forth the disciplining actions of the market for corporate control. In practice, a substantially larger premium is required to cover the expenses represented by the

inherent uncertainty in determining private values, the expense (sometimes substantial) of attempting a takeover, and the possibility that the attempt many fail. In
fact, as the studies cited later in the text note, it was usually necessary to pay a
substantial premium over the current market price to actually attract enough shareholders to close the transaction.

25. For an enthusiastic statement of this position from one of the major proponents of the finance model, see Jensen, "Eclipse of the Public Corporation."

26. Michael C. Jensen and Richard S. Ruback, "The Market for Corporate Control:
The Scientific Evidence," *Journal of Financial Economics* 11, no. 1–4 (1983): 5–50.

27. Gregg A. Jarrell, James A. Brickley, and Jeffrey M. Netter, "The Market for
Corporate Control: The Empirical Evidence Since 1980," *Journal of Economic Perspectives* 2, no. 1 (1988): 49–67, p. 53.

28. Some authors suggest that the market for managers and the product market
can also play a governance role. The market for managers presumably rewards
efficient managers and punishes the slackers. The product market is the ultimate
mechanism for rewarding efficient companies and punishing inefficient ones. However, the market for managers is least effective at disciplining shirking managers who
don't wish to change jobs and product market success or failure may take a long time
to reach its logical conclusion. See George Bittlingmayer, "The Market for Corporate
Control (Including Takeovers)," in *Encyclopedia of Law and Economics,* ed. Boudewijn
Bouckaert and Gerrit De Geese (Northampton, Mass.: E. Elgar, 1999).

29. Blair, *Ownership and Control,* p. 107.

30. S. J. Grossman and O. D. Hart, "Takeover Bids, The Free Rider Problem and
the Theory of the Firm," *Bell Journal of Economics* 11, no. 1 (1980): 42–64.

31. A "prisoner's dilemma" refers to a situation where agreement would be better
for the parties than disagreement, but where the nature of the situation makes
agreement difficult or impossible to achieve.

32. Pauline O'Sullivan, "Governance by Exit: An Analysis of the Market for Corpo-
rate Control," in *Corporate Governance: Economic, Management, and Financial Issues,* ed.
Kevin Keasey, Steve Thompson, and Mike Wright (New York: Oxford University
Press, 1997), 122–146, p. 123.

33. A. Shleifer and R. Vishny, "Equilibrium Short Horizons of Investors and
Firms," *American Economic Review* 80, no. 2 (May 1990): 148–53.

34. Andrei Shleifer and Lawrence H. Summers, "Breach of Trust in Hostile Takeovers," in *Corporate Takeovers: Causes and Consequences,* ed. Alan J. Auerbach (Chicago:
National Bureau of Economic Research, 1988), 33–56. However, in a comment on
this essay published in the same volume, Oliver Williamson argues that the reduction
in wages represented the end of "rent sharing" in a regulated industry and that after
deregulation a similar reduction would have occurred in any case because of market
forces in the more competitive industry.

35. Ross, Westerfield, and Jaffe, "From Corporate Finance," p. 58.

36. In an article in the *Financial Times,* David Hale, chief global economist for
Zurich Financial Services, Chicago, asserted that the market value of America On-
Line was greater than all of the transportation companies — rail, truck, and air — in
the country. Perhaps the market is efficiently valuing the transportation industry
and this one company, even though the company has yet to show positive earnings
(David Hale, "Personal View: U.S. Cycle Theory," *The Financial Times,* February 17,
1999, p. 20). See also Charles P. Kindleberger, *Manias, Panics, and Crashes: A History of
Financial Crises,* revised ed. (New York: Basic Books, 1989).

37. *Institutional Investment Report* (New York: Conference Board, 1998), table 6,
p. 18.

38. Poison pills are various finance measures that increase the cost of the takeover
and that automatically go into effect when a company receives an unwanted takeover

bid. Classified boards elect a fraction of their members every year rather than the entire board. This makes it harder for a bidder to mount a proxy campaign to replace an existing board with one favorable to the bidder. Dual-class stock issues give more votes per share to one class of stockholders—expected to be favorable to management—while giving fewer votes to other classes of stockholders.

39. In 1982, in *Edgar v. MITE Corp.* the Supreme Court effectively invalidated the previous (first-generation) antitakeover statutes. After 1982, states passed second-generation antitakeover statutes that were generally accepted by the courts, particularly after the 1987 case *CTS v. Dynamics Corp of America,* in which the court upheld an Indiana takeover law (Jonathan M. Karpoff and Paul H. Malatesta, "The Wealth Effects of Second-Generation State Takeover Legislation," *Journal of Financial Economics* 25, no. 2 [1989]: 291–322).

40. Rulings from the Delaware chancellery court are particularly important because so many companies are incorporated in that state. See Charles M. Elson, "Courts and Boards: The Top 10 Cases," *Directors & Boards* 22, no. 1 (1997): 26–36. Elson cites the following three Delaware cases as particularly strengthening management (and boards) ability to prevent unwanted takeovers: *Unocal Corp. v. Mesa Petroleum Co.,* 493 A. ed. 946 (Del. 1985), *Moran v. Household International Inc.,* 500 A.2d 1346 (Del. 1985), and *Revlon Inc. v. MacAndrews & Forbes Holding Inc.,* 506 A.2d 173 (Del. 1985).

41. Monks and Minow, *Corporate Governance,* p. 215.

42. See Appendix 3-1 of Blair, *Ownership and Control,* pp. 116–121, for a list of proposed reforms.

Chapter 5. Critiques of the Financial Model

1. Even in an article lamenting layoffs at AT&T, Secretary of Labor Robert Reich recognizes that "any chief executive who hesitates before doing everything possible to maximize returns to shareholders risks trouble" (Reich, "How to Avoid These Layoffs?" *New York Times,* January 4, 1995, p. A13).

2. See Chapter 3.

3. Quoted in Mansel G. Blackford and K. Austin Kerr, *Business Enterprise in American History,* 3rd ed. (Boston: Houghton Mifflin, 1994), p. 252.

4. T. Donaldson and L. E. Preston, "The Stakeholder Theory of the Corporation: Concepts, Evidence and Implications," *Academy of Management Review* 20, no. 1 (1995): 65–91, as quoted in Shann Turnbull, "Corporate Governance: Its Scope, Concerns and Theories," *Corporate Governance* 5, no. 4 October (1997): 180–205. See also John R. Boatright, "Staking Claims: The Role of Stakeholders in the Contractual Theory of the Firm" (ASSA Meetings, Chicago, Ill.: 1998), for an interesting critique of contractian theory.

5. Margaret M. Blair, *Ownership and Control: Rethinking Corporate Governance for the Twenty-First Century* (Washington, D.C.: Brookings Institution, 1995), p. 219; Boatright, "Staking Claims," p. 2, makes similar arguments, suggesting that there is little agreement among the proponents of stakeholder theory about the terms and conditions of what or who is a legitimate stakeholder.

6. Donaldson and Preston, "The Stakeholder Theory," pp. 75–77.

7. Many such claims and an economic analysis behind them is found in Michael Meeropol, *Surrender: How the Clinton Administration Completed the Reagan Revolution* (Ann Arbor: University of Michigan Press, 1998).

8. George David Smith and Davis Dyer, "The Rise and Transformation of the American Corporation," in *The American Corporation Today,* ed. Carl Kaysen (New York: Oxford University Press, 1996), 28–73, p. 57.

9. For a textbook discussion, see Archie B. Carroll, *Business and Society* (Cincinnati, Oh.: South-Western, 1989).

10. Cited in Blair, *Ownership and Control,* p. 205; pp. 3, 335 in Adolph A. Berle and Gardiner C. Means, *The Modern Corporation and Private Property* (New York: Macmillan, 1932).

11. See Mark J. Roe, "The Corporation and the Law, 1959–1994," in Kaysen, *The American Corporation Today,* p. 103.

12. William M. Evan and R. Edward Freeman, "A Stakeholder Theory of the Modern Corporation: Kantian Capitalism," in *Ethical Issues in Business,* ed. Thomas Donaldson and Patricia H. Wehan (Upper Saddle River, N.J.: Prentice Hall, 1993), 166–171, pp. 97–106.

13. Kevin Keasey, Steve Thompson, and Mike Wright, "Introduction: The Corporate Governance Problem — Competing Diagnoses and Solutions," in *Corporate Governance: Economic, Management, and Financial Issues,* ed. Kevin Keasey, Steve Thompson, and Mike Wright (New York: Oxford University Press, 1997), p. 9.

14. Boatright, "Staking Claims," p. 2.

15. Keasey, et al., *Corporate Governance,* pp. 26–28. The argument is a form of what in other venues is called "sweat equity."

16. Cited in Blair, *Ownership and Control,* p. 322. This view is also shared by Ronald Gilson, "Cooperate Governance and Economic Efficiency: When Do Institutions Matter?" (Columbia and Stanford Universities, Schools of Law and Business, 1995).

17. It is not clear in Blair's work why firm specific human-capital investments (often made by both employee and employer jointly in various proportions) itself is a form of residual risk, although if linked to firm profitability in terms of bonus or incentive wages, then the status of residual risktaker is obvious.

18. This position has been criticized on the basis that many skills are industry or process specific, not just firm specific. Such a view would not necessarily draw different conclusions regarding the importance of employee stakeholding claims. Often this is referred to as "match"-specific human capital, which certainly would include a specific firm, but would also include any industry where skills and knowledge "match."

19. As the following quotation shows, Berle and Means were acutely aware of this problem. "If we are to assume that the desire for *personal profit* is the prime force motivating control, we must conclude that the interests of control are different from and often radically opposed to those of ownership; that the owners most emphatically will not be served by a profit-seeking controlling group. In the operation of the corporation, the controlling group even if they own a large block of stock, can serve their own pockets better by profiting at the expense of the company than by making profits for it." Exploitation of shareholders can come from other shareholders as well as from managers (Adolph A. Berle and Gardiner C. Means, *The Modern Corporation and Private Property,* revised ed. [New York: Macmillan, 1967], p. 114).

20. Monks and Minow, *Corporate Governance,* pp. 268–70.

21. Margaret M. Blair and Lynn A. Stout, "A Team Production Theory of Corporate Law," (unpublished, 1998), p. 23.

22. Cited in Blair, *Ownership and Control,* p. 276.

23. Boatright, "Staking Claims," p. 4.

24. Berle and Means, *The Modern Corporation,* pp. 3, 355, cited by Boatright, "Staking Claims," p. 7.

25. Oliver E. Williamson, *The Economic Institutions of Capitalism* (New York: Free Press, 1985), pp. 3–7.

26. Oliver Williamson, "Corporate Finance and Corporate Governance, Economic Analysis and Policy" (Berkeley: University of California, December 1987), p. 16.

27. Williamson, *The Economic Institutions of Capitalism,* p. 3. Transaction costs are defined as the "costs of running the economic system, parallel with the idea of friction in physics" (p. 19).

28. Oliver E. Williamson and Janet Bercovitz, "The Modern Corporation as an Efficiency Instrument: The Comparative Contracting Perspective," in *The American Corporation Today,* ed. Carl Kaysen (New York: Oxford University Press, 1996), 327–359, p. 331.

29. Williamson, *The Economic Institutions of Capitalism.* See chapters on vertical integration and "credible commitments" for examples.

30. Opportunism may occur, for example, when an automobile company requires a supplier to make a part using an expensive die that is only valuable in manufacturing that particular part. The supplier will be reluctant to invest in the die because it fears that the automobile company will exploit it once it has made the investment. The solution is to have the automobile company buy the die for the supplier to use.

31. Herbert Simon, *Administrative Behavior,* 2nd ed. (New York: MacMillan, 1957), p. xxiv, as quoted in Williamson and Bercovitz, "The Modern Corporation." See also Williamson, *The Economic Institutions of Capitalism,* pp. xii–xiii; 30.

32. Williamson, *The Economic Institutions of Capitalism,* pp. 32, 45.

33. Armen A. Alchian, "Uncertainty, Evolution, and Economic Theory," in *Industrial Organization,* ed. Oliver E. Williamson (Brookfield, Vt.: E. Elgar, 1990), 23–33, p. 23 (emphasis in original).

34. Williamson and Bercovitz, "The Modern Corporation," pp. 327, 330.

35. Williamson, *The Economic Institutions of Capitalism,* p. xii.

36. Williamson and Bercovitz, "The Modern Corporation," p. 333.

37. Williamson, *The Economic Institutions of Capitalism,* p. 320

38. Williamson and Bercovitz, "The Modern Corporation," pp. 336–37; 344; 347.

39. Williamson, *The Economic Institutions of Capitalism,* p. 298. In this model, he suggests that "Most constituencies are better advised to perfect their relation to the firm at the contracting interface at which firm and constituencies stake their main bargain." He opposes the variety of proposals to place a plurality of interest groups on the board (p. 300).

40. Williamson, "Corporate Finance," p. 2.

41. The Coase problem is stated in Ronald H. Coase's seminal article, "The Nature of the Firm," *Economica N. S.* 4 (1937): 386–405.

42. Williamson, "Corporate Finance," p. 5.

Chapter 6. Does Ownership Matter?

1. Robert A. G. Monks and Nell Minow, *Corporate Governance* (Cambridge, Mass.: Basil Blackwell, 1995), p. 1. The authors are also very aware of the macro view of corporate governance presented below.

2. Kevin Keasey and Mike Wright, "Issues in Corporate Accountability and Governance," *Accounting and Business Research* 23, no. 91a (1993): 291–303, p. 2.

3. *United States 1996, OECD Economic Surveys* (Paris: Organization for Economic Co-operation and Development, 1996).

4. For a discussion of this and other reasons for the concern with corporate governance in the 1980s, see Margaret M. Blair, *Ownership and Control: Rethinking Corporate Governance for the Twenty-First Century* (Washington, D.C.: Brookings Institution, 1995), pp. 6–11.

5. "Why Corporate Governance," Sacramento, Calif., November 7, 1989, as quoted in George A. Steiner and John F. Steiner, *Business, Government, and Society,* 7th ed. (New York: Random House, 1994), p. 641.

6. "Global Governance Principles," agenda item 19, CalPERS Investment Committee, December 16, 1996.

7. It is recognized that both industry- and economy-wide trends that are beyond the control of even the most talented manager also affect economic performance. But it is central to the hypothesis that, ceteris paribus, better-managed firms should be more profitable than poorly managed ones.

8. Blair, *Ownership and Control,* pp. 6–11.

9. For a discussion of the history and possible explanations for the market for corporate control, see George Bittlingmayer, "The Market for Corporate Control (Including Takeovers)," in *Encyclopedia of Law and Economics,* ed. Boudewijn Bouckaert and Gerrit De Geese (Northampton, Mass.: E. Elgar, 1999).

10. For example, Rappaport views the market for corporate control as one of the most effective governance mechanisms available to shareholders (Alfred Rappaport, "The Staying Power of the Public Corporation," *Harvard Business Review* 68, no. 1 [1990]: 96–104).

11. Pauline O'Sullivan, "Governance by Exit: An Analysis of the Market for Corporate Control," in *Corporate Governance: Economic, Management, and Financial Issues,* ed. Kevin Keasey, Steve Thompson, and Mike Wright (New York: Oxford University Press, 1997), 122–146, p. 122.

12. However, hostile takeovers are not dead, especially in Europe after the emergence of European Union currency, which began in January 1999. On February 18, 1999, Olivetti launched a hostile takeover of Telecom Italy, the recently privatized telephone company in Italy (Paul Betts and James Blitz, "Olivetti's 36 Billion Pound Bid Spurned by Italian Rival," *Financial Times,* February 22, 1999, p. 1).

13. P. Asquith, "Merger Bids, Uncertainty and Shareholder Returns," *Journal of Financial Economics* 11, no. 1–4 (1983): 51–83.

14. Julian R. Franks and Colin Mayer, "Hostile Takeovers and the Correction of Managerial Failure," *Journal of Financial Economics* 40, no. 1 (1996): 163–81.

15. Randal Morck, Andrei Shleifer, and Robert W. Vishny, "Characteristics of Targets of Hostile and Friendly Takeovers," in *Corporate Takeovers: Causes and Consequences,* ed. Alan J. Auerbach (Chicago: National Bureau of Economic Research, 1988), pp. 101–136.

16. Gregg A. Jarrell, James A. Brickley, and Jeffry M. Netter, "The Market for Corporate Control: The Empirical Evidence Since 1980," *Journal of Economic Perspectives* 2, no. 1 (1988): 49–67, p. 51.

17. R. J. Limmack, "Corporate Mergers and Shareholder Wealth Effects 1997–1986," *Accounting and Business Research* 21, no. 83 (1991): 239–51.

18. W. H. Mikkelson and R. S. Ruback, "An Empirical Analysis of the Interfirm Equity Investment Process," *Journal of Financial Economics* 14, no. 4 (1985): 523–53.

19. C. G. Holderness and D. P. Sheehan, "Raiders or Saviors? The Evidence of Six Controversial Investors," *Journal of Financial Economics* 14, (December 1985): 555–79.

20. In an event study, the researcher identifies an event (e.g., announcement of a takeover bid) and then compares the market return on the stock to a benchmark such as the S&P 500. If there is a statistically significant difference in return before and after the event, the difference is attributed to the event and represents a measure of the financial market's judgement about the event. Several difficulties with event studies are evident. First, it is often difficult to identify the "event" precisely and misspecification of the event can have a substantial impact on results. Second, it is often difficult to control for other factors that might influence relative performance. This becomes particularly important when trying to identify events that affect stock value for more than a few days. Finally, identical events may result in opposite market reactions. For example, adoption of an antitakeover measure may

depress stock price because it is seen as making a takeover less likely. Alternatively, it may increase stock price if it is viewed as a signal management thinks takeover activity is about to begin and the device is part of a program to get the highest price possible for the company. Despite these shortcomings, event studies are widely used to study the kind of phenomenon discussed here.

21. Michael C. Jensen and Richard S. Ruback, "The Market for Corporate Control: The Scientific Evidence," *Journal of Financial Economics* 11, no. 1–4 (1983): 5–50, p. 16.

22. Cited in Jarrell, Brickley, and Netter, "The Market for Corporate Control," p. 53. The explanation for this secular decline is usually given as either increased competition among bidders or an increased ability to bargain for a larger share of the premium by target firms on behalf of their shareholders.

23. Eugene P. H. Furtado and Vijay Karan, "Causes, Consequences and the Shareholder Wealth Effects of Management Turnover: A Review of the Empirical Evidence," *Financial Management* 19, no. 2 (1990): 60–75.

24. D. J. Ravenscraft and E. M. Scherer, *Mergers, Sell-Offs and Economic Efficiency* (Washington, D.C.: Brookings Institution, 1987).

25. E. Herman and L. Lowenstein, "The Efficiency Effects of Hostile Takeovers," in *Knights, Raiders and Targets: The Impact of Hostile Takeovers*, ed. John C. Coffee Jr., Louis Lowenstein, and Susan Rose Ackerman (Oxford: Oxford University Press, 1988), and A. D. Cosh, K. Lee, and A. Singh, "Institutional Investment, Mergers and the Market for Corporate Control," *International Journal of Industrial Organizations* 7, no. 1 (1989): 73–100.

26. Sanjai Bhagat, Andrei Shleifer, and Robert W. Vishny, "Hostile Takeovers in the 1980s: The Return to Corporate Specialization," in *Brookings Papers on Economic Activity: Microeconomics*, ed. Martin Neil Baily and Clifford Winston (Washington, D.C.: Brookings Institution, 1990), 1–84, p. 2.

27. P. M. Healy, K. G. Palepu, and R. S. Ruback, "Does Corporate Performance Improve After Mergers," *Journal of Financial Economics* 31, no. 2 (1992): 135–75, and Sherry L. Jarrell, "Do Takeovers Generate Value? Evidence on the Capital Market's Ability to Assess Takeovers" (Ph.D. dissertation, University of Chicago, 1991), cited in Roberta Romano, ed., *Foundations of Corporate Law* (New York: Oxford University Press, 1993), p. 265.

28. Romano, *Foundations of Corporate Law*, p. 264.

29. Pauline O'Sullivan, "Governance by Exit," p. 135.

30. The finance literature considers the cost and benefits of the market for corporate control to shareholders and employees. It generally doesn't consider the cost that changes in control might have to individuals or communities that may have made investments in schools and other public services or that businesses may have made based on the continued presence of a plant in a community. These concerns were a part of the popular culture — see the movie *Other People's Money*, the novel *Bonfire of the Vanities*, or the investigative book *Barbarians at the Gate*. Popular concerns may have played an important political role in the antitakeover legislation that many states enacted in response to hostile takeovers.

31. Andrei Shleifer and Lawrence H. Summers, "Breach of Trust in Hostile Takeovers," in *Corporate Takeovers: Causes and Consequences*, ed. Alan J. Auerbach (Chicago: National Bureau of Economic Research, 1988), 33–56.

32. Bhagat, Shleifer, and Vishny, "Hostile Takeovers," p. 2.

33. Romano, *Foundations of Corporate Law*, p. 266.

34. Roberta Romano, "A Guide to Takeovers: Theory, Evidence and Regulation," *Yale Journal on Regulation* 9, no. 1 (1992): 119–180, p. 142.

35. Steven Kaplan, "Management Buyouts: Evidence on Taxes as a Source of Value," *Journal of Finance* 44, no. 3 (1989): 611–32.

36. Bhagat, Shleifer, and Vishny, "Hostile Takeovers," p. 2 (emphasis in original).

37. Michael Jensen, Steven Kaplan, and Laura Stiglin, "The Effects of LBOs on Tax Revenues," *Tax Notes* 42, no. 6 (1989): 727–33.

38. Steven N. Kaplan, "The Evolution of U.S. Corporate Governance: We Are All Henry Kravis Now" (paper presented at the Power and Influence of Pension and Mutual Funds, New York University, Stern School of Business, February 21, 1997).

39. Romano, *Foundations of Corporate Law,* p. 266.

40. California Public Employee' Retirement System, *Corporate Governance Core Principles & Guidelines*, April 13, 1998, p. 4, mimeo.

41. Adam Bryant, "CalPERS Draws a Blueprint for its Concept of an Ideal Board," *New York Times,* June 17, 1997, p. D1.

42. "Report of the NACD Blue Ribbon Commission on Director Compensation," (Washington, D.C.: National Association of Corporate Directors, 1995), and "Statement on Corporate Governance" (New York: The Business Roundtable, 1997).

43. "Draft OECD Principles of Corporate Governance: Ad Hoc Task Force on Corporate Governance," Fiscal and Enterprise Affairs Directorate for Financial Markets (Paris: Organization for Economic Co-operation and Development, 1999), p. 10.

44. "1995 Board Index: Board Trends and Practices at Major American Corporations," (SpencerStuart, 1995), p. 14.

45. "1996 Board Index: Board Trends and Practices at Major American Corporations," (SpencerStuart, 1996).

46. Some researchers differentiate between inside directors (current officers of the company), affiliated outside directors (former officers and other persons with a commercial relationship to the firm), and independent directors (those who don't fall into either of the other two classes).

47. Report of the NACD, p. 10.

48. California Public Employees' Retirement System, *Corporate Governance Core Principles and Guidelines*, Appendix B-1, "Definition of Independent Director," April 13, 1998, mimeo.

49. Sanjai Bhagat and Bernard Black, "The Relationship Between Board Composition and Firm Performance," in *Comparative Corporate Governance: The State of the Art and Emerging Research*, ed. Klaus Hopt, et al. (Oxford: Clarendon Press, 1998), 281–306, p. 282.

50. The National Association of Corporate Directors urges that boards set a substantial target for stock ownership by each director (Report of the NACD, pp. 9–15).

51. Kathleen Day, "Frank Carlucci and the Corporate Whirl," *Washington Post*, February 7, 1993, p. H1.

52. Judith H. Dobrzynski, "When Directors Play Musical Chairs," *New York Times*, November 17, 1996, Section 3, p. 9.

53. Bhagat and Black, "The Relationship Between Board Composition and Firm Performance," p. 291.

54. Corporate law assigns the decisions of the management of the company to the hired managers. Within this area, management has wide latitude for its actions. It assigns to the board of directors (as representatives of the shareholders) the monitoring and evaluation of management and grants to the board the ability to replace management should results be unsatisfactory.

55. For a more extensive discussion of the proxy process and the proxy guidelines of institutional investors, see Chapter 2.

56. Jonathan M. Karpoff, Paul M. Malatesta, and Ralph A. Walkling, "Corporate Governance and Shareholder Initiatives: Empirical Evidence," *Journal of Financial Economics* 42, no. 3 (1996): 365–95.

57. See Table 2.2 in Chapter 2.

58. Karpoff, Malatesta, and Walkling, "Corporate Governance," pp. 372–73. This result holds for the three different events-dates the authors tested: initial press announcement, proxy mailing, or meeting date.

59. Willard T. Carleton, James M. Nelson, and Michael S. Weisbach, "The Influence of Institutions on Corporate Governance through Private Negotiations: Evidence from TIAA-CREF," *Journal of Finance* 53, no. 4 (1998): 1335–62.

60. Speech to "Relational Investing" conference sponsored by The Institutional Investor Project, Center for Law and Economic Studies, Columbia University School of Law, May 6–7, 1993, New York, New York.

61. Stephen L. Nesbitt, "Long-term Rewards From Shareholder Activism: A Study of the 'CalPERS' Effect," *Continental Bank Journal of Applied Corporate Finance* 6, Spring (1994): 75–80. For a review of the CalPERS 1992 target firms and the criteria used to select them, see James P. Hawley, Andrew T. Williams, and John U. Miller, "Getting the Herd to Run: Shareholder Activism at the California Public Employees' Retirement System (CalPERS)," *Business and the Contemporary World* 6, no. 4 (1994): 26–48.

62. Stephen L. Nesbitt, "The 'CalPERS Effect' on Target Company Share Prices," September 8, 1996. Presented at a conference on The Power and Influence of Pension and Mutual Funds, February 21, 1997, Stern School of Business, New York University.

63. Claire E. Crutchley, Carl D. Hudson, and Marlin R. H. Jensen, "Shareholder Wealth Effects of CalPERS' Activism," *Financial Services Review* 7, no. 1 (1998): 1–10. The authors actually divided CalPERS targeting program into three periods: 1987–1990, 1990–1994, and 1994–1998. The first period focused on traditional corporate governance topics. The second period used many of the tools of the first, but targeted firms because they were underperformers. In the third period, underperformers were still targeted, but the engagement technique switched from a more confrontational one to a "quiet diplomacy" approach in which CalPERS tried to negotiate directly with management out of the glare of the press. The text compares the first and third periods.

64. Michael P. Smith, "Shareholder Activism by Institutional Investors: Evidence from CalPERS," *Journal of Finance* 51, no. 1, March (1996): 227–52.

65. John D. Wagster and Andrew K. Prevost, "Wealth Effects of the CalPERS' 'Hit List' to SEC Changes in the Proxy Rules" (Wayne State University: School of Business Administration, 1996).

66. In addition to liberalizing the communication provisions of Rule 14a-21a, the SEC also placed a positive requirement on companies to better explain and justify executive compensation in their annual reports (Wagster and Prevost, "Wealth Effects," p. 7). For a discussion of the 1992 reforms, the details of this liberalization are discussed in more detail in Chapter 8.

67. Examples include the Teachers Insurance and Annuity Association-College Retirement Equities Fund (TIAA-CREF), State of Wisconsin Investment Board (SWIB), and the New York City Combined Funds. See particularly the study of informal communications between TIAA-CREF and portfolio companies by Carleton, Nelson, and Weisbach, "The Influence of Institutions on Corporate Governance through Private Negotiations."

68. Presumably Pickens felt that support from small shareholders by broadening the support for good corporate governance, including the opposition to antitakeover measures, might help his own program of corporate acquisitions.

69. Deon Strickland, Kenneth W. Wiles, and Marc Zenner, "A Requiem for the USA: Is Small Shareholder Monitoring Effective," *Journal of Financial Economics*, 40, no. 2 (1996): 319–38.

70. Note the free-rider problem here. Total wealth generated greatly exceeded the

cost of the program to USA, but the real question is how much of the wealth gain accrued to USA members who bore the cost. See, for example, CalPERS' analysis of this for their activities in which they conclude that the gains in appreciation in their own portfolio outweigh the expense (CalPERS Legal Office, "Memo to Members of the Investment Committee," August 14, 1995). The free-rider problem is compounded in this situation. CalPERS and others claim gains resulting in both individual firms that have been targeted and in market-wide improvement by "keeping the herd running."

71. The Council of Institutional Investors is an association of public pension funds, Taft-Hartley funds and, recently, some private pension funds. Through the executive director, Sara Teslick, the council has been very active in promoting institutional investor activism and corporate governance reform. The focus list of poorly performing funds serves as a coordinating device for investor activism. It is particularly useful to those institutions that would like to be active, but lack the resources to identify appropriate targets.

72. Tim C. Opler and Jonathan Sokobin, "Does Coordinated Institutional Activism Work? An Analysis of the Activities of the Council of Institutional Investors" (Ohio State University: Fisher College of Business, 1997), pp. 9, 14.

73. Sunil Wahal, "Pension Fund Activism and Firm Performance," *Journal of Financial and Quantitative Analysis* 31, no. 1 (1996): 1–23. The public pension funds are from California, Colorado, New York, Pennsylvania, Wisconsin, and Florida. The sample also includes TIAA-CREF.

74. This group is largely made up of underperforming firms and reflects a marked shift in the tactics institutional investors used to select target firms. In 1990 and before, virtually all of the firms were subject to proxy proposals. After 1990, some institutions began to target firms for performance reasons only and did not propose proxies for those firms. Of the 50 targets (some firms may have been targeted by more than one institution or more than once during the period by the same institution), 48 were after 1990.

75. Monks and Minow, *Corporate Governance*, p. 153. The six companies were General Motors, American Express, Westinghouse, IBM, Eastman Kodak, and Borden Inc.

76. Joseph A. Grundfest, "Just Vote No: A Minimalist Strategy for Dealing with Barbarians Inside the Gates," *Stanford Law Review* 45, no. 4 (1993): 857–973.

77. In the "April coup" referred to in the quotation, GM board member John Smale replaced CEO Robert Stempel as chairman of the board's executive committee. At that time, the board also demoted two of Stempel's lieutenants and made other changes in senior management. In late October, rumors of Stempel's termination began to circulate and on November 2 he was replaced.

78. Jonathan M. Karpoff, "The Impact of Shareholder Activism on Target Companies: A Survey of Empirical Findings," (University of Washington: School of Business, 1998).

79. Bernard S. Black, "Shareholder Activism and Corporate Governance in the United States," in *The New Palgrave Dictionary of Economics and the Law*, ed. Peter Newman (New York: Macmillan Stockton Press, 1998), 459–65, p. 459.

80. Leslie Scism, "Teachers' Pension Plan to give Firms Tough Exams," *Wall Street Journal*, October 6, 1993, p. C1. Also see Hawley and Williams, "Getting the Herd to Run."

81. However, some observers think that institutional investors might be moving back toward a greater use of proxy proposals after a number of years of more "quiet" activism. It may be that their influence with portfolio companies is enhanced by the glare (or potential glare) of press coverage (Personal communication, Kenneth Birch, Investor Responsibility Research Center).

Chapter 7. Models of Monitoring and Corporate Governance

1. Exceptions are individuals who own large blocks of stock in particular firms, or individuals such as Warren Buffet who manage closed-end investment funds.

2. See John C. Coffee, Jr., "Liquidity versus Control: The Institutional Investor as Corporate Monitor," *Columbia Law Review* 91, no. 6 (1991): 1277–1368.

3. Bernard S. Black, "Agents Watching Agents: The Promise of Institutional Investor Voice," *UCLA Law Review* 39, no. 4 (1992): 811–93, p. 831. See also Bernard S. Black, "Institutional Investors and Corporate Governance: The Case for Institutional Voice," *Journal of Applied Corporate Finance* 5, no. 5 (1992): 19–32; and Michael Gerlach, *Alliance Capitalism* (Berkeley: University of California Press, 1992), pp. 63–159, for a discussion of the keiretsu form of organization.

4. For alternative characterizations of the liquidity-control spectrum, see Ronald Gilson, "Cooperate Governance and Economic Efficiency: When Do Institutions Matter?" (Columbia and Stanford Universities, Schools of Law and Business, 1995), pp. 13–16, p. 21; *OECD Economic Surveys, Italy 1995* (Paris: Organization for Economic Co-operation and Development, 1995), p. 51; Michael E. Porter, "Capital Choices: Changing the Way America Invests in Industry" (Washington, D.C.: U.S. Council on Competitiveness, 1992), p. 66.

5. Rafael La Porta, Florencio Lopez-de-Silanes, Andrei Schleifer, and Robert W. Vishny, "Corporate Ownership Around the World," NEBR Working Paper 6625 (Cambridge, Mass., National Bureau of Economic Research, 1998).

6. See Robert A. G. Monks, "Relationship Investing," *Corporate Governance* 2, no. 2 (1994): 58–76.

7. John Pound, "The Rise of the Political Model of Corporate Governance and Corporate Control," *New York University Law Review* 68, no. 5 (1993): 1003–71, p. 1007. Pound advocates that "insurgents use public processes to educate voters [shareholders] and propose alternatives to the policies of incumbents" through both formal mechanisms (e.g., proxy fights), but more importantly through "informal, political mechanisms to supplant, and even replace, the extreme measure of the formal voting challenge" (p. 1008). For Pound and others, "lobbying" through informal means becomes an extremely important means of monitoring and effecting change.

8. See Willard T. Carleton, James M. Nelson, and Michael S. Weisbach, "The Influence of Institutions on Corporate Governance through Private Negotiations: Evidence from TIAA-CREF," *Journal of Finance* 53, no. 4 (1998): 1335–62. For a discussion of informal (and other forms of) monitoring in the U.K., see John Holland, "Influence and Intervention by Financial Institutions in their Investee Companies," *Corporate Governance* 6, no. 4 (1998): 249–64.

9. Willard T. Carleton, James M. Nelson, and Michael S. Weisbach, "The Influence of Institutions on Corporate Governance," p. 1009. See pp. 1011–38 for an elaboration of the formal and informal models.

10. Joseph A. Grundfest, "Just Vote No: A Minimalist Strategy for Dealing with Barbarians Inside the Gates," *Stanford Law Review* 45, no. 4 (1993): 857–973, p. 95. He adds: "takeover[s] seem an imprecise and therefore imperfect means of identifying and ousting incompetent managers."

11. See Black, "Agents Watching Agents," p. 831, and Black, "Institutional Investors and Corporate Governance," pp. 19–32.

12. Mark J. Roe, *Strong Managers, Weak Owners: The Political Roots of American Corporate Finance* (Princeton, N.J.: Princeton University Press, 1994), pp. 11–12. Notable failures of the "crisis board" were in Westinghouse, Sears, IBM, and American Express, and GM over a protracted number of years. The various "corporate coups" of 1992 and 1993 at these and other firms were a result of institutional investors pressuring boards. One result was the restructuring of many of these boards.

13. Porter, "Capital Choices," pp. 44–45.

14. Public funds were joined somewhat later, albeit in a very quiet way, by some large indexed funds, such as Wells Fargo's Nikko Fund and Fidelity. Recently Well's Nikko Fund was taken over by Barclays PLC.

15. John Pound, "The Rise of the Political Model of Corporate Governance and Corporate Control," p. 1041. See also Bernard S. Black, "Shareholder Passivity Re-examined," *Michigan Law Review* 89, no. 3 (1990): 520–608, pp. 575–91. Joseph Grundfest calculates the benefits and costs of a particular type of activism and finds positive benefits for institutions that hold as little of 1% of the outstanding stock of a company (Joseph A. Grundfest, "Just Vote No," pp. 912–13).

16. For further elaboration and examples see James P. Hawley, Andrew T. Williams, and John U. Miller, "Getting the Herd to Run: Shareholder Activism at the California Public Employees' Retirement System (CalPERS)," *Business and the Contemporary World* 6, no. 4 (1994): 26–48. We make the point that the key element in targeting specific underperformers is rounding up the stray firms (underperformers) by making examples of them in order to keep the herd as a whole moving. Thus, there is believed to be simultaneously firm-specific and general market effects to this type of monitoring.

17. See Coffee, "Liquidity vs. Control," p. 1286.

18. Richard Koppes and Maureen L. Reilly, "An Ounce of Prevention: Meeting the Fiduciary Duty to Monitor an Index Fund through Relationship Investing," *Journal of Corporation Law* 20, no. 3 (1995): 413–49, p. 418. Koppes and Reilly suggest that institutional activist are not traders, and thus not price takers (as the capital assets pricing model assumes), "precisely because they have the power to affect the returns that they realize. Returns, in other words, are endogenous to their actions . . . the marketplace is no longer regulating itself . . . today's investor does not enjoy the luxury of a perfectly competitive capital market" (pp. 443–44).

19. Black, "Agents Watching Agents," p. 21.

20. Mark J. Roe, *Strong Managers, Weak Owners*, p. 244.

21. This point may be of particular importance concerning the alleged conflicts of interests of some public funds due to provincial political pressures; this is discussed below. See Joseph A. Grundfest, "Subordination of American Capital," *Journal of Financial Economics* 27, no. 1 (1990): 89–114, pp. 106–7; and Roe, *Strong Managers Weak Owners*, for a discussion of the Jeffersonian distrust of economic concentration.

22. Black, "Institutional Investors and Corporate Governance," p. 21.

23. Portfolio holdings could be reduced to about 100 firms without sacrificing the benefits of diversification with little increase of risk. See Richard Brealey and Stewart C. Myers, *Principles of Corporate Finance*, 4th ed. (New York: McGraw-Hill, 1991).

24. Thomas W. Briggs, "Shareholder Activism and Insurgency Under the New Proxy Rules," *The Business Lawyer* 50, no. 1 (1994), p. 111. Briggs adds, referring to the 1992 loosening of the SEC communication rules, that "The SEC's reforms probably do not go far enough. Shareholder free speech of all sorts, especially speech advocating action, continues to be chilled by the proxy rules and by Section 13(d)" (p. 147).

25. See James P. Hawley and Andrew T. Williams, "The Westinghouse Corporation and Institutional Investor Activism" (paper presented at the International Association for Business and Society, Vienna, Austria, June 26–29, 1995).

26. Grundfest, "Just Vote No," p. 905.

27. Mark J. Roe, *Strong Managers, Weak Owners*, p. 246.

28. John Pound, "The Rise of the Political Model of Corporate Governance and Corporate Control," pp. 1046–61. See also Robert A. G. Monks and Nell Minow, *Corporate Governance* (Cambridge, Mass.: Basil Blackwell, 1995), pp. 148–53. See also the text of the "New Compact Between Owners and Directors" in Monks and Minow,

Corporate Governance, pp. 532–36, as a good example of Pounds' idea of increasing sophistication of the "political" idea.

29. F. Hawthorne, "What the New SEC Rules do for Activism," *Institutional Investor,* April 1993, p. 47, as quoted in Monks and Minow, *Corporate Governance,* p. 456. Monks argues that there is no single panacea for adequate monitoring. He sites seven aspects of governance that when taken together (but not singly) can begin to provide adequate governance and monitoring. They are: 1) an enlightened CEO; 2) stronger corporate charters; 3) independent directors; 4) well-structured boards; 5) independent experts; 6) a free press; and 7) multiple external constraints such as economic factors, tax and regulatory schemes, and social values and ethics (Robert A. G. Monks, *The Emperor's Nightingale* [Reading, Mass.: Addison-Wesley, 1998], pp. 52–57).

30. Mark Latham, "Corporate Monitoring: New Shareholder Power Tool," *Financial Analysts Journal* 54, no. 5 (1998): 9–15.

31. Kevin Keasey, Steve Thompson, and Mike Wright, *Corporate Governance: Economic, Management, and Financial Issues* (New York: Oxford University Press, 1997), p. 9. If self-perpetuating and an oligarchy, then the principal-agent model is irrelevant since the interests of the board are entirely self-centered and the shareholders satisfied purely pragmatically.

32. Mark Latham, "The Corporate Monitoring Firm," *Corporate Governance* 7, no. 1 (1999): 12–20.

33. Latham, "Corporate Monitoring: New Shareholder Power Tool," pp. 9–11.

34. Latham, "Corporate Monitoring: New Shareholder Power Tool," p. 12.

35. Monks, *The Emperor's Nightingale,* pp. 146–58.

36. Robert Denham and Michael E. Porter, "Lifting All Boats" (Washington, D.C.: Competitiveness Policy Council, 1995), pp. 45–48. See Black, "Institutional Investors and Corporate Governance," and Black, "Agents Watching Agents," for a discussion of different configurations of voice. See also Robert A. G. Monks, "Corporate Governance in the Twenty-First Century, A Preliminary Outline," available online at http://www.lens-library.com/info/cg21.html, accessed April 18, 1999.

37. Steve Hammerick, "CalPERS Adds to Arsenal," *Pensions and Investments,* October 27, 1997, pp. 2, 56.

38. Phyllis Feinberg, "CalPERS Proposes Ambitious Plan of Action," *Pensions and Investments,* November 30, 1998, p. 12.

39. Richard C. Ferlauto, "Labor's Growing Shareholder Activism Agenda," *Pensions and Investments,* March 23, 1998, p. 12, and Barry B. Burr, "Labor's Role in Capital Markets," *Pensions and Investments,* September 12, 1998, p. 12.

40. For an overview of labor fund activism, see Stewart J. Schwab and Randal S. Thomas, "Realigning Corporate Governance: Shareholder Activism by Labor Unions," *Michigan Law Review* 96, no. 4 (1998): 1018–94, Randall S. Thomas and Kenneth J. Martin, "Should Labor be Allowed to Make Shareholder Proposals?" *Washington Law Review* 73, no. 41 (1998): 41–80, and Marleen A. O'Connor, "Organized Labor as Shareholder Activist: Building Coalitions to Promote Worker Capitalism," *University of Richmond Law Review* 31, no. 5 (1997): 1345–98.

41. Joann S. Lublin, "Oklahoma Count Affirms Holders' Right to Pursue a Binding Bylaw Proposal," *Wall Street Journal,* January 28, 1999, p. B2.

42. Indeed, "The Relationship Investing Conference" was the title of a major conference held by Columbia University Law School in May 1993 in New York City.

43. CalPERS committed itself to a "limited concept of relationship investing," the details of which have yet to be made public or perhaps even acted on. It may be modeled on CalPERS over 40% ownership in Calletus, a real-estate holding company (Richard Koppes, Memo to Members of the Board of Administration, CalPERS, August 1, 1995, Sacramento, Calif., p. 3).

44. Monks and Minow, *Corporate Governance,* p. 161.

45. Robert T. Kleiman, Kevin Nathan, and Joel M. Shulman, "Are There Payoffs for 'Patient' Corporate Investors?" *Mergers and Acquisitions* 28, no. 5 (1994): 34–41, pp. 34–35, 37, and 40–41. Koppes and Reilly, "An Ounce," p. 41, make a distinction between "private equity" partnerships defined as "large block [investment] in a specific firm with active participation," while defining "relationship investing" as involving "substantial ownership, long-term commitment, and reciprocity between owner and management." These different definitions illustrate the nascent quality of the governance movement.

46. See, for instance, various issues of the journal *Corporate Governance,* which focus to a large degree on board of director issues. Also see "Code of Best Practices: Report of the Committee on the Financial Aspects of Corporate Governance" (London: Cadbury Commission, Gee & Co., Ltd., 1992), also known as "The Cadbury Report." See Ira Millstein, "Corporate Governance" (Paris: Organization for Economic Cooperation and Development, 1998), pp. 105–7 for an extensive list of corporate governance codes and country standards.

47. See Edward Jay Epstein, *Who Owns the Corporation* (New York: Twentieth Century Fund: Priority Press, 1986).

48. Interview with Dale Hansen, CEO, California Public Employees' Retirement System CalPERS, April 6, 1993.

49. Joann S. Lublin and Elizabeth MacDonald, "Panel to Propose Boosting Independence and Power of Board Audit Committees," *Wall Street Journal,* January 8, 1999, p. A3.

50. "Corporate Governance," special supplement to *The Economist,* January 29, 1994, pp. 14–15. See also Ada Demb and Franz-Federick Neubauer, *The Corporate Board: Confronting the Paradoxes* (New York: Oxford University Press, 1992), and Jay W. Lorsch and Elizabeth MacIver, *Pawns or Potentates: The Reality of America's Corporate Boards* (Cambridge, Mass.: Harvard Business School Press, 1989).

51. Monks, *The Emperor's Nightingale,* p. 54.

52. Paul G. Stern, quoted in Margaret M. Blair, *Ownership and Control: Rethinking Corporate Governance for the Twenty-First Century* (Washington, D.C.: Brookings Institution, 1995), p. 77.

53. *Economist,* "Corporate Governance," p. 15.

54. See "Annual Review of the Best and the Worst Boards," *Business Week,* November 25, 1996, 82–106.

55. See Walter J. Salmon, "Crisis Prevention: How to Gear Up Your Board," *Harvard Business Review* 71, no. 1 (1993): 68–75, p. 69, for a discussion on adequate board information access.

56. See Gerald F. Davis, "Agents Without Principles? The Spread of the Poison Pill through the Intercorporate Network," *Administrative Science Quarterly* 36, no. 2 (1991): 45–80, for a discussion on the cultural "embeddedness and interconnectedness" of the "intercorporate environment." Davis provides an interesting critique of agency theory as ignoring the interorganizational aspects of the firm, thereby relying on what he calls an "undersocialized" view of managerial action divorced from its social context, e.g., board interlocks and interlocking information flows. We might title such an approach the social interlock agency theory perspective.

57. Monks and Minow, *Corporate Governance,* p. 192.

58. The growing problem of massive stock option issues diluting the value of firms' profits and share value is widely discussed, and largely beyond the scope of this work. See, for instance, Phillip Coggan, "U.S. Profits Overstated by a Third, Says Report," *Financial Times,* April 17, 1998, p. 1, and Richard Waters, "Crowing King Gong," *Financial Times,* March 3, 1998, p. 21. See also Paul M. Sheer and Barbara Tierney,

"Shareholders Block General Datacomm From Reducing Employee Option Price," *Wall Street Journal*, February 8, 1999, p. A10.

59. "1995 Board Index: Board Trends and Practices at Major American Corporations," (SpencerStuart, 1995). This study finds that 56% of the corporations surveyed provided grants or options to their outside directors (p. 28).

60. "Why Corporate Governance Today? A Policy Statement," (Sacramento, Calif.: California Public Employees' Retirement System, 1995), p. 14.

61. "Report of the NACD Blue Ribbon Commission on Director Compensation," (Washington, D.C.: National Association of Corporate Directors, 1995).

62. The following sections broadly follow James P. Hawley and Andrew T. Williams, "The Corporate Board of Directors as Philosopher Kings: The NACD Blue Ribbon Report on Director Professionalism," *Business and the Contemporary World* 9, no. 2 (1997): 299–324.

63. The corporate governance literature often classifies directors as "independent or outside director," "inside or executive director," and, sometimes, "gray or affiliated outside director." The latter category would refer to directors who have a business relationship but not an employment relationship with the firm. A director who was also the director of the corporation's major bank would be a "gray" director.

64. "Report of the NACD Blue Ribbon Commission on Director Compensation," (Washington, D.C.: National Association of Corporate Directors, 1995), p. 10.

65. The details of the ADM situation are presented in John A. Byrne, "The Best and Worst Boards," *Business Week*, November 25, 1996, pp. 82–98.

66. Bruce Orwall and Joann S. Lublin, "If a Company Prospers, Should Its Directors Behave by the Book?" *Wall Street Journal*, February 24, 1997, p. A1.

67. "Report of the NACD Blue Ribbon Commission on Director Compensation," p. vii (emphasis added).

68. Michael S. Weisbach, "Outside Directors and CEO Turnover," *Journal of Financial Economics* 20, no. 1–2 (1998): 431–60.

69. See James P. Hawley, "Political Voice, Fiduciary Activism and the Institutional Ownership of U.S. Corporations: The Role of Public and Non-Corporate Pension Funds," *Sociological Perspectives* 38, no. 3 (1995): 415–35.

70. For a review of initiatives and an evaluation of outcomes, see Tim C. Opler and Jonathan Sokobin, "Does Coordinated Institutional Activism Work? An Analysis of the Activities of the Council of Institutional Investors" (Ohio State University, Fisher College of Business, 1997), and Jonathan M. Karpoff, Paul M. Malatesta, and Ralph A. Walkling, "Corporate Governance and Shareholder Initiatives: Empirical Evidence," *Journal of Financial Economics* 42, no. 3 (1996): 365–95.

71. Monks and Minow suggest the major concern should be "for shareholders to assert and exercise control over the selection and ordering of priorities of the board through some kind of collective action vehicle . . . [such as] the shareholder committee. . . . The mere fact that the directors will know that they have been chosen by investors should make them more responsive to shareholder concerns" (Monks and Minow, *Corporate Governance*, pp. 224–25).

72. "Report of the NACD Blue Ribbon Commission on Director Compensation," p. 5.

73. Albert O. Hirschman, *Exit, Voice and Loyalty* (Cambridge, Mass.: Harvard University Press, 1970). "Exit" is leaving a situation, e.g., selling one's stock position. "Voice" involves staying and trying to change an unsatisfactory situation, e.g., trying to influence a board to adopt particular policies.

74. *The Economist*, "Corporate Governance," pp. 14–15. John Pound, "The Rise of the Political Model of Corporate Governance and Corporate Control," *New York University Law Review* 68, no. 5 (1993): 1003–71, p. 1007.

75. Michael C. Jensen, "The Modern Industrial Revolution, Exit and the Failure of

Internal Control Systems," in *Studies in International Corporate Finance and Governance Systems*, ed. Donald H. Chew (New York: Oxford University Press, 1997), 18–37, p. 35.

Chapter 8. Policy Currents

1. Robert Denham and Michael E. Porter, "Lifting All Boats" (Washington, D.C.: Competitiveness Policy Council, 1995), p. 33. See also Mark J. Roe, *Strong Managers, Weak Owners: The Political Roots of American Corporate Finance* (Princeton, N.J.: Princeton University Press, 1994).

2. Bernard S. Black, "Disclosure, Not Censorship: The Case for Proxy Reform," *Journal of Corporation Law* 17, no. 1 (1991): 49–86, p. 49.

3. Bernard S. Black, "Next Steps in Proxy Reform," *Journal of Corporation Law* 18, no. 1 (1992): 1–55, p. 53.

4. Denham and Porter, "Lifting All Boats," p. 34.

5. Louis Lowenstein, "Financial Transparency and Corporate Governance: You Manage What You Measure," *Columbia Law Review* 96, no. 5 (1996): 1335–62, p. 1334. Similar transparency problems, if in lesser degree, affect U.S. capital markets as the collapse and subsequent rescue of Long Term Capital Management in 1998–99 illustrates.

6. See, for instance, John C. Coffee, Jr., "Liquidity Versus Control: The Institutional Investor as Corporate Monitor," *Columbia Law Review* 91, no. 6 (1991): 1277–1368, pp. 1329–36.

7. Denham and Porter, "Lifting All Boats," p. 35.

8. Black, "Next Steps in Corporate Governance Reform."

9. Thomas W. Briggs, "Shareholder Activism and Insurgency Under the New Proxy Rules," *Business Lawyer* 50, no. 1 (1994), pp. 111–26, 135, 147. For a positive view, see, for example, Richard Koppes and Maureen L. Reilly, "An Ounce of Prevention: Meeting the Fiduciary Duty to Monitor an Index Fund Through Relationship Investing," *Journal of Corporation Law* 20, no. 3 (1995): 413–49. It should be noted that it was CalPERS' and Koppes' initiative in 1989 to petition the SEC to change its rules that provides another important example of the political strength of public funds. See James P. Hawley and Andrew T. Williams, "The Westinghouse Corporation and Institutional Investor Activism" (paper presented at the International Association for Business and Society, Vienna, Austria, June 26–29, 1995), for a discussion of the first use of this newly deregulated freedom in fall 1992 in the Westinghouse case.

10. Denham and Porter, "Lifting All Boats," p. 37. See also Bernard S. Black, "Shareholder Passivity Reexamined," *Michigan Law Review* 89, no. 3 (1990): 520–608, pp. 542–45, 550–51.

11. Denham and Porter, "Lifting All Boats," pp. 38–39.

12. See Steven L. Willborn, "Public Pensions and the Uniform Management of Public Employee Retirement Systems Act," *Rutgers Law Review* 51, no. 1 (1998): 141–72, for a general overview of the relation between fiduciary duty and information transparency and diversification.

13. Roe, *Strong Managers, Weak Owners*, p. 274. See also Black, "Shareholder Passivity Reexamined," pp. 536–42; Margaret M. Blair, *Ownership and Control: Rethinking Corporate Governance for the Twenty-First Century* (Washington, D.C.: Brookings Institution, 1995), pp. 68–76; Denham and Porter, "Lifting All Boats," pp. 41–42; and Robert A. G. Monks and Nell Minow, *Corporate Governance* (Cambridge, Mass.: Basil Blackwell, 1995), pp. 154–55.

14. Coffee, "Liquidity Versus Control," pp. 1339–42. He also notes that should a

majority of the market come to be held by indexed portfolios, at some point the market becomes significantly less than optimally efficient. Making a clear distinction between traders and investors might thus add greater liquidity to the market should present trends continue.

15. Coffee, "Liquidity Versus Control," pp. 1345–47; Denham and Porter, "Lifting All Boats," pp. 39–40; and Michael E. Porter, "Capital Choices: Changing the Way America Invests in Industry" (Washington, D.C.: U.S. Council on Competitiveness, 1992), p. 85. Porter argues that in order to effectively monitor institutions should be provided with insider information, but should be prevented from voting on it since they are long-term holders and have no short-term interest.

16. Coffee, "Liquidity versus Control," p. 1343.

17. Black, "Disclosure, Not Censorship," p. 50; and Coffee, "Liquidity Versus Control," p. 1362.

18. John Pound, "The Rise of the Political Model of Corporate Governance and Corporate Control," *New York University Law Review* 68, no. 5 (1993): 1003–71, p. 1041.

19. Norma M. Sharara and Anne E. Hoke-Witherspoon, "The Evolution of the 1992 Shareholder Communication Proxy Rules and Their Impact on Corporate Governance," *Business Lawyer* 49, no. 1 (1993): 327–58, p. 355.

20. Black, "Disclosure, Not Censorship," p. 2. See also Briggs, "Shareholder Activism," p. 147.

21. Sharara and Hoke-Witherspoon, "The Evolution of the 1992 Shareholder Communication Proxy Rules," pp. 349–58.

22. Quoted in Marleen A. O'Connor, "Organized Labor as Shareholder Activist: Building Coalitions to Promote Worker Capitalism," *University of Richmond Law Review* 31, no. 5 (1997): 1345–98, pp. 1363–65.

23. O'Connor, in "Organized Labor as Shareholder Activist," points out that the various attempts to pressure the SEC to permit high-performance workplace practice resolutions (some linking to CEO pay) were on the whole unsuccessful.

24. Michael Schroeder, "Groups United to Oppose SEC's Effort to Shift Stance on Shareholder Issues," *Wall Street Journal*, October 23, 1997, p. 12; and Michael Schroeder, "SEC Backs Off on Shareholder Resolution Curbs," *Wall Street Journal*, October 20, 1997, p. 3. See also Merrill B. Stone, "Final Shareholder Proposal Rules Fall Short of Reform," *National Law Journal* 20, no. 43 (1988): B9, at *http://web.lexis-nexis.com*.

25. Michelle McCann, "Shareholder Proposal Rule: Cracker Barrel in Light of Texaco," *Boston College Law Review* 39, no. 4 (1998): 965–91.

26. Ricki Fulman, "Investors' Council Meets with SEC," *Pensions and Investments*, April 20, 1998, p. 38.

27. Joann S. Lublin, "Oklahoma Count Affirms Holders' Right to Pursue a Binding Bylaw Proposal," *Wall Street Journal*, January 28, 1999, p. B2.

28. The legislative history of the act makes clear that the intent was not to impose additional fiduciary duties on institutional investors to act as lead plaintiffs (Richard M. Phillips and Gilbert C. Miller, "The Private Securities Litigation Reform Act of 1995: Rebalancing Litigation Risks and Rewards for Class Action Plaintiffs, Defendants and Lawyers," *Business Lawyer* 51, no. 4 [1996]: 1009–69, p. 1040). The act has a number of other important provisions, in particular a "safe harbor" provision for "forward looking" statements by firms, in particular concerning future product announcements. For a highly critical review, see John C. Coffee, Jr., "The Future of the Private Securities Litigation Reform Act; or, Why the Fat Lady Has Not Yet Sung," *Business Lawyer* 51, no. 4 (1996): 975–1007.

29. John W. Avery, "Securities Litigation Reform: The Long and Winding Road to the Private Securities Litigation Reform Act of 1995," *Business Lawyer* 51, no. 2

(1996): 335–78, pp. 337, 373–75. With some exceptions the court is mandated to appoint the class member that has the largest financial interest in the case.

30. Joseph A. Grundfest and Michael A. Perino, "Securities Litigation Reform: The First Year's Experience" (Stanford, Calif.: Stanford Law School, 1997), found at: *http://securities.stanford.edu/report,* p. 30, accessed March 30, 1999.

31. Avery, "Securities Litigation Reform," p. 374, fn. 259.

32. Elliot J. Weiss and John S. Berckerman, "Let the Money do the Monitoring," *Yale Law Review* 104, no. 8 (1995): 2053–2127, p. 2054.

33. For example, CalPERS recovered about $3.1 million in 1993 and $2.7 million in 1994. (Weiss and Berckerman, "Let the Money Do the Monitoring," p. 2054). See also Grundfest and Perino, "Securities Litigation Reform," for data by type of case and category of plaintiff.

34. In *Weiser v. Grace,* the court held that CalPERS, as a large institutional investor, "should be allowed a voice in the ongoing discovery and settlement discussions, and not simply given the opportunity to object at the end" (quoted in Grundfest and Perino, "Securities Litigation Reform," p. 35). They comment, "It demonstrates that institutional investor participation need not be limited to the role of lead plaintiff" in order to be both effective and their leading role recognized.

35. John C. Coffee, Jr., "The Future of the Private Securities Litigation Reform Act, pp. 975–1007; and Coffee, "Liquidity Versus Control," pp. 1348–51.

36. Denham and Porter, "Lifting All Boats," p. 41. See also Bernard S. Black, "Agents Watching Agents: The Promise of Institutional Investor Voice," *UCLA Law Review* 39, no. 4 (1992): 811–93, pp. 822–23; Blair, *Ownership and Control,* pp. 195 et seq.; Porter, "Capital Choices," p. 79; and Mark J. Roe, "The Modern Corporation and Private Pensions," *UCLA Law Review* 41, no. 1 (1993): 75–116, pp. 97–99.

37. Carl W. Kester, "Industrial Groups as Systems of Contractual Governance," *Oxford Review of Economic Policy* 8, no. 3 (1992), pp. 82–83.

38. Coffee, "Liquidity Versus Control."

39. Denham and Porter, "Lifting All Boats," pp. 52–53.

40. Koppes and Reilly, "An Ounce of Prevention," pp. 429, 447–48. A delegate is a formal or informal representative to a firm, or having a relation with a firm (e.g., on the board), and acts as an intermediary between the firm and an institution. Thus, monitoring a delegate is part of prudence.

41. Denham and Porter, "Lifting All Boats," p. 53.

42. Blair, *Ownership and Control,* pp. 116–117, 193.

43. Coffee, "Liquidity Versus Control."

44. Denham and Porter, "Lifting All Boats," pp. 41–42.

45. Blair, *Ownership and Control,* p. 193.

46. "Corporate Governance, Improving Competitiveness and Access to Capital in Global Markets: Report to the OECD by the Business Sector Advisory Group on Corporate Governance" (Organization for Economic Co-operation and Development, 1998), pp. 62–63.

47. Kester, "Industrial Groups as Systems," p. 40; and Porter, "Capital Choices," p. 86.

48. Porter, "Capital Choices," pp. 80, 86–87, 91. As part of Porter's concern for restructuring the mission and strategy of firms, he offers a number of accounting concepts that would measure long-term value by standards other than current stock price, e.g., worker training and other human capital investments. In turn he argues that it is important to bring employees directly into governance by giving them some form of ownership stake.

49. See Blair, *Ownership and Control,* p. 121; and Denham and Porter, "Lifting All Boats," p. 80.

50. Blair, *Ownership and Control,* pp. 118–20, 197–98. Many, but not all of these

proposals are supported by the U.K.'s Cadbury Commission Report's recommendations. For a list of country codes see "Corporate Governance, Improving Competitiveness."

51. Coffee, "Liquidity Versus Control," p. 1338; Koppes and Reilly, "An Ounce of Prevention," p. 445; and Denham and Porter, "Lifting All Boats," pp. 88–89.

52. Coffee, "Liquidity Versus Control," pp. 1359–60.

53. See also Ronald Gilson and Reinier Kraakman, "Reinventing the Outside Director: An Agenda for Institutional Investors," *Stanford Law Review* 43 (1991): 863–906, for a discussion of this issue.

54. Bernard S. Black, "Institutional Investors and Corporate Governance: The Case for Institutional Voice," *Journal of Applied Corporate Finance* 5, no. 5 (1992): 19–32.

55. Robert A. G. Monks, "Corporate Governance in the Twenty-First Century: A Preliminary Outline" available online at: http://www.lens-library.com/info/doc_list.html, p. 22, accessed May 7, 1999.

56. Black, "Institutional Investors and Corporate Governance," p. 845. "White squire funds" developed during the hostile takeover period in the 1980s to provide capital and support to firms in danger of takeover bids.

57. Monks and Minow, *Corporate Governance*, pp. 20–21; and Porter, "Capital Choices," p. 70.

58. Roberta Romano, "Public Pension Fund Activism in Corporate Governance Reconsidered," *Columbia Law Review* 93, no. 4 (1993): 795–853, pp. 799, 840–851. It is not clear how Romano views the impact of defined-contribution plans indexed portfolios since there is a tendency in the latter to create specialized funds, indexes of indexes.

59. Monks and Minow, *Corporate Governance*, pp. 20–21.

60. For a background discussion of the growth and nature of ESOPs, see Joseph Raphael Blasi and Douglas Lynn Kruse, *The New Owners: The Mass Emergence of Employee Ownership in Public Companies and What it Means to American Business* (New York: Harper Business, 1991).

61. Denham and Porter, "Lifting All Boats," pp. 61–64.

Chapter 9. Summary and Conclusions

1. Adolph A. Berle and Gardiner C. Means, *The Modern Corporation and Private Property*, revised ed. (New York: Macmillan, 1967), p. 8.

2. See Tables 3.3 and 3.4.

3. "*Institutional Investment Report*," (New York: Conference Board, 1998), p. 10.

4. See also Table 3.4.

5. See Chapter 1.

6. "Institutional Investment Report," p. 21.

7. Richard Koppes and Maureen L. Reilly, "An Ounce of Prevention: Meeting the Fiduciary Duty to Monitor an Index Fund Through Relationship Investing," *Journal of Corporation Law* 20, no. 3 (1995): 413–49.

8. *Foundations of Corporate Law*, ed. Roberta Romano, Interdisciplinary Readers in Law (New York: Oxford University Press, 1993), p. 266.

9. This is not to say that other forces, some external to the U.S. economy such as low raw material prices resulting from the financial collapse of some countries in Southeast Asia, haven't also contributed to the superior economic performance over this period.

10. Quoted in Leslie Scism, "Teachers' Pension Plan to Give Firms Tough Exams," *Wall Street Journal*, October 6, 1993, p. C1.

11. "Why Corporate Governance Today? A Policy Statement" (Sacramento, Calif.: California Public Employees' Retirement System, 1995), p. 14.

12. "Statement of Procedures and Policies for Voting Proxies" (New York: New York City Combined Funds, 1987), p. 18.

13. However, the guidelines explicitly reject proxy proposals that seek to give stockholders the right to designate the beneficiary of charitable contributions in proportion to shares owned. Although the guidelines don't provide the rational for this position, it would certainly be a plausible outcome of a cost-benefit calculation on the issue ("Statement of Proceedings," p. 18).

14. Interview with Kim Johnson, general counsel, Colorado Public Employee Retirement System, December 4, 1997.

15. See Bernard S. Black, "Shareholder Passivity Reexamined," *Michigan Law Review* 89, no. 3 (1990): 520–608.

16. Interview with Kim Johnson, general counsel, Colorado Public Employee Retirement System, December 4, 1997.

17. Interview with Richard M. Schlefer, Director CREF Corporate Governance, and Peter Clapman, Senior Vice-President and Chief Counsel, Investments, December 16, 1997.

18. Lilli A. Gordon, "Active Investing in the U.S. Equity Market: Past Performance and Future Prospects: A Report Prepared for the California Public Employees' Retirement System" (Cambridge, Mass.: Gordon Group, 1993).

19. California Public Employees' Retirement System, "Company Responses to Request for Board Governance Self-Evaluation," May 31, 1995.

20. Mitchel Benson, "Fund Warns Maxxam Not to Log," *Wall Street Journal*, February 19, 1997, p. CA1.

21. "The general issue is how companies deal with safety, not just as a social issue, but as one affecting their viability and attractiveness as an investment" (Interview with Richard M. Schlefer, Director CREF Corporate Governance, and Peter Clapman, Senior Vice-President and Chief Counsel, Investments, December 16, 1997).

22. See Roberta Romano, "Public Pension Fund Activism in Corporate Governance Reconsidered," *Columbia Law Review* 93, no. 4 (1993): 795–853.

23. Claire E. Crutchley, Carl D. Hudson, and Marlin R. H. Jensen, "Shareholder Wealth Effects of CalPERS' Activism," *Financial Services Review* 7, no. 1 (1998): 1–10.

24. Personal communication from Ken Birtch, Investors Responsibility Research Center, January 19, 1999.

Bibliography

Reports and Surveys

"1995 Board Index: Board Trends and Practices at Major American Corporations." SpencerStuart, 1995.

"1996 Board Index: Board Trends and Practices at Major American Corporations." SpencerStuart, 1996.

"1997 Annual Report." New York City, Teachers Insurance and Annuity Association — College Retirement Equities Fund, 1998.

"Annual Review of the Best and the Worst Boards." *Business Week*, November 25, 1996, 82–106.

The Brancato Report on Institutional Investment. Fairfax, Va.: Victoria Group, various issues.

"Code of Best Practices: Report of the Committee on the Financial Aspects of Corporate Governance." London, Cadbury Commission, Gee & Co., 1992.

"Company Relations with Institutional Investors." The Conference Board, 1994.

"Corporate Governance." Special supplement, *Economist*, January 29, 1994.

"Corporate Governance, Improving Competitiveness and Access to Capital in Global Markets: Report to the OECD by the Business Sector Advisory Group on Corporate Governance." Organization for Economic Co-operation and Development, April 1998.

"Draft OECD Principles of Corporate Governance: Ad Hoc Task Force on Corporate Governance." Paris, Organization for Economic Co-operation and Development, February 5, 1999.

Global Shareholder. Washington, D.C.: Investor Responsibility Research Council, various issues.

"High-Performance Workplaces: Implicitions for Investment Research and Active Investing Strategies." Cambridge, Mass.: Gordon Group, May 30, 1994.

"Institutional Investment Report." New York, The Conference Board, June 1998.

"Institutional Investment Report." New York, The Conference Board, August 1998.

"Interpretive Bulletin 94-1 (Title 29)." 32606–32608. Federal Register, U.S. Government Printing Office, June 23, 1994.

"Interpretive Bulletin 94-2 (Title 29)." 38860–38864. Federal Register, U.S. Government Printing Office, July 29, 1994.

"Investment Outlook Scoreboard." *Business Week*, December 29, 1997, 161–88.

"Memo to Members of the Investment Committee." Sacramento, Calif.: Public Employees' Retirement System Legal Office, August 14, 1995.

OECD Economic Surveys, Italy 1995. Paris: Organization for Economic Co-operation and Development, 1995.
OECD Economic Surveys, Germany 1995. Paris: Organization for Economic Co-operation and Development, 1995.
"Poison Pill Bylaw Proposals Pending at 14 Companies." *Corporate Governance Highlights* 10, no. 2 (1999): 5.
"Report of the NACD Blue Ribbon Commission on Director Compensation." Washington, D.C.: National Association of Corporate Directors, 1995.
"Semi-Annual Report: College Retirement Equities Fund." New York: College Retirement Equities Fund, June 30, 1998.
"Share and Share Unalike." *Economist*, August 7, 1999, pp. 18–20.
"Statement of Procedures and Policies for Voting Proxies." New York: New York City Combined Funds, November (last amended June 1998) 1987.
"Statement on Corporate Governance." New York City, The Business Roundtable, September 1997.
"Uniform Management of Public Employee Retirement Systems Act (1977)." National Conference of Commissioners of Uniform State Laws, December 11, 1997.
United States 1996, OECD Economic Surveys. Paris, France: Organization for Economic Co-operation and Development, 1996.
"Why Corporate Governance Today? A Policy Statement." Sacramento, Calif.: California Public Employees' Retirement System, August 14, 1995.

Books and Articles

Alchian, Armen A. "Uncertainty, Evolution, and Economic Theory." In *Industrial Organization*, edited by Oliver E. Williamson. Brookfield, Vt.: E. Elgar, 1990, pp. 23–33.
Amihud, Y., and B. Lev. "Risk Reduction as a Managerial Motive for Conglomerate Mergers." *Bell Journal of Economics* 12, no. 2 (1981): 605–17.
Anand, Vineeta. "Defined Benefit Assets Surge 20.3%." *Pension & Investments*, March 22, 1999, pp. 1, 45.
Asquith, P. "Merger Bids, Uncertainty and Shareholder Returns." *Journal of Financial Economics* 11, no. 1–4 (1983): 51–83.
Avery, John W. "Securities Litigation Reform: The Long and Winding Road to the Private Securities Litigation Reform Act of 1995." *Business Lawyer* 51, no. 2 (1996): 335–78.
Beauchamp, Tom L., and Norman E. Bowie. *Ethical Theory and Business*. 3rd ed. Englewood Cliffs, N.J.: Prentice Hall, 1979.
Benson, Mitchel. "Fund Warns Maxxam Not to Log." *Wall Street Journal*, February 19, 1997, p. CA1.
Berle, Adolph A. "For Whom Are Corporate Managers Trustees: A Note." *Harvard Law Review* 45 (1932): 1365–72.
Berle, Adolph A., and Gardiner C. Means. *The Modern Corporation and Private Property*. New York: Macmillan, 1932.
———. *The Modern Corporation and Private Property*. Revised ed. New York: Macmillan, 1967.
Betts, Paul, and James Blitz. "Olivetti's 36 Billion Pound Bid Spurned by Italian Rival." *Financial Times*, February 22, 1999, p. 1.
Bhagat, Sanjai, and Bernard Black. "The Relationship Between Board Composition and Firm Performance." In *Comparative Corporate Governance: The State of the Art and Emerging Research*, edited by Klaus Hopt, Mark Roe, Eddy Wymeersch, and Stefan Prigge. Oxford: Clarendon Press, 1998, pp. 281–306.

Bhagat, Sanjai, Andrei Shleifer, and Robert W. Vishny. "Hostile Takeovers in the 1980s: The Return to Corporate Specialization." In *Brookings Papers on Economic Activity: Microeconomics*, edited by Martin Neil Baily and Clifford Winston. Washington, D.C.: Brookings Institution, 1990, pp. 1–84.

Bittlingmayer, George. "The Market for Corporate Control (Including Takeovers)." In *Encyclopedia of Law and Economics*, edited by Boudewijn Bouckaert and Gerrit De Geese. Northampton, Mass.: E. Elgar, 1999.

Black, Bernard S. "The Value of Institutional Investor Monitoring: The Empirical Evidence." *UCLA Law Review* 39, no. 4 (1992): 895–939.

———. "Agents Watching Agents: The Promise of Institutional Investor Voice." *UCLA Law Review* 39, no. 4 (1992): 811–93.

———. "Disclosure, Not Censorship: The Case for Proxy Reform." *The Journal of Corporation Law* 17, no. 1 (1991): 49–86.

———. "Institutional Investors and Corporate Governance: The Case for Institutional Voice." *Journal of Applied Corporate Finance* 5, no. 5 (1992): 19–32.

———. "Next Steps in Corporate Governance Reform: 13(d) Rules and Control of Person Liability." In *Modernizing U. S. Securities Regulation: Economic and Legal Perspectives*, edited by Kenneth Lehn and Robert Kamphuis. Burr Ridge, Ill.: Irwin, 1992.

———. "Next Steps in Proxy Reform." *The Journal of Corporation Law* 18, no. 1 (1992): 1–55.

———. "Shareholder Activism and Corporate Governance in the United States." In *The New Palgrave Dictionary of Economics and the Law*, edited by Peter Newman, 459–65. New York: Macmillan Stockton Press, 1998.

———. "Shareholder Passivity Reexamined." *Michigan Law Review* 89, no. 3 (1990): 520–608.

Blackford, Mansel G., and K. Austin Kerr. *Business Enterprise in American History*. 3rd ed. Boston: Houghton Mifflin, 1994.

Blair, Margaret M. "Firm Specific Human Capital and the Theory of the Firm." New York, Columbia University School of Law, November 22, 1996.

———. *Ownership and Control: Rethinking Corporate Governance for the Twenty-First Century*. Washington, D.C.: Brookings Institution, 1995.

———. "Survey of Empirical Evidence on the Effects of 'Relationship Investing' on Corporate Performance: a report prepared for the Subcouncil on Capital Allocation." Washington, D.C., Competitiveness Policy Council, December 22, 1994.

Blair, Margaret M., and Lynn A. Stout. "A Team Production Theory of Corporate Law." unpublished manuscript, March 16, 1998.

Blasi, Joseph Raphael, and Douglas Lynn Kruse. *The New Owners: The Mass Emergence of Employee Ownership in Public Companies and What It Means to American Business*. New York: Harper Business, 1991.

Boatright, John R. "Staking Claims: The Role of Stakeholders in the Contractual Theory of the Firm." ASSA Meetings, Chicago, January 1998.

Brandeis, Louis D. *Other People's Money and How the Bankers Use It*. New York: Harper & Row, 1967.

Brealey, Richard, and Stewart C. Myers. *Principles of Corporate Finance*. 4th ed. New York: McGraw-Hill, 1991.

Briggs, Thomas W. "Shareholder Activism and Insurgency Under the New Proxy Rules." *The Business Lawyer* 50, no. 1 (1994): 99–149.

Bryant, Adam. "CalPERS Draws a Blueprint for its Concept of an Ideal Board." *New York Times*, June 17, 1997, p. D1.

Burch, Philip, Jr. *The Managerial Revolution Reassessed: Family Control in America's Large Corporations, Lexington Books*. Lexington, Mass.: D. C. Heath, 1972.

Burr, Barry B. "Labor's Role in Capital Markets." *Pensions and Investments*, September 12, 1998, p. 12.

Byrne, John A. "The Best and Worst Boards." *Business Week*, November 25, 1996, pp. 82–98.

Carleton, Willard T., James M. Nelson, and Michael S. Weisbach. "The Influence of Institutions on Corporate Governance through Private Negotiations: Evidence from TIAA-CREF." *Journal of Finance* 53, no. 4 (1998): 1335–62.

Carroll, Archie B. *Business and Society*. Cincinnati, Ohio: South-Western, 1989.

Chandler, Alfred D. *The Visible Hand: The Managerial Revolution in American Business*. Cambridge, Mass.: Belknap Press of Harvard University Press, 1977.

Clapman, Peter C. "Independent Board Key to Firm Management." *Pensions and Investments*, April 20, 1998, p. 12.

Clarkson, Max B. E. *The Corporation and its Stakeholders*. Toronto: University of Toronto Press, 1999.

Coase, Ronald H. "The Nature of the Firm." *Economica N. S.* 4 (1937): 386–405.

Coffee, John C., Jr. "The Future of the Private Securities Litigation Reform Act; or, Why the Fat Lady has not Yet Sung." *Business Lawyer* 51, no. 4 (1996): 975–1007.

——— . "Liquidity Versus Control: The Institutional Investor as Corporate Monitor." *Columbia Law Review* 91, no. 6 (1991): 1277–1368.

Coggan, Phillip. "U.S. Profits Overstated by a Third, Says Report." *Financial Times*, April 17, 1998, p. 1.

Cosh, A. D., K. Lee, and A. Singh. "Institutional Investment, Mergers and the Market for Corporate Control." *International Journal of Industrial Organizations* 7, no. 1 (1989): 73–100.

Cox, Edwin Burk. *Trends in the Distribution of Stock Ownership*. Philadelphia: University of Pennsylvania Press, 1963.

Crutchley, Claire E., Carl D. Hudson, and Marlin R. H. Jensen. "Shareholder Wealth Effects of CalPERS' Activism." *Financial Services Review* 7, no. 1 (1998): 1–10.

Davis, Gerald F. "Agents Without Principles? The Spread of the Poison Pill through the Intercorporate Network." *Administrative Science Quarterly* 36, no. 2 (1991): 45–80.

Day, Kathleen. "Frank Carlucci and the Corporate Whirl." *Washington Post*, February 7, 1993, p. H1.

Demb, Ada, and Franz-Frederick Neubauer. *The Corporate Board: Confronting the Paradoxes*. New York: Oxford University Press, 1992.

Denham, Robert, and Michael E. Porter. "Lifting All Boats." Washington, D.C.: Competitiveness Policy Council, 1995.

Dobrzynski, Judith H. "When Directors Play Musical Chairs." *New York Times*, November 17, 1996, section 3, p. 9.

Donaldson, Lex, and James H. Davis. "Board and Company Performance — Research Challenges the Conventional Wisdom." *Corporate Governance* 2, no. 3 (1994).

Donaldson, T., and L. E. Preston. "The Stakeholder Theory of the Corporation: Concepts, Evidence and Implications." *Academy of Management Review* 20, no. 1 (1995): 65–91.

Drucker, Peter. *The Unseen Revolution: How Pension Fund Socialism Came to America*. New York: Harper and Row, 1979.

Eisenberg, Melvin Aron. "The Structure of Corporation Law." *Columbia Law Review* 89, no. 7 (1989): 1461–1525.

Elson, Charles M. "Courts and Boards: The Top 10 Cases." *Directors & Boards* 22, no. 1 (1997): 26–36.

Epstein, Edward Jay. "The Last Days of Armand Hammer." *New Yorker*, September 23, 1996, p. 36.

———. *Who Owns the Corporation.* New York: Twentieth Century Fund Priority Press, 1986.

Evan, William M., and R. Edward Freeman. "A Stakeholder Theory of the Modern Corporation: Kantian Capitalism." In *Ethical Issues in Business,* edited by Thomas Donaldson and Patricia H. Wehan. Upper Saddle River, N.J.: Prentice-Hall, 1993, pp. 166–71.

Fama, Eugene F. "Agency Problems and the Theory of the Firm." *Journal of Political Economy* 88, no. 21 (1980): 288–307.

Farrer, Janathan, and Ian M. Ramsay. "Director Share Ownership and Corporate Performance-Evidence from Australia." *Corporate Governance* 6, no. 4 (1998): 233–48.

United States Federal Trade Commission. *National Wealth and Income, 69th Cong., 1st sess. Senate. Doc. 126.* Washington, D.C.: U.S. Government Printing Office, 1926.

Feinberg, Phyllis. "CalPERS Proposes Ambitious Plan of Action." *Pensions and Investments,* November 30, 1998, p. 12.

Ferlauto, Richard C. "Labor's Growing Shareholder Activism Agenda." *Pensions and Investments,* March 23, 1998, p. 12.

Franks, Julian R., and Colin Mayer. "Hostile Takeovers and the Correction of Managerial Failure." *Journal of Financial Economics* 40, no. 1 (1996): 163–81.

Friedman, Benjamin M. "Economic Implications of Changing Share Ownership." National Bureau of Economic Research, 1995.

Friedman, Milton. *Capitalism and Freedom.* Chicago: University of Chicago Press, 1992.

Fulman, Ricki. "Investors Council Meets with SEC." *Pensions and Investments,* April 20, 1998, p. 38.

Furtado, Eugene P. H., and Vijay Karan. "Causes, Consequences and the Shareholder Wealth Effects of Management Turnover: A Review of the Empirical Evidence." *Financial Management* 19, no. 2 (1990): 60–75.

Galbraith, John Kenneth. *American Capitalism: The Concept of Countervailing Power.* Boston: Houghton Mifflin, 1956.

Gerlach, Michael. *Alliance Capitalism.* Berkeley: University of California Press, 1992.

Ghilarducci, Teresa. *Labor's Capital: The Economics and Politics of Private Pensions.* Cambridge Mass.: MIT Press, 1992.

Ghilarducci, Teresa, James Hawley, and Andrew T. Williams. "Labor's Interests and the Evolution of Corporate Governance." *Journal of Law and Society* 24, no. 1 (1997): 56–43.

Gilson, Ronald. "Cooperate Governance and Economic Efficiency: When Do Institutions Matter?" Columbia and Stanford Universities, Schools of Law and Business, 1995.

Gilson, Ronald, and Reinier Kraakman. "Reinventing the Outside Director: An Agenda for Institutional Investors." *Stanford Law Review* 43 (1991): 863–906.

Gompers, Paul A., and Andrew Metrick. "How Are Large Institutions Different from Other Investors? Why Do These Differences Matter?" Cambridge, Mass.: Harvard Business School Working Paper, August 1998.

Goodpaster, Kenneth E. "Business Ethics and Stakeholder Analysis." *Business Ethics Quarterly* 1, no. 1 (1991): 53–73.

Gordon, Lilli A. "Active Investing in the U.S. Equity Market: Past Performance and Future Prospects: A Report Prepared for the California Public Employees' Retirement System." Cambridge, Mass.: Gordon Group, January 11, 1993.

Gordon, Lilli A., and John Pound. "Governance Matters: An Empirical Study of the Relationship Between Corporate Governance and Corporate Performance." John F. Kennedy School of Government, 1991.

Gould, Carole. "Fund Watch: At the 401(k) Forefront." *New York Times,* December 31, 1995, Section 3, p. 4.

Greider, William. *Who Will Tell the People? The Betrayal of American Democracy.* New York: Simon & Schuster, 1992.

Grossman, S. J., and O. D. Hart. "Takeover Bids, the Free Rider Problem and the Theory of the Firm." *Bell Journal of Economics* 11, no. 1 (1980): 42–64.

Grundfest, Joseph A. "Just Vote No: A Minimalist Strategy for Dealing with Barbarians Inside the Gates." *Stanford Law Review* 45, no. 4 (1993): 857–973.

———. "Subordination of American Capital." *Journal of Financial Economics* 27, no. 1 (1990): 89–114.

Grundfest, Joseph A., and Michael A. Perino. "Securities Litigation Reform: The First Year's Experience." Stanford, Calif., Stanford Law School, February 27, 1997.

Hale, David. "Personal View: U.S. Cycle Theory." *Financial Times*, February 17, 1999, p. 20.

Hammerick, Steve. "CalPERS Adds to Arsenal." *Pensions and Investments*, October 27, 1997, p. 2.

Hansmann, H. B. *The Ownership of Enterprise.* Cambridge, Mass.: Harvard University Press, 1996.

———. "Ownership of the Firm." In *New Palgrave Dictionary of Economics and the Law*, edited by Peter Newman. New York: Macmillan, 1998, pp. 735–42.

Harbrecht, S. J., Paul P. *Pension Funds and Economic Power.* New York: The Twentieth Century Fund, 1959.

Hart, Oliver. "Corporate Governance: Some Theory and Implications." *Economic Journal* 105 (1995): 678–89.

———. *Firms, Contracts and Financial Structure.* Oxford: Clarendon Press, 1995.

Hasnas, John. "The Normative Theories of Business Ethics: A Guide for the Perplexed." *Business Ethics Quarterly* 8, no. 1 (1998): 19–42.

Hawley, James P. "Political Voice, Fiduciary Activism and the Institutional Ownership of U.S. Corporations: The Role of Public and Non-Corporate Pension Funds." *Sociological Perspectives* 38, no. 3 (1995): 415–35.

Hawley, James P., and Andrew T. Williams. "The Corporate Board of Directors as Philosopher Kings: The NACD Blue Ribbon Report on Director Professionalism." *Business and the Contemporary World* 9, no. 2 (1997): 299–324.

———. "The Westinghouse Corporation and Institutional Investor Activism." Paper presented at the International Association for Business and Society, Vienna, June 26–29, 1995.

Hawley, James P., Andrew T. Williams, and John U. Miller. "Getting the Herd to Run: Shareholder Activism at the California Public Employees' Retirement System (CalPERS)." *Business and the Contemporary World* 6, no. 4 (1994): 26–48.

Hawthorne, F. "What the New SEC Rules do for Activism." *Institutional Investor*, April 1993, p. 47.

Hayek, F. "The Corporation in a Democratic Society: In Whose Interests Ought It and Will It be Run?" In *Business Strategy*, edited by H. I. Ansoff. New York: Penguin, 1977, pp. 225–39.

Hayes, Robert H., and William J. Abernathy. "Managing Our Way to Economic Decline." *Harvard Business Review* 58, July–August (1980): 67–77.

Healy, P. M., K. G. Palepu, and R. S. Ruback. "Does Corporate Performance Improve After Mergers." *Journal of Financial Economics* 31, no. 2 (1992): 135–75.

Herman, E., and L. Lowenstein. "The Efficiency Effects of Hostile Takeovers." In *Knights, Raiders and Targets: The Impact of Hostile Takeovers*, edited by Louis Lowenstein, John C. Coffee, Jr., and Susan Rose Ackerman. Oxford: Oxford University Press, 1988.

Hilferding, Rudolf. *Finance Capital.* Translated by Morris Watnick and Sam Gordon. London: Routledge & Kegan Paul, 1981.

Hirschman, Albert O. *Exit, Voice and Loyalty*. Cambridge, Mass.: Harvard University Press, 1970.

Holderness, C. G., and D. P. Sheehan. "Raiders or Saviors? The Evidence of Six Controversial Investors." *Journal of Financial Economics* 14, December (1985): 555–79.

Holland, John. "Influence and Intervention by Financial Institutions in Their Investee Companies." *Corporate Governance* 6, no. 4 (1998): 249–64.

Ip, Greg. "New Paradigm View for Stocks Is Bolstered." *Wall Street Journal*, September 13, 1999, p. C1.

Jarrell, Gregg A. "The Wealth Effects of Litigation by Targets: Do Interests Diverge in a Merger." *Journal of Law and Economics* 28, no. 1 (1985): 151–77.

Jarrell, Gregg A., James A. Brickley, and Jeffry M. Netter. "The Market for Corporate Control: The Empirical Evidence Since 1980." *Journal of Economic Perspectives* 2, no. 1 (1988): 49–67.

Jarrell, Sherry L. "Do Takeovers Generate Value? Evidence on the Capital Market's Ability of Assess Takeovers." Ph.D. dissertation, University of Chicago, 1991.

Jensen, Michael C. "Eclipse of the Public Corporation." *Harvard Business Review* 67, no. 5 (1989): 61–74.

———. "The Modern Industrial Revolution, Exit and the Failure of Internal Control Systems." In *Studies in International Corporate Finance and Governance Systems*, edited by Donald H. Chew. New York: Oxford University Press, 1997, pp. 32–34.

———. "Takeovers: Their Causes and Consequences." *Journal of Economic Perspectives* 2, no. 1 (1998): 43–64.

Jensen, Michael C., and William H. Meckling. "Theory of the Firms: Managerial Behavior, Agency Costs and Ownership Structure." *Journal of Financial Economics* 3, no. 4 (1976): 305–60.

Jensen, Michael C., and Richard S. Ruback. "The Market for Corporate Control: The Scientific Evidence." *Journal of Financial Economics* 11, no. 1–4 (1983): 5–50.

Jensen, Michael, Steven Kaplan, and Laura Stiglin. "The Effects of LBOs on Tax Revenues." *Tax Notes* 42, no. 6 (1989): 727–33.

Kaplan, Steven. "Management Buyouts: Evidence on Taxes as a Source of Value." *Journal of Finance* 44, no. 3 (1989): 611–32.

Kaplan, Steven N. "The Evolution of U.S. Corporate Governance: We Are All Henry Kravis Now." Paper presented at the Power and Influence of Pension and Mutual Funds, New York University, Stern School of Business, February 21, 1997.

Karpoff, Jonathan M. "The Impact of Shareholder Activism on Target Companies: A Survey of Empirical Findings." University of Washington, School of Business, September 8, 1998.

Karpoff, Jonathan M., and Paul H. Malatesta. "The Wealth Effects of Second-Generation State Takeover Legislation." *Journal of Financial Economics* 25, no. 2 (1989): 291–322.

Karpoff, Jonathan M., Paul M. Malatesta, and Ralph A. Walkling. "Corporate Governance and Shareholder Initiatives: Empirical Evidence." *Journal of Financial Economics* 42, no. 3 (1996): 365–95.

Kaysen, Carl, ed. *The American Corporation Today*. New York: Oxford University Press, 1996.

Keasey, Kevin, Steve Thompson, and Mike Wright, ed. *Corporate Governance: Economic, Management, and Financial Issues*. New York: Oxford University Press, 1997.

———. "Introduction: The Corporate Governance Problem — Competing Diagnoses and Solutions." In *Corporate Governance: Economic, Management, and Financial Issues*, edited by Kevin Keasey, Steve Thompson, and Mike Wright. New York: Oxford University Press, 1997.

Keasey, Kevin, and Mike Wright. "Issues in Corporate Accountability and Governance." *Accounting and Business Research* 23, no. 91a (1993): 291–303.

Keller, Morton. "The Making of the Modern Corporation." *Wilson Quarterly* 21, no. 4 (1997): 58–69.

Kester, Carl W. "Industrial Groups as Systems of Contractual Governance." *Oxford Review of Economic Policy* 8, no. 3 (1992): 24–44.

Kimmel, Lewis H. *Share Ownership in the United States*. Washington, D.C.: Brookings Institution, 1952.

Kindleberger, Charles P. *Manias, Panics, and Crashes: A History of Financial Crises*. Revised ed. New York: Basic Books, 1989.

Kleiman, Robert T., Kevin Nathan, and Joel M. Shulman. "Are There Payoffs for 'Patient' Corporate Investors?" *Mergers and Acquisitions* 28, no. 5 (1994): 34–41.

Koppes, Richard. "International Corporate Governance." Sacramento, Calif.: CalPERS, March 22, 1995.

———. "Memo to Members of the Board of Administration, CalPERS." Sacramento, Calif., 1995.

Koppes, Richard, and Maureen L. Reilly. "An Ounce of Prevention: Meeting the Fiduciary Duty to Monitor an Index Fund Through Relationship Investing." *Journal of Corporation Law* 20, no. 3 (1995): 413–49.

La Porta, Rafael, Florencio Lopez-de-Silanes, Andrei Shleifer, and Robert W. Vishny. "Corporate Ownership Around the World." NBER Working Paper 6625. Cambridge, Mass., National Bureau of Economic Research, 1998.

———. "Law and Finance." *Journal of Political Economy* 106, no. 6 (1998): 1113–55.

Latham, Mark. "The Corporate Monitoring Firm." *Corporate Governance* 7, no. 1 (1999): 12–20.

———. "Corporate Monitoring: New Shareholder Power Tool." *Financial Analysts Journal* 54, no. 5 (1998): 9–15.

Lazonick, William. "The Anglo-Saxon Corporate System." In *The Corporate Triangle: The Structure and Performance of Corporate Systems in a Global Economy*, edited by P. H. Admiraal. Malden, Mass.: Blackwell, 1997, pp. 1–35.

Limmack, R. J. "Corporate Mergers and Shareholder Wealth Effects 1997–1986." *Accounting and Business Research* 21, no. 83 (1991): 239–51.

Lindblom, Charles E. *Politics and Markets*. New York: Basic Books, 1997.

Lorsch, Jay W., and Elizabeth MacIver. *Pawns or Potentates: The Reality of America's Corporate Boards*. Cambridge, Mass.: Harvard Business School Press, 1989.

Lowenstein, Louis. "Financial Transparency and Corporate Governance: You Manage What You Measure." *Columbia Law Review* 96, no. 5 (1996): 1335–62.

Lublin, Joann S. "CalPERS Considers Seeking Board Seats." *Wall Street Journal*, December 26, 1997, p. A3.

———. "Oklahoma Count Affirms Holders' Right to Pursue a Binding Bylaw Proposal." *Wall Street Journal*, January 28, 1999, p. B2.

Lublin, Joann S., and Elizabeth MacDonald. "Panel to Propose Boosting Independence and Power of Board Audit Committees." *Wall Street Journal*, January 8, 1999, p. A3.

Lucas, Robert E. "On the Mechanics of Economic Development." *Journal of Monetary Economics* 22, no. 1 (1998): 3–42.

Manne, H. G. "Mergers and the Market for Corporate Control." *Journal of Political Economy* 73 (1965): 110–20.

Marcil, Sharon, and Peg O'Hara. "Voting by Institutional Investors on Corporate Governance Issues in the 1987 Proxy Season." Washington, D.C.: Investors Responsibility Research Center, October 1987.

Markoff, John. "Hewlett-Packard Picks Rising Star at Lucent as Its Chief Executive." *New York Times*, July 20, 1999, p. C1.

Marshall, Alfred. *Industry and Trade.* London: Macmillan, 1920.

McCann, Michelle. "Shareholder Proposal Rule: Cracker Barrel in Light of Texaco." *Boston College Law Review* 39, no. 4 (1998): 965–91.

McConnell, John J., and Henri Servaes. "Additional Evidence on Equity Ownership and Corporate Value." *Journal of Financial Economics* 27, no. 2 (1990): 595–612.

Meeropol, Michael. *Surrender: How the Clinton Administration Completed the Reagan Revolution.* Ann Arbor: University of Michigan Press, 1998.

Mikkelson, W. H., and R. S. Ruback. "An Empirical Analysis of the Interfirm Equity Investment Process." *Journal of Financial Economics* 14, no. 4 (1985): 523–53.

Millstein, Ira M. "Corporate Governance." Paris: Organization for Economic Cooperation and Development (OECD), 1998.

Millstein, Ira M., and Paul W. MacAvoy. "The Active Board of Directors and Performance of the Large Publicly Traded Corporation." *Columbia Law Review* 98, no. 5 (1998): 1283–1321.

Monks, Robert A. G. "Corporate Governance in the Twenty-First Century, A Preliminary Outline." Lens, Inc. www.lens-inc.com, 1995.

———. *The Emperor's Nightingale.* Reading, Mass.: Addison-Wesley, 1998.

———. "Relationship Investing." *Corporate Governance* 2, no. 2 (1994): 58–76.

Monks, Robert A. G., and Nell Minow. *Corporate Governance.* Cambridge, Mass.: Basil Blackwell, 1995.

———. *Watching the Watchers: Corporate Governance in the Twenty-First Century.* Cambridge, Mass.: Blackwell Publishers, 1996.

Morck, Randal, Andrei Shleifer, and Robert W. Vishny. "Characteristics of Targets of Hostile and Friendly Takeovers." In *Corporate Takeovers: Causes and Consequences,* edited by Alan J. Auerbach. Chicago: National Bureau of Economic Research, 1988, pp. 101–36.

Nesbitt, Stephen L. "Long-term Rewards from Shareholder Activism: A Study of the 'CalPERS' Effect." *Continental Bank Journal of Applied Corporate Finance* 6, Spring (1994): 75–80.

Noe, Thomas H., and Michael J. Rebello. "The Design of Corporate Boards: Composition, Compensation, Factions, and Turnover." Georgia State University, Department of Finance, College of Business Administration, March 1996.

O'Connor, Marleen A. "Organized Labor as Shareholder Activist: Building Coalitions to Promote Worker Capitalism." *University of Richmond Law Review* 31, no. 5 (1997): 1345–98.

Opler, Tim C., and Jonathan Sokobin. "Does Coordinated Institutional Activism Work? An Analysis of the Activities of the Council of Institutional Investors." Ohio State University, Fisher College of Business, August 1997.

Orwall, Bruce. "Disney Holders Decry Payouts at Meeting." *Wall Street Journal,* February 26, 1997, p. A3.

Orwall, Bruce, and Joann S. Lublin. "If a Company Prospers, Should Its Directors Behave by the Book?" *Wall Street Journal,* February 24, 1997, p. A1.

O'Sullivan, Pauline. "Governance by Exit: An Analysis of the Market for Corporate Control." In *Corporate Governance: Economic, Management, and Financial Issues,* edited by Kevin Keasey, Steve Thompson, and Mike Wright. New York: Oxford University Press, 1997, pp. 122–46.

Pearlstein, Steven. "No More Mr. Nice Guy: Corporate America Has Done an About-Face in How It Pays and Treats Employees." *Washington Post Weekly Edition,* December 18–24, 1995.

Phillips, Richard M., and Gilbert C. Miller. "The Private Securities Litigation Reform Act of 1995: Rebalancing Litigation Risks and Rewards for Class Action Plaintiffs, Defendants and Lawyers." *The Business Lawyer* 51, no. 4 (1996): 1009–69.

Porter, Michael E. "Capital Choices: Changing the Way America Invests in Industry." Washington, D.C.: U.S. Council on Competitiveness, 1992.

Poterba, James M., and Andrew A. Samwick. "Stock Ownership Patterns, Stock Market Fluctuations and Consumption." *Brookings Papers on Economic Activity*, no. 2 (1995): 295–372.

Pound, John. "The Rise of the Political Model of Corporate Governance and Corporate Control." *New York University Law Review* 68, no. 5 (1993): 1003–71.

Pozen, R. C. "Institutional Investors: The Reluctant Activists." *Harvard Business Review* 72, no. 1, January–February (1994): 140–49.

Prahalad, C. K. "Corporate Governance or Corporate Value Added? Rethinking the Primacy of Shareholder Value." In *Studies in International Corporate Finance and Governance Systems*, edited by Donald H. Chew. Oxford: Oxford University Press, 1997, pp. 46–57.

Rappaport, Alfred. "The Staying Power of the Public Corporation." *Harvard Business Review* 68, no. 1 (1990): 96–104.

Rauch, James E. "Productivity Gains from Geographic Concentration of Human Capital: Evidence from Cities." *Journal of Urban Economics*, 34, no. 3 (1993): 380–400.

Ravenscraft, D. J., and E. M. Scherer. *Mergers, Sell-Offs and Economic Efficiency*. Washington, D.C.: Brookings Institution, 1987.

Reich, Robert. "How to Avoid These Layoffs?" *New York Times*, January 4, 1995, p. A13.

Reichelstein, Stefan. "Agency." In *The New Palgrave Dictionary of Money and Finance*, edited by Peter Newman, Murray Milgate, and John Eatwell. London: Macmillan, 1992.

Reid, S. R. *Mergers, Managers, and the Economy*. New York: McGraw-Hill, 1968.

Roe, Mark J. "The Corporation and the Law, 1959–1994." In *The American Corporation Today*, edited by Carl Kaysen. New York: Oxford University Press, 1996, pp. 102–27.

———. "The Modern Corporation and Private Pensions." *UCLA Law Review* 41, no. 1 (1993): 75–116.

———. *Strong Managers Weak Owners: The Political Roots of American Corporate Finance*. Princeton, N.J.: Princeton University Press, 1994.

Romano, Roberta. "External Governance Structures: The Market for Corporate Control." In *Foundations of Corporate Law*, edited by Roberta Romano. New York: Oxford University Press, 1993, pp. 229–233.

———. "A Guide to Takeovers: Theory, Evidence and Regulation." *Yale Journal on Regulation* 9, no. 1 (1992): 119–80.

———. "Public Pension Fund Activism in Corporate Governance Reconsidered." *Columbia Law Review* 93, no. 4 (1993): 795–853.

Romano, Roberta, ed. *Foundations of Corporate Law*. New York: Oxford University Press, 1993.

Ross, Stephen A., Randolph W. Westerfield, and Jeffrey F. Jaffe. "From Corporate Finance." In *Foundations of Corporate Law*, edited by Roberta Romano. New York: Oxford University Press, 1993, pp. 45–62.

Salmon, Walter J. "Crisis Prevention: How to Gear Up Your Board." *Harvard Business Review* 71, no. 1 (1993): 68–75.

Schroeder, Michael. "Groups United to Oppose SEC's Effort to Shift Stance on Shareholder Issues." *Wall Street Journal*, October 23, 1997, p. 12.

———. "SEC Backs Off on Shareholder Resolution Curbs." *Wall Street Journal*, October 20, 1997, p. 3.

Schuster, E. "Fiduciary." In *The New Palgrave Dictionary of Money and Finance*. New York: Macmillan, 1992, p. 22.

Schwab, Stewart J., and Randall S. Thomas. "Realigning Corporate Governance: Shareholder Activism by Labor Unions." *Michigan Law Review* 96, no. 4 (1998): 1018–94.

Scism, Leslie. "Teachers' Pension Plan to Give Firms Tough Exams." *Wall Street Journal*, October 6, 1993, p. C1.

Serwer, Andrew E. "Mr. Price Is on the Line." *Fortune*, December 9, 1996, p. 70.

Sharara, Norma M., and Anne E. Hoke-Witherspoon. "The Evolution of the 1992 Shareholder Communication Proxy Rules and Their Impact on Corporate Governance." *Business Lawyer* 49, no. 1 (1993): 327–58.

Sheer, Paul M., and Barbara Tierney. "Shareholders Block General Datacomm from Reducing Employee Option Price." *Wall Street Journal*, February 8, 1999, p. A10.

Shleifer, Andrei, and Lawrence H. Summers. "Breach of Trust in Hostile Takeovers." In *Corporate Takeovers: Causes and Consequences*, edited by Alan J. Aurebach. Chicago: National Bureau of Economic Research, 1988, pp. 33–56.

Shleifer, A., and R. Vishny. "Equilibrium Short Horizons of Investors and Firms." *American Economic Review* 80, no. 2 (1990): 148–53.

———. "Management Entrenchment: The Case of Manager-Specific Investments." *Journal of Financial Economics* 25, no. 1 (1989): 123–39.

Simon, Herbert. *Administrative Behavior*. 2nd ed. New York: Macmillan, 1957.

Smith, Adam. *Wealth of Nations*. Cannan ed. New York: Modern Library, 1937.

Smith, George David, and Davis Dyer. "The Rise and Transformation of the American Corporation." In *The American Corporation Today*, edited by Carl Kaysen. New York: Oxford University Press, 1996, pp. 28–73.

Smith, Michael P. "Shareholder Activism by Institutional Investors: Evidence from CalPERS." *Journal of Finance* 51, no. 1 (March 1996): 227–52.

Stapledon, Geof P. *Institutional Shareholders and Corporate Governance*. Oxford: Oxford University Press, 1996.

Steiner, George A., and John F. Steiner. *Business, Government, and Society*. 7th ed. New York: Random House, 1994.

Stone, Merrill B. "Final Shareholder Proposal Rules Fall Short of Reform." *National Law Journal* 20, no. 43 (1988): B9.

Strickland, Deon, Kenneth W. Wiles, and Marc Zenner. "A Requiem for the USA: Is Small Shareholder Monitoring Effective." *Journal of Financial Economics*, 40, no. 2 (1996): 319–38.

Strouse, Jean. "The Unknown J. P. Morgan." *New Yorker*, November 23, 1998, p. 13.

Temin, Peter. "The Stability of the American Business Elite." *Industrial and Corporate Change* 8, no. 2 (1999): 189–209.

Thomas, Randall S., and Kenneth J. Martin. "Should Labor Be Allowed to Make Shareholder Proposals?" *Washington Law Review* 73, no. 41 (1998): 41–80.

Turnbull, Shann. "Corporate Governance: Its Scope, Concerns and Theories." *Corporate Governance* 5, no. 4 October (1997): 180–205.

U.S. Census Bureau. *Statistical Abstract of the United States: 1998*. Washington, D.C.: U.S. Government Printing Office, 1998.

Wagster, John D., and Andrew K. Prevost. "Wealth Effects of the CalPERS' 'Hit List' to SEC Changes in the Proxy Rules." Wayne State University, School of Business Administration, August 22, 1996.

Wahal, Sunil. "Pension Fund Activism and Firm Performance." *Journal of Financial and Quantitative Analysis* 31, no. 1 (1996): 1–23.

Waters, Richard. "Crowing King Gong." *Financial Times*, March 3, 1998, p. 21.

Weidenbaum, Murray, and Steven Vogt. "Takeovers and Stockholders." *California Management Review* 29, no. 4 (1987): 157–68.

Weisbach, Michael S. "Outside Directors and CEO Turnover." *Journal of Financial Economics* 20, no. 1–2 (1998): 431–60.

Weiss, Elliot J., and John S. Berckerman. "Let the Money Do the Monitoring." *Yale Law Review* 104, no. 8 (1995): 2053–2127.

Whitley, Richard. *Business Systems in East Asia.* Thousands Oaks, Calif.: Sage, 1995.

Willborn, Steven L. "Public Pensions and the Uniform Management of Public Employee Retirement Systems Act." *Rutgers Law Review* 51, no. 1 (1998): 141–72.

Williamson, Oliver E. "Corporate Finance and Corporate Governance, Economic Analysis and Policy." Berkeley: University of California, December 1987.

———. *The Economic Institutions of Capitalism.* New York: Free Press, 1985.

———. *Industrial Organization.* Brookfield, Vt.: E. Elgar, 1990.

———. "Managerial Discretion and Business Behavior." *American Economic Review* 63, no. 5 (1963): 1033–57.

———. "On the Governance of the Modern Corporation." *Hofstra Law Review* 8, no. 1 (1979): 63–98.

———. "Organization Form, Residual Claimants, and Corporate Control." *Journal of Law and Economics* 26, no. 2 (1983): 351–74.

———. "Transaction-Cost Economics: The Governance of Contractual Relations." *Journal of Law and Economics* 22, no. 2 (1979): 233–61.

Williamson, Oliver E., and Janet Bercovitz. "The Modern Corporation as an Efficiency Instrument: The Comparative Contracting Perspective." In *The American Corporation Today*, edited by Carl Kaysen. New York: Oxford University Press, 1996, pp. 327–59.

Index

Acknowledgments

The principal ideas in this book were first developed as part of a background document on corporate governance commissioned by the Organization for Economic Organization and Development (OECD) in 1996. Later that year, the OECD paper won first prize in the Lens Fund's international corporate governance paper competition, encouraging us further and supporting additional research. For this publication the manuscript has been thoroughly revised, expanded, and updated.

Many individuals have provided invaluable assistance in a variety of ways. In particular the following people have read all or portions of the manuscript, made suggestions, comments, and criticisms, and have pointed us in directions we might not have otherwise gone: Peter Jarrett, Edwin Epstein, Nelson Shelton, Gail Pasyna, Eric Halpern, Joseph Grundfest, Bernard Black, Ronald Gilson, John Cioffi, Michael Riech, Teresa Ghilarducci, Richard Koppes, Dale Hanson, Rauf Gonenc, Mats Iasksson, and Jon Lukomnik. The authors would specially like to acknowledge the principals of Lens, Inc., Robert Monks and Nell Minow, for the suggestion in their book *Corporate Governance* that institutional investors might have the interests of universal owners. For her research assistance in 1998–99, we are indebted to Jerazeth Lopez.

At different times the authors had the pleasure of working on the manuscript at the Judge Institute of Management at the University of Cambridge, England, and wish to thank the many scholars for their support and critical feedback. In particular, the authors would like to thank Sandra Dawson, the Director of the Judge Institute, and Philip Stiles and John Hendry for providing a congenial, supportive, and stimulating work environment during which substantial portions of the manuscript were drafted.

We are deeply grateful for financial assistance to the Alfred P. Sloan Foundation, the Saint Mary's College Graduate Business Alumni Fund, and the Saint Mary's College Faculty Development Fund.